Language, Interaction
and Social Cognition

Language, Interaction and Social Cognition

edited by

Gün R. Semin and Klaus Fiedler

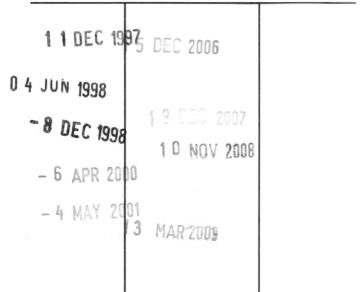

Chapters 1, 4 and 5, and editorial arrangement © Gün R. Semin and Klaus Fiedler 1992
Chapter 2 © Myron Rothbart and Marjorie Taylor 1992
Chapter 3 © Glenn D. Reeder, John B. Pryor and Bogdan Wojciszke 1992
Chapter 6 © David L. Hamilton, Pamela A. Gibbons, Steven J. Stroessner and Jeffrey W. Sherman 1992
Chapter 7 © Anne Maass and Luciano Arcuri 1992
Chapter 8 © C. Douglas McCann and E. Tory Higgins 1992
Chapter 9 © Fritz Strack and Norbert Schwarz 1992
Chapter 10 © Terry Kit-fong Au 1992
Chapter 11 © William J. McGuire and Claire V. McGuire 1992
Chapter 12 © Carl F. Graumann 1992

First published 1992

SAGE Publications Ltd
6 Bonhill Street
London EC2A 4PU

SAGE Publications Inc
2455 Teller Road
Newbury Park, California 91320

SAGE Publications India Pvt Ltd
32, M-Block Market
Greater Kailash – I
New Delhi 110 048

British Library Cataloguing in Publication Data

Language, Interaction and Social Cognition
  I. Semin, G.R.   II. Fiedler, Klaus
  302.2

  ISBN 0–8039–8530–4

Library of Congress catalog card number 92–053697

Typeset by Mayhew Typesetting, Rhayader, Powys
Printed in Great Britain by Biddles Ltd., Guildford, Surrey

Contents

Acknowledgements

We would like to thank the Volkswagen Stiftung for the generous grant that enabled the workshop on which this volume is based. We would also like to thank Catrin Finkenauer for her assistance in running the workshop.

Gün R. Semin and Klaus Fiedler

The Contributors

Luciano Arcuri, University of Padua, Italy
Terry Kit-fong Au, University of California, Los Angeles, USA
Klaus Fiedler, University of Mannheim, Germany
Pamela A. Gibbons, University of California, Santa Barbara, USA
Carl F. Graumann, University of Heidelberg, Germany
David L. Hamilton, University of California, Santa Barbara, USA
E. Tory Higgins, Columbia University, New York, USA
Anne Maass, University of Padua, Italy
C. Douglas McCann, York University, Ontario, Canada
Claire V. McGuire, Yale University, USA
William J. McGuire, Yale University, USA
John B. Pryor, Illinois State University, USA
Glenn D. Reeder, Illinois State University, USA
Myron Rothbart, University of Oregon, USA
Norbert Schwarz, Zentrum für Umfragen, Methoden und Analysen
    (ZUMA), Mannheim, Germany
Gün R. Semin, Free University of Amsterdam, the Netherlands
Jeffrey W. Sherman, University of California, Santa Barbara,
    USA
Fritz Strack, University of Trier, Germany
Steven J. Stroessner, University of California, Santa Barbara, USA
Marjorie Taylor, University of Oregon, USA
Bogdan Wojciszke, University of Gdansk, Poland

1
Introduction

Gün R. Semin and Klaus Fiedler

The interest in social psychology, conceived broadly, and language presents a rather unusual and heavily punctured history. However bizarre it sounds, this concern predates the history of experimental psychology. Its origins can be located in the middle of the nineteenth century, to the then emerging concentration of the relationship between *Völkerpsychologie* and language (Lazarus and Steinhal, 1860). Indeed, a journal with that precise label (*Völker-. psychologie und Sprachwissenschaft*) was founded in 1860.

The focal concern was that one could not appreciate human functioning within the then prevailing elementaristic psychology. The critique stated that an elementaristic psychology was decontextualized from its social and more distinctly cultural frame. The theme about contextualizing social psychology in the late sixties and early seventies (for example, Israel & Tajfel, 1972) is one which resembles in some of its features this earlier debate. The comparative element, cultural psychology, is a theme which has gained credence in recent years (see, *inter alia*, Shweder, 1990; Cole, 1990; Jahoda, 1992; Wertsch, 1991). In contrast, interest in the social psychological implications of language can be traced back over a number of decades; it is only recently that a tradition of the 'social psychology of language' has emerged (cf., for example, Giles and Coupland, 1991; Giles and Robinson, 1990) This is somewhat surprising in view of the fact that much of our behaviour essentially involves communication and is manifested in language use. What is more surprising in this context is that within this emerging tradition the interplay of language and *social cognition* has occupied a minor role to date, and it is only very recently that interest in this field has begun to grow (for example, Brown and Fish, 1983; Hoffman et al., 1984; Hoffman et al., 1986; Semin and Greenslade, 1985). A precursor of this type of orientation is to be found in Fritz Heider's classic, *The Psychology of Interpersonal Relations* (1958). Language provides the medium in which social knowledge in general and knowledge about interpersonal relations in particular are mapped, and this was in large part the agenda in Heider's (1958) work. Knowledge about the world and social reality are generated, articulated and communicated through the medium of language. This is not to deny or question the relevance of non-verbal communication. However, it is difficult if not impossible to imagine how systematic and coherent communication could be sustained only by non-verbal means. Knowledge about the world in general but also about social interaction and social reality are mapped into language in an integral way. Language does not only contain the distilled or crystallized knowledge of generations before us; it enables us to structure our present by bringing the past to bear upon it, and also furnishes a medium by which bridges to the future may be built.

One could argue that the question of why language has been neglected in social psychology and related areas is somewhat misleading. It is misleading mainly because there are large pockets of research that are concerned with language, though they are not identified as such. For instance, there is a long-standing tradition that has its origins in the crossroads of person perception and taxonomic models in personality (cf. Semin, 1990), and that has been concerned with identifying the underlying structure of trait terms (adjectives). The problem has been that such research has been concerned with attempts to identify the intrapsychological implications of such structures: what is the structure of personality, or what does it tell us about the way in which people process information? The neglected partner has been language, and if it was introduced it was introduced in opposition. Are the consistent patterns merely a reflection of 'certain language conventions', 'mere semantic patterns' with no psychological reality? The issue that has been largely ignored is that language conventions, semantic patterns and wording effects are an integral part of cognition in social context, which is generally referred to in terms of an interface or dialectical relationship between language and psychological reality. For instance, Cattell has noted that

> The position we shall adopt is a very direct one . . . making only the one assumption that all aspects of human personality which are or have been of importance, interest, or utility have already been recorded in the substance of language. For, throughout history, the most fascinating subject of general discourse, and also that in which it has been most vitally necessary to have adequate, representative symbols, has been human behaviour. Necessity could not possibly have been barren where so little apparatus is required to permit the birth of invention. (Cattell, 1943, p. 483)

The current expression of this perspective can be found in

taxonomic approaches to personality that utilize Cattell's view as a general guiding principle. This view is now termed the 'sedimentation' or 'lexical' hypothesis (see Goldberg, 1981, 1989) and is assumed to even predate Cattell (that is, Galton, 1884). The important point with regard to this and other related work is that the perspective guiding this research has not attempted to incorporate an explicit language-based angle to the regularly and systematically patterned factorial solutions of trait terms. Nevertheless, it is in principle possible to advance at least semantic arguments for the regular factorial solutions, as has been done, however controversially, by Shweder (the systematic distortion hypothesis, Shweder, 1982).

But there are other approaches (more directly within current social psychological work on social cognition) that can equally well be treated as furnishing a language-based approach to social cognitive processes. This is work that is concerned with what Schneider (1991: 548ff) subsumes in his recent review of social cognition under 'structural differences among traits'. These studies suggest systematic differences between different traits (adjectives) with respect to different inferential processes. Essentially, this work is concerned with identifying propertics or parameters of adjectives that invite differential inferences or delimit cognitive processes in certain ways. One example is Rothbart and Park's (1986) suggestion that there are systematic differences between adjectives in terms of the ease or difficulty with which they can be confirmed. Adjectives with a negative semantic valence are easy to acquire (for example, you need few instances of confirmatory behaviours to infer the property 'dishonest' in a person) and difficult to get rid of (that is, you need many instances of disconfirming evidence). The reverse is found for positively valenced adjectives. You need many confirming instances of evidence to be seen as having a property such as 'honest', and just a few or even one to lose it. With some qualifications, this research has been replicated (Funder and Dobroth, 1987). Rothbart and Park's work is intellectually related to earlier work by Reeder and his colleagues (for example, Reeder and Brewer, 1979; Reeder, 1979) showing that the higher diagnosticity of negative behaviours is typical for morality-related behaviour. An opposite pattern holds for ability-related behaviour, where positive evidence (success) is often more diagnostic than negative evidence (failure).

The point within the perspective of the interface between language and social cognition is that obviously these differences are related to certain properties of traits (not only semantic valence or social desirability: see Rothbart and Park, 1986), but there is no explicit or implicit anchoring of such trait inferences in some linguistic framework. In contrast, other approaches were developed from considerations about the linguistic properties of adjectives (such as their morphological relations to different verb classes), which attempt to elucidate the nature of trait terms and their socio-cognitive meanings (see Semin and Fiedler, 1991; and Chapter 2 below, by Semin and Fiedler, for recent elaborations on interpersonal verbs). Further work in the adjective domain examines other systematic properties of trait terms with regard to stability, causality, duration, hierarchical relations and breadth (Chaplin et al., 1988; Hampson et al., 1986; John et al., 1991). Yet again, there is other work on properties of adjectives addressing trait classes as they relate to behavioural manifestations (see, for example, Reeder and Brewer, 1979; Reeder, 1979; Reeder et al., 1982; Reeder et al., 1977). These strands of research are also developed with internal criteria; that is, psychological criteria about the properties of traits. Consequently, no externally identifiable markers of the distinguished classes or properties of adjectives are explicated – for instance, in terms of specific semantic, morphological, or other linguistic criteria that are independent of the intrapsychological (cognitive inference) measures.

In conceiving of the interface between language, social interaction and cognition, one can think of different foci of analysis. One of the important elements that has occupied centre stage in social psychology is how knowledge is mapped into categories and how a potentially infinite universe is managed by introducing categories that make the complexity of our universe manageable. This focus on the cognitive properties of social categories is a fundamental enterprise in terms of understanding how our social world is divided. Part 1 of this volume is devoted to this basic issue.

It is also important to understand whether and how the way in which social interaction and interpersonal relations are mapped into diverse categories is reflected in language. Thus, the theme of Part 2 is whether there are social or extra-individual representations or 'carriers' of the categories we find in interpersonal language and whether these display systematic intrapsychological processes (such as cognitive inferences).

The next question is how people strategically employ devices such as different categories, or category names. This cuts to the heart of the matter of how different social psychological phenomena are maintained, manifested and transmitted. Obviously, there may be certain regularities in the way specific linguistic categories are manifested, but this does not mean that the particular uses of such categories are constrained in discourse. Any social event is open to multiple descriptions, multiple interpretations. Thus, the choice of terms and their strategic use mediates different messages about the same empirical event. It is here that we move from the examination of how distinct types of knowledge are mapped into language to the examination of how distinct types of social psychological phenomena are expressed by differential use of linguistic devices. These issues are addressed in Parts 2, 3 and 4 of this volume.

Finally, in Part 5, the analysis of language as a repertoire of social knowledge is broadened to include the uses of certain syntactic forms in addition to lexical substance. In general, the extent to which cognitive processes may be constrained by syntactic rules seems to be much less understood at present than the substantial, semantic constraints addressed in the earlier chapters.

The manner in which the themes of each part are fleshed out by the individual contributions to this volume is as follows. The two contributions in Part 1 examine properties of categories in the social domain. The emphasis is on the relationship between social categories and social reality. One of the interesting questions in this regard is the types of inferential potentials that different categories acquire and the reasons as well as the implications of these differences for social cognition. As Rothbart and Taylor (Chapter 2) point out, certain social categories carry extraordinary inferential power. In examining how and why certain linguistic labels or symbols map rich inductive information, they utilize a conceptual bridge that brings together Gordon Allport's classic work on the *Nature of Prejudice* (1954) and recent developments on categorization (such as Medin, 1989) employing both diachronic and synchronic perspectives of analysis. Reeder, Pryor and Wojciszke (Chapter 3) examine the behaviour–trait inference relationship by proposing a four-part typology that suggests differential patterns of relationships between traits and their behavioural manifestations. In doing so, they advance a model that furnishes a systematic basis for differentiating between different trait categories governed by different inferential schemes that guide inferences from behaviours to traits or dispositions and vice versa.

The two contributions in the next part, employ a taxonomic model of interpersonal verbs and adjectives, which is derived on the basis of genuinely linguistic criteria that are independent of the cognitive–social phenomena the model is intended to account for. The model was developed in order to examine how different features of interpersonal relationships are marked in language.

Chapter 4 (Semin & Fiedler) presents some of these properties of word classes and then examines how underlying features of attribution are anchored in interpersonal language. The main argument developed in the fifth chapter (Fiedler and Semin) is that the differential use of linguistic styles in communication are responsible for a variety of attributional phenomena. Thus, the intention is to draw attention to the extra-individual element, namely the medium that carries attributional phenomena, rather than merely to focus on intrapsychological phenomena. Fiedler and Semin also elaborate on the issue of the dialectical relationship between inter- and intrapsychological phenomena, namely language and cognition, emphasizing that the issues cannot be understood with the unidirectional causality assumptions that have prevailed for a long time in the domain of linguistic relativity.

The contribution of language to the maintenance and transmission of stereotypes is the theme of Part 3, 'Language, intergroup relations and stereotypes'. Despite the substantial amount of research that characterizes the domain of stereotypes and intergroup relations, the properties of the communication process itself, namely the type of language used to describe ingroup and outgroup, has never been the subject of systematic research until recently (Maass et al., 1989). Maass and Arcuri, in Chapter 7, introduce a model of how stereotypes are sustained and transmitted by identifying distinct properties of communication. They find that the differential use of abstract or concrete communicative styles by ingroup members to describe ingroup and outgroup members serves distinct functions. The work by Hamilton, Gibbons, Stroessner and Sherman (Chapter 6) also focuses on the relationship between stereotypes and language in the context of communication – that is, spontaneous language use. They examine the diverse linguistic options that are available to a communicator and how the communicator strategically deploys these options in relevant intergroup or stereotype contexts.

Chapters 8 and 9 in Part 4 are devoted to 'Communication and social cognition' in the context of dyadic situations involving communicators and recipients. The common denominator of these two chapters is their reliance on the Gricean (1975) principle of *cooperative communication*. Thus, communicators have to shape their messages according to the informational needs of the recipients, who in turn have to figure out the communicators' intentions from obvious as well as more subtle aspects of the message. The focus here is on actual communication rather than language as a system or structure. The intriguing contention of McCann and Higgins in Chapter 8 is that a communicator's attempts to shape a verbal message in accordance with the recipients' needs and expectations will not only affect message content itself but will also feed back to change cognitive representations within the communicator. Thus, aside from the permanent representation of social knowledge within language as a system, cognitive information processing may even depend on strategic short-term variations in language use. Strack and Schwarz's contribution (Chapter 9) addresses communication in standardized questioning situations (such as interviews or questionnaires) involving survey researchers and respondents as interactants. Although these standardized procedures were developed to control or eliminate language effects that might obscure the result, Strack and Schwarz show that such standard formats cannot prevent respondents from adhering to the norm of cooperative communication, interpreting subtle cues such as question order or response alternatives to infer what kind of information the researcher wants to get.

Part 5, 'Words, reasoning and presuppositions in social cognition', begins with a contribution by Terry Au (Chapter 10), who examines criticisms of research on linguistic relativity, using the issue of counterfactual reasoning as a vehicle. While the alleged absence of markers for counterfactuals in Chinese and the alleged deficits of Chinese people in counterfactual reasoning have been considered as prime evidence for linguistic relativity, Au provides abundant evidence that Chinese people engage in counterfactual reasoning as much as people in other linguistic communities. This is because everyday life creates multiple opportunities to use counterfactual thinking if only to experience emotions such as regret or gratitude, or to fantasize and enjoy fictions and dramas. Cognition as well as language reflect these opportunities and, in fact, a closer look at language shows that linguistic markers for counterfactuals do exist, although in the form of more subtle devices. Similarly, Chapter 11 by McGuire and McGuire is concerned with seemingly arbitrary word-order regularities in kinship and food terms as well as series of adjective attributes. To say 'mother and father', 'apples and oranges', and 'white silk dress' instead of 'father and mother', 'oranges and apples', or 'silk white dress' does not appear at first sight to serve an obvious function or to reflect some rational principle. However, closer analysis reveals that such word orderings may reflect cognitive or affective factors such as phonological ease, cognitive availability or affective involvement. At the same time, we learn that linguistic regularities reflect manifold influences and change with time and social context, therefore evading a simple and invariant explanation. However, even when the origins of such word-order regularities are complex and difficult to understand, deviations from such rules may be utilized in communication to convey subtle information. The closing chapter by Grauman addresses the important issue of perspectivity in communication, and reports studies based on a theory of perspectivity developed by the author. The main line of the argument revolves around a fundamental question of whether all knowledge is perspectival. After discussing the problem of perspectivity as it is found in language, literature, cognition and language use, he presents empirical work of how perspectivity influences text production, comprehension, memory and the relationship between speaker and hearer perspectives.

Thus, the aim of this volume is to introduce considerations about language in a more systematic way into social cognition and communication processes. In a different sense, it is an attempt to introduce the social into social cognition, and to start by pointing out one possible response to the question posed by David Schneider in his *Annual Review* lament: 'Where, oh where, is the social in social cognition?' (1991: 553). We think that the beginnings of an answer can be found in research on the dialectical relationship between language and social cognition. Even if this means at times that one has to exaggerate the one or the other element in this dialectic.

References

Allport, G. W. (1954) *The Nature of Prejudice*. Cambridge, MA: Addison-Wesley.

Brown, R. and Fish, D. (1983) The Psychological causality implicit in language. *Cognition*, 14: 233–274.

Cattell, R. B. (1943) The description of personality: Basic traits revolved into clusters. *Journal of Abnormal and Social Psychology*, 38: 476–506.

Chaplin, W. F., John, O. and Goldberg, L. R. (1988) Conceptions of states and traits: Dimensional attributes with ideals as prototypes. *Journal of Personality and Social Psychology*, 54: 541–557.

Cole, M. (1990) Cultural psychology: A once and future discipline? In J. J. Berman (ed.), *Nebraska Symposium on Motivation: Cross-Cultural Perspectives* (vol. 37). Lincoln, NE: University of Nebraska Press.

Funder, D. C. and Dobroth, K. M. (1987) Differences between traits: Properties associated with interjudge agreement *Journal of Personality and Social Psychology*, 52: 409–418.

Galton, F. (1884) Measurement of character. *Fortnightly Review*, 36: 179–185.

Giles, H. and Coupland, N. (1991) *Language: Contexts and Consequences*. Oxford: Open University Press.

Giles, H. and Robinson, W. P. (1990) *Handbook of Social Psychology and Language*. Chichester: Wiley.

Goldberg, L. R. (1981) Language and individual differences: The search for universals in personality lexicons. In L. Wheeler (ed.), *Review of Personality and Social Psychology*, vol. 2. Beverly Hills, CA: Sage.

Goldberg, L. R. (1989) Standard markers of the big five structure. Paper presented at the Workshop on Personality Language, University of Groningen, June 1989.

Grice, P. (1975) Logic and conversation. In P. Cole and M. Morgan (eds), *Syntax and Semantics*. New York: Academic Press.

Hampson, S. E., John, O. and Goldberg, L. R. (1986) Category breadth and hierarchical structure in personality: Studies of asymmetries in judgments of trait implications. *Journal of Personality and Social Psychology*, 51: 37-54.

Heider, F. (1958) *The Psychology of Interpersonal Relations*. New York: Wiley.

Hoffman, C., Lau, I. and Johnson, D. R. (1986) The linguistic relativity of person cognition: An English-Chinese comparison. *Journal of Personality and Social Psychology*, 51: 1097-1105.

Hoffman, C., Mischel, W. and Baer, J. S. (1984) Language and person cognition: Effects of communicative set on trait attribution. *Journal of Personality and Social Psychology* 46: 1029-1043.

Israel, J. and Tajfel, H. (1972) *The Context of Social Psychology*. London and New York: Academic Press.

Jahoda, G. (1992) *Crossroads Between Culture and Mind*. Hemel Hempstead: Harvester-Wheatsheaf.

John, O. P., Hampson, S. E. and Goldberg, L. R. (1991) The basic level in personality-trait hierarchies: Studies of trait use and accessibility in different contexts. *Journal of Personality and Social Psychology*, 60: 348-361.

Lazarus, M. and Steinhal, R. (1860) Einladende Gedanken über Völkerpsychologie und Sprachwissenschaft. *Zeitschrift für Volkerpsychologie und Sprachwissenschaft*, 1: 1-73.

Maass, A., Salvi, D., Arcuri, L. and Semin, G. R. (1989) Language use in intergroup contexts. *Journal of Personality and Social Psychology*, 57: 981-993.

Medin, D. L. (1989) Concepts and conceptual structure. *American Psychologist*, 44: 1469-1481.

Reeder, G. D. (1979) Context effects for attributions of ability. *Personality and Social Psychology Bulletin*, 5: 65-68.

Reeder, G. D. and Brewer, M. B. (1979) A schematic model of dispositional attribution in interpersonal perception. *Psychological Review*, 86: 61-79.

Reeder, G. D., Henderson, D. J. and Sullivan, J. J. (1982) From dispositions to behaviors. The flip side of attribution. *Journal of Research in Personality*, 16: 355-375.

Reeder, G. E., Messick, D. M. and Van Avermaet, E. (1977) Dimensional asymmetry in attributional inference. *Journal of Experimental Social Psychology*, 13: 46 57.

Rothbart, M. and Park, B. (1986) On the confirmability and disconfirmability of trait concepts. *Journal of Personality and Social Psychology*, 50: 131-142.

Schneider, D. (1991) Social cognition. *Annual Review of Psychology*, 42: 527-561.

Semin, G. R. (1990) Personality and everyday language. In G. R. Semin and K. J. Gergen (eds), *Everyday Understanding: Social and Scientific Implications*, pp. 151-175. London and Beverly Hills: Sage.

Semin, G. R. and Fiedler, K. (1991) The linguistic category model, its bases, applications and range. In W. Stroebe and M. Hewstone (eds), *European Review of Social Psychology*, vol. 2. Chichester: Wiley.

Semin, G. R. and Greenslade, L. (1985) Differential contributions of linguistic factors to memory based ratings: Systematizing the systematic distortion hypothesis. *Journal of Personality and Social Psychology*, 49: 1713-1723.

Shweder, R. A. (1982) Fact and artifact in trait perception: The systematic distortion hypothesis. In B. A. Maher and W. B. Maher (eds), *Progress in Experimental Personality Research*, vol. 2. New York: Academic Press.

Shweder, R. A. (1990) Cultural psychology – what is it? In J. W. Stigler, R. A. Shweder and H. Gilbert (eds), *Cultural Psychology: Essays on Comparative Human Development*. New York: CUP.

Wertsch, J. V. (1991) *Voices of the Mind*. Hemel Hempstead: Harvester–Wheatsheaf.

PART 1

SOCIAL CATEGORIES AND SOCIAL REALITY

2

Category Labels and Social Reality: Do We View Social Categories as Natural Kinds?

Myron Rothbart and Marjorie Taylor

The goal of this paper is to re-examine a very old social psychological question: why do our labels for social categories possess such extraordinary power? Gordon Allport's *Nature of Prejudice* refers to some labels as

> exceedingly salient and powerful. They tend to prevent alternative classification, or even cross-classification . . . 'labels of primary potency' . . . act like shrieking sirens, deafening us to all finer discriminations that we might otherwise perceive. (Allport, 1954: 179)

This brief quote from Allport contains a wealth of ideas about the nature of category labels. It suggests that labels differ in their potency, possess disproportionate power, obscure within-category differences, imply exclusivity from other categories, and have a reality above and beyond what is justified by the real-world correlates of that label. Although it is often quite difficult in practice to determine whether our perception of an object is disproportionately influenced by our knowledge of the object's category membership, Allport's observations strike us as enormously insightful. The general question we pose in this chapter is: What are some of the possible psychological mechanisms that may lead to the phenomena Allport describes?

The argument we propose in this paper utilizes a distinction between 'natural kind' categories (such as *birds, fish, gold*, and *daffodils*) and 'human artifact' categories (such as *chair, bicycle, sweater*, and *house*). We argue that people are inclined to view categories of natural kinds as less arbitrary than those of artifact kinds because natural kinds are believed to possess underlying essences that make one category different from another. With respect to the important question of how people represent social categories, we believe that whereas social categories are in reality more like human artifacts than natural kinds, they are often perceived as more like natural kinds than human artifacts. The implicit assumption that social categories, like natural kind categories, possess an underlying essence has a number of important implications. These include a tendency to infer deep essential qualities on the basis of surface appearance, a tendency to treat even independent categories as if they were mutually exclusive, and a tendency to imbue even arbitrary categorizations with deep meaning.

Distinctions among Types of Categories

Advances in thinking about categorization are often motivated by the recognition of important distinctions between different types of categories. For example, Rosch and her colleagues (Rosch and Mervis, 1975; Rosch et al., 1976) revolutionized research on categorization by pointing out the differences between real world categories used by people in everyday life (such as *dog, chair*) and categories based on an arbitrary selection of defining features (such as *large red circle*). Rosch showed that the former reflect structure in the world and are not defined by necessary and sufficient features. Thus, her work demonstrated that categories like *large red circle* do not provide a good model for the groupings that humans find meaningful, and research using such categories is limited in what it can reveal about human classification systems.

The distinction between natural kinds (such as *tiger, gold*) and human artifacts (such as *car, sweater*) is the focus of our discussion in this chapter. Rosch's conclusions about category structure tended to collapse this distinction, but the differences between natural kinds and artifacts have been an important topic in philosophical analyses of categories (for example, Kripke, 1972; Putnam, 1975; Schwartz, 1978) and have recently been shown to be important psychologically (for example, Gelman, 1988; Gelman and O'Reilly, 1988; Keil, 1989). One way to capture this distinction is to consider the types of objects and substances that exist in the world that are relatively or potentially independent of the behaviors and beliefs of humans (natural kinds), compared with categories that reflect human needs and desires (artifacts) (Keil, 1989). It is possible to imagine the existence of tigers and gold in a world with no humans, but not the existence of cars and sweaters. The distinction between naturally occurring objects and substances and the artifacts created by humans should probably be viewed as continuous rather than discrete (Keil, 1989) (humans might create a new species of animal by genetic engineering or nonhuman animals might develop their own artifacts such as a stick in removing grubs from a tree stump); nonetheless the natural kind / artifact distinction has important psychological implications.

There are a number of characteristics distinguishing natural kinds from artifacts (Gelman and Coley, 1991; Keil, 1989); however, we think the crux of the distinction has to do with differences in inductive potential. Natural kinds are perceived as having relatively homogeneous exemplars and as capturing deep underlying similarities among exemplars (Gelman, 1988). Thus, one of the most fundamental characteristics of natural kinds is their rich inductive potential. In contrast, the inductive potential of most artifact categories is relatively limited because members of an artifact category share few properties beyond the ones directly relevant to the function they were created to fulfill (Gelman, 1988). For the purpose of our discussion, we will describe this difference between natural kinds and artifacts in more detail and then outline a closely related psychological phenomenon – namely, the belief that natural kinds have an underlying essence fundamental to category membership.

Inductive Potential
An important function of categorization is to allow one 'to go beyond the information given.' Although theoretical knowledge is important for all categories (Murphy and Medin, 1985), Gelman and Coley (1991) point out that categories differ in the extent to which they capture theoretically meaningful distinctions (also see Markman, 1989). According to Quine (1977) and other philosophers (for example, Putnam, 1975), natural kinds are laden in theory such that category membership allows the induction of a potentially infinite amount of information about an exemplar. For example, when an object is categorized as a tiger, we expect the object to have the appearance of other tigers, but also to have a similar habitat, method of hunting, caring for its young, life expectancy, and internal body structure. Many of the features shared by the exemplars of a natural kind category are not immediately obvious, and thus we might also expect that an exemplar of the category *tiger* will be like other tigers in ways not known by most people (such as body temperature).

Although artifacts share a set of functional properties, they are usually free to vary in many ways and thus have less inductive potential than natural kinds. According to Gelman:

> as long as the function is carried out, then all else can vary, including shape, material, and internal parts. With new technology, artifacts can be made of new materials (such as plastic), can change size (for example, tape recorders have gotten smaller), or can change overall shape and internal parts (e.g., airplanes). With shifting fashions, artifacts can change style and color (e.g., hats, cars). Someone can invent an entirely new subtype of an artifact (witness the dramatic changes in computers over the past 30 years). In contrast, natural kinds are constrained by their genetic or molecular structure to reach a certain size, to have a certain color, to have a certain set of parts. (1988: 70).

Gelman's intuitions were supported by her research showing that people rate natural kinds as more homogeneous than artifacts. It is interesting that preschool children who have very little knowledge of biology also expect the exemplars of a natural kind to share many deep underlying similarities (Gelman and Markman, 1986), and by at least seven years of age, children are willing to draw more inferences on the basis of membership in a natural kind than membership in an artifact category (Gelman, 1988).

The exemplars of a natural kind category are assumed to be similar in so many ways that scientific disciplines evolve to study them (Carey, 1985). In fact, special scientific knowledge may be required to identify exemplars of a natural kind because deep underlying characteristics rather than superficial perceptual features are often assumed to be the ones most critical for category membership. Most people rely on experts to distinguish gold from other yellow metals, diamonds from cut glass, or cheetahs from leopards, a phenomenon Putnam (1975, 1988) calls the 'linguistic division of labor.' The assumption that natural kinds have deep underlying similarities is also demonstrated in our routine acceptance of anomalous members in natural kind categories. For example, dolphins look very much like fish, but we accept the scientific wisdom that categorizes them as mammals. Because the basis for category membership rests on deep underlying non-obvious structure, it is possible to ignore violations of the usual appearance of a category member. For example, an animal born to tiger parents that had long white hair and no ears or tail would nonetheless be categorized as a tiger. It might not look like other tigers, but we would include it in the category because its lineage would be more important than its perceptual characteristics for determining category membership.

Artifact categories do not capture deep underlying similarities to the same degree as natural kinds. According to Schwartz:

there is no underlying nature of pencils, nor is there the presumption of such a nature. What makes a pencil are superficial characteristics such as a certain form and function. There is nothing underlying about these features. They are analytically associated with the term 'pencil,' not disclosed by scientific investigation. (1978: 571)

This point is consistent with our intuition about the role of experts in identifying exemplars of a category. As mentioned earlier, experts may often play a role in natural kind categorization even for familiar categories such as *bird* or *gold*; however, most people rely on their own intuitions rather than those of experts when it comes to determining membership in familiar artifact categories. For example, scientific discoveries led to the categorization of a dolphin as a mammal and a penguin as a bird, but it is difficult to imagine a discovery of any kind that would affect the way we categorize an object as a chair or sweater. As Schwartz points out,

If a scientist were interested in chairs as a subject of scientific study and got himself a good specimen and started to examine it closely in order to discover the nature of chairs, we would think he was crazy. Compare this with a zoologist interested in snakes, who obtains a fine specimen and begins to dissect it . . . (1978: 573)

Malt (1989) has tested this contrast between natural kinds and artifact categories in a series of experiments examining the acceptability of sentences containing a variety of hedges (such as 'technically,' 'by definition,' and so on). She found that subjects judge the hedge 'according to experts' to make sense when the sentence refers to a natural kind (such as 'According to experts, that's an apple.'), but not when the sentence refers to an artifact category (such as 'According to experts, that's a shirt.'). In addition, subjects were given a task in which they selected an appropriate response to a scenario involving a difficult-to-categorize natural kind (for example, a tree that seemed to be halfway between a lemon tree and an orange tree) or artifact (for example, a garment that seemed halfway between a blouse and a shirt). For the natural kind scenarios, subjects tended to choose the response. 'We would have to ask an expert to tell which it is.' For the artifact scenarios, subjects chose the response, 'Well, I guess you can call it whichever you want.' Malt's results indicate that there are clear differences in people's intuitions about the role experts play in the categorization of natural kinds and artifacts.

The difference between natural kinds and artifacts in inductive potential and the role of experts are important, although probably less discrete than we have implied. For example, there are artifacts (such as computers) that are a closer fit to the way we have described natural kinds than artifacts (see Keil, 1989, for a discussion of special cases). In addition, it is true that artifacts can be the topic of study (for example, an antique dealer would be considered an expert on some types of artifacts) (Gelman, 1988). Although it is important to note then the natural kind / artifact distinction is more continuous than categorical, the psychological evidence shows that people expect familiar natural kinds such as *dog* and *fish* to differ from everyday artifact categories such as *chair* and *cup* with respect to induction potential. We will continue by discussing belief in essence, which we view as closely related to the perception of richness in inductive potential.

Psychological Essentialism
The classical theory that concepts have necessary and defining features has been seriously challenged by the work of Rosch and her colleagues (Rosch and Mervis, 1975; Rosch et al., 1976). It appears to be difficult, however, to give up the idea that categories, especially natural kind categories, have some core essence essential for all exemplars. Recently, Medin and his colleagues (Medin, 1989; Medin and Ortony, 1989) have considered the tendency to endow categories with essences as an interesting psychological phenomenon (also see Malt, 1989).

> People act as if things (e.g., objects) have essences or underlying natures that make them the thing they are. Furthermore, the essence constrains or generates properties that may vary in their centrality. One of the things that theories do is to embody or provide causal linkages from deeper properties to more superficial or surface properties. (Medin, 1989: 1476)

According to Medin, psychological essentialism may play an important role in how we think about many kinds of categories, including artifacts (like chairs and tables) as well as natural kinds. However, our intuition is different. We think that a belief in an underlying essence necessary to category membership would be most likely when it is possible to speculate that this essence is related to something like substance, genetic code, innate potential, or molecular structure. Thus, as Gelman and Coley suggest, essentialism would be a particularly important characteristic of natural kinds. We think essentialism would play a less important role for artifact categories because it is difficult to imagine what the essence of an artifact category might be like.[1] There is something much less compelling about the possibility of an essence for wastebaskets (one of the examples used by Medin) than for birds or gold. Our view is that this difference is due, in part, to the fact that natural kinds are associated with particular substances (for example, gold is assumed to have a particular atomic structure), whereas the substances of artifacts are often quite variable (for example, a wastebasket can be made of wood, metal, plastic, etc.) (Gelman, 1988). It should be pointed out, however, that Medin's claim is not that objects have essences, just that people think they do. What we are further suggesting is that people's assumption of essentialism would be most likely to affect their thinking about a category when their theoretical knowledge suggests possibilities, even vague ones, for what the essence might be like.

According to Medin and Ortony (1989), psychological essentialism also includes the idea that deep essential properties may often be related to more superficial perceptual characteristics. Thus, perceptual characteristics can often provide a useful heuristic for identifying objects in a given category. As Medin and Ortony point out, appearances are usually not misleading. One might assume there are reasons why a dog looks the way it does, linked to its essential identity as a dog. If an object looks a lot like a dog, it will probably turn out to be a dog. According to Medin and Ortony (1989), people believe perceptual appearances are specified by the deep underlying criteria for inclusion in the category. The dog-like appearance may be causally related to the essence that is crucial for category membership. Our acceptance of anomalous members, however, indicates that the noncritical nature of perceptual attributes is recognized. In the case of artifacts, perceptual appearances are related to the function of the artifact (for example, a chair has a particular sort of shape because it was designed for human bodies) rather than to an underlying genetic code. If a coffee pot is altered to have the appearance and function of a bird-feeder, it becomes a birdfeeder. Compare this with the case of a skunk surgically altered to have the appearance of a raccoon. Keil (1989) found that by nine years of age, children report that the coffee pot can be altered to become a birdfeeder, but a skunk cannot be transformed into a raccoon, even with a dramatic surgical change in appearance.

One implication of psychological essentialism is that there is a single correct way to identify an object, with this identity persisting over time (Markman, 1989). It does not make sense to talk about an object having more than one essence or changing its essence. This idea is also consistent with Lakoff's (1987) discussion of taxonomic arguments among biologists. According to Lakoff's analysis, the implicit belief seems to be that 'taxonomies, after all, divide things into kinds, and it is taken for granted that there is only one correct division of the natural world into natural kinds' (1987: 119; see also Dawkins, 1986). One can think of essence as part of the objective physical world waiting to be discovered.

However, as Medin (1989) has pointed out, arguments have been made suggesting that objects require as many essences as there are possible descriptions. Medin gives the example of an object being described as a piece of rock, a paperweight and an ashtray, and therefore requiring at least three essences. We would argue that the essence of an object pertains to its natural kind identity (for example, rock), not to its artifact identities (that is, paperweight or ashtray); however, ruling out essences for artifacts does not solve the problem of multiple essences. Natural kind objects can be described at several levels of abstraction (kangaroo, marsupial, mammal, animal) and thus could be said to have a number of potential essences (but see Gelman and Coley, 1991, for a discussion of natural kinds as basic level categories). Once again, however, it is important to note that Medin's claim (and ours) is that people *think* objects have essences, not that this is an epistemologically sound position.

Despite the fact that there may be a number of possible essences for an object depending upon how the object is currently being categorized, the idea of essence suggests that people may tend to treat the current categorization of the object as reflecting its one true identity. This hypothesis has very important implications for social categorization. To be consistent with research investigating a closely related idea in the area of children's word learning strategies, we call this hypothesis the assumption of mutual exclusivity (Markman, 1987, 1989; Markman and Wachtel, 1988). According to mutual exclusivity, people may think of objects as belonging to non-overlapping categories. Markman suggests that natural kinds are assumed to be mutually exclusive because of their rich inductive potential.

> People may further constrain natural kind and other richly structured categories, viewing them as mutually exclusive or unique. This derives both from the amount of information and the special status of the information conveyed by natural kinds. If so many properties are implied by a given natural kind category, it is unlikely that an object could qualify for membership in two unrelated natural kinds. (1989: 115)

We would add that the case for mutual exclusivity is considerably strengthened by a belief in an essence fundamental to category membership.

In summary, we do not claim an essence can be specified or even that essences actually exist, but we do assert that a belief in essence exists. People's reliance on experts for the identification of natural kinds (the linguistic division of labor) suggests a belief in essentialism is not disturbed by an inability to specify the exact nature of an essence. In fact, a belief in essentialism could remain intact even if no expert was able to describe the essence of a particular category, because the possibility exists that there could be advances in science relevant to its discovery. In contrast, the possibility that scientific investigation might reveal new information about the essence of an everyday artifact category such as *chair* or *toaster* seems unlikely or even anomalous.

It is interesting to note that Allport commented on the issue of essentialism more than 30 years ago. When describing the consequences of 'the principle of least effort' in categorization, he argued:

> that a *belief in essence* develops. There is an inherent 'Jewishness' in every Jew. The 'soul of the Oriental,' 'Negro blood,' . . . 'the passionate Latin' – all represent a belief in essence. A mysterious mana (for good or ill) resides in a group, all of its members partaking thereof. (Allport, 1954: 173–174)

We agree there is something almost mystical about psychological essentialism, given that our belief in essences persists in the face of very little clear understanding. Perhaps part of our belief is that essences may be ultimately unknowable, like a spirit or soul. The relevant point for our discussion, however, is that although the essence of a natural kind category is only vaguely understood, people may not be deterred from assuming it exists and this belief has important psychological consequences.

Are Social Categories Like Natural Kinds?

How can we best conceive of the nature of social categories? Are they more like natural kind or human artifact categories? It may be instructive to consider the social categories occupied by the authors of this paper. One is female, the other male; both are North American, but one is a citizen of Canada and the other a citizen of the United States; one is a distant descendant of ancestors who emigrated from Britain and the other is a first-generation American, with parents born in Eastern Europe; both are psychologists, but one is a developmental and the other a social psychologist; neither is religious, but one was raised a Baptist, and the other a Jew; one is a member of the American Horse Show Association, the other a member of the American Civil Liberties Union; one is a quilter, the other a woodworker; one prefers chocolate and the other vanilla ice cream. Some of these categories are a result of personal choice, others are imposed by circumstance; at least one of these distinctions has a biological component, most others probably have none; some of these categories require effort, achievement and recognition for membership, others require little or no effort. Some are matters of self-definition; some are of considerable personal and social importance, others are trivial.

At first glance, it would appear that some of these categories appear more like natural kinds and others more like human artifacts. If so, which characteristics do we use to make this judgment? We believe there are at least two dimensions along which social categories vary that are most relevant to the perception of natural kind structures: *inductive potential*, and *unalterability*.

Inductive Potential As we have described, membership in a natural kind category provides a wealth of information about category members. With respect to social categories, some categories are *assumed* to be rich in meaning, others impoverished in their associations. To the extent that category membership is assumed to predict diverse and important knowledge of the person's other attributes, it is central in character; to the extent that category membership is assumed to predict little or nothing else of interest about the person, it is peripheral in character. Thus, gender and race are often treated as central categories, preference for chocolate versus vanilla as peripheral, and membership in the AHSA or ACLU or status as a Baptist or Methodist somewhere in between. As we will argue, however, the level of inductive potential for social categories is not a fixed attribute, and shows enormous variability across circumstances.

Unalterability It is implicit in the basic character of natural kind structures, and reinforced by psychological essentialism, that category status cannot be altered. A fish cannot become a bird, and vice versa. In the domain of social categories, alterability refers to the ease with which an individual or group can acquire or shed a category label. Gender, race, and caste would be at the extreme unalterable end of this continuum, with purely voluntary associations (such as membership in the AHSA or ACLU) at the other extreme, and with achievement related categories (professional status) somewhere in between. However, as we will argue shortly, the alterability or unalterability of many social categories refers to our perception of category attributes, rather than to some invariant and objective reality.

Categories most likely to be thought of as having characteristics similar to natural kinds would be those that are high in both unalterability and perceived inductive potential. We argue that social categories that meet these requirements are still quite unlike natural kinds. However, we will claim that people have a strong tendency to view social categories as natural kinds. Even social categories that are alterable and low in inductive potential may, under certain circumstances, be incorrectly assumed to have the characteristics of natural kinds.

Before proceeding with this argument, it is important to clarify an issue regarding our level of analysis. We strongly suspect that the proclivity to view many social categories as natural kinds is due to the fact that in addition to their social categories, humans are 'natural kind' objects (see Lingle et al., 1984). Since we are biological entities, could it not be argued that social categories such as gender and, perhaps to a lesser extent, race are biological, and therefore unalterable (as well as possessing rich inductive potential)? In our view, the issue is not whether men and women have different physical morphologies, but whether the biological differences between groups are important predictors of behaviour by virtue of the underlying biology rather than by virtue of our social assumptions of what *ought* to go with the observed physical differences. We do not wish to argue that biological factors are unimportant in influencing behaviour. It is conceivable to us that even preferences for vanilla or chocolate ice cream may be related, albeit in a complex manner, to underlying biological/temperamental differences between individuals. However, the important issue is the extent to which it is appropriate to think of social categories as having the characteristics of natural kinds; that is, as having an unalterable 'essence' with rich inductive potential.

We cannot answer this question, of course, without full knowledge of the relationship between our biological nature and its direct effects on behavior. That knowledge does not exist at present, and it is not clear whether we will ever be able to specify the precise contributions of biology and culture when accounting for *group* differences. What we can argue, however, is that social categories with the appearance of unalterability and rich inductive potential may not necessarily be unalterable and central. More accurately, although unalterability and inductive potential are thought of as fixed qualities for natural kind categories, we have strong reason to believe that social categories thought of as unalterable and central can, under different circumstances, be thought of as alterable and peripheral. We wish to make this argument more fully by discussing the dynamic nature of social categories.

The Inductive Potential of Social Categories

A major difference between natural kinds and social categories concerns inductive potential. As we have mentioned, natural kinds have rich inductive potential because they reflect deep underlying regularities in nature that are stable over time. The perceived inductive potential of social categories, however, reflects social values and beliefs and is variable across cultures and over time.

This point is evident when we examine naturally occurring, protracted conflicts, such as those in the Middle East, South Africa, or Northern Ireland. In analyzing any one of these conflicts, there is a tendency to view the particular dimensions underlying a conflict as *inherently* conflict-inducing. For example, in those conflicts where differences in religion are paramount, there is an assumption that those differences inexorably lead to conflict. This bias ignores the fact that the same differences in other contexts may be considered insubstantial, and that meaningless differences in one's own society may be associated with profound conflict elsewhere. This problem has been put into perspective by Jonathan Swift and Sigmund Freud.

In 1735, Jonathan Swift published *Gulliver's Travels*, in which he introduced us to two warring nations, the Little-Endians and the Big-Endians, who shared a long history of violent conflict (Swift, 1735/1977). The Little-Endians preferred to break their eggs on the small end, and the big-Endians preferred to break their eggs on the large end. By satirizing the centuries of war between the Protestants and the Catholics as tantamount to the difference between breaking one's egg on the large or small side, Swift provided us with a powerful insight. One cannot predict the magnitude of social meaning, or the magnitude of conflict, from the inherent magnitude of category differences. Differences of trivial magnitude can, under proper circumstances generate profound conflict, and the reverse prediction is also plausible: differences of considerable magnitude may generate little or no conflict.[2]

In 1922, Freud published *Group Psychology and the Analysis of the Ego*, and introduced us to the concept of the narcissism of small differences:

> Every time two families become connected by a marriage, each of them think itself superior to or of better birth than the other. Of two neighboring towns each is the other's most jealous rival; every little canton looks down upon the others with contempt. Closely related races keep one another at arm's length; the South German cannot endure the North German, the Englishman casts every kind of aspersion upon the Scot, the Spaniard despises the Portuguese. We are no longer astonished that greater differences should lead to an almost insuperable

repugnance. Such as the Gallic people feel for the German, the Aryan for the Semite, and the white races for the colored. (1922/1959: 33).

The fact that trivial differences can become profound is supported by Sherif's classic work on the Robber's Cave experiments (Sherif et al., 1961/1988). White middle-class boys were virtually randomly divided into two groups of campers at a state park, and named themselves on the basis of their location in the park ('Rattlers' and 'Eagles'). Relations between groups were defined at first as competitive, then cooperative, with profound correspondent effects on intergroup attitudes. This research is in the spirit of Swift and Freud as it argues that one does not need a long history of value conflict or belief conflict to establish hostility between two groups. Nor does one need 'real' differences, such as cultural, language, or physical differences, to establish conflict. In Sherif's view, what one needs is self-defined groups (however arbitrary) and competition over limited resources. What makes Sherif's view somewhat complex is that the competition need not be over life and limb, but can be competition in setting up tents, cleaning one's cabin, or on the baseball field.

The view that competition is a necessary condition for bias against the outgroup has been challenged by the now classic work of Tajfel, Rabbie, and others, using the minimal group paradigm (Billig and Tajfel, 1973; Rabbie and Horwitz, 1969; Tajfel, 1970). With this paradigm, subjects are labeled along a putatively arbitrary dimension (under- versus over-estimator of dots, a preferrer of Klee versus Kandinsky, or a 'blue' versus 'green' subject). The effect of this labeling is to induce a more favorable view of own versus other group, and a more favorable allocation of resources to one's own group. Competition is not a necessary condition for this bias against the outgroup, but mere categorization is. What makes competition so powerful, we suspect, is that it continually activates the use of us versus them distinction, given the zero sum nature of the interaction.

The observations of Swift, Freud, Tajfel, and Rabbie all point to the fact that physical, religious, cultural, or language differences are not necessary conditions for ingroup bias. Virtually any basis for separating individuals into mutually exclusive groups can produce the same effects. Two arguments require emphasis, however. One is that such peripheral distinctions as preferring chocolate to vanilla ice cream can become the basis for profound psychological distinctions *under the appropriate circumstances*. Such superficial differences could then potentially be taken as diagnostic of critical underlying differences. Although it is difficult to imagine people going to war over preferences in ice cream, a change in perspective to that of Swift or Freud might help us to understand why the Khmer Rouge, a rurally based Cambodian political group, slaughtered so many urban Cambodians, or why centuries of war characterized the relations between Protestants and Catholics.[3]

The Alterability of Social Categories

Although for natural kind structures, category membership is by definition unalterable (a fish cannot become a bird), the same is not true for many social categories. We nonetheless tend to perceive social categories as unalterable, and construct biological or quasi-biological concepts to convey that inexorability. To illustrate this point it is instructive to consider different meanings associated with the category *Jew*.

In the Early Christian era, Jews were considered to be a group who, along with many others, had not yet chosen Christianity (Schweitzer, 1971). Jews who embraced Christianity were treated as any other Christian, with conversion having approximately the same status as one moving from Methodism to Presbyterianism today. Conversion was a voluntary act, with minimum effort, allowing one to shed the category *Jew* and adopt the category *Christian*. However, in Spain, by the fourteenth and fifteenth centuries, a Jew who converted to Catholicism was treated as a Catholic who was still a Jew. This group was given the name of Marranos (swine, in Spanish), and became a target of the Spanish Inquisition. Conversion from Jew to Catholic no longer meant shedding one's status as a Jew. By the 1930s, in Nazi Germany, Jewishness was then considered fully a racial attribute, and defined in the Nuremburg Laws by heredity (existence of at least one Jewish grandparent).[4]

This historical excursion shows that the meaning of a social category is not invariant. In the history of the Jews, the meaning of the category was clearly on the extreme alterable end of the continuum in the Early Christian era, but moved to the unalterable end in the Nazi period.[5]

To summarize our argument thus far, although we cannot specify with certainty that social categories have little or no biological component (and therefore no 'natural kind' basis), we suspect that the direct contribution of biological factors to *group* differences in behaviour is minimal. What we can say with confidence is that social categories that appear to have strong natural kind qualities, that is, that appear unalterable and rich in inductive potential, may be the same categories that under different circumstances appear highly alterable and low in inductive potential. The literature on social conflict, and particularly the minimal group paradigm, suggests that distinctions that are highly central in one circumstance are peripheral in another, and that arbitrary, peripheral distinctions can become central under appropriate conditions. In different historical epochs, the category *Jew* has been viewed variably as alterable by volition or genetically unalterable.

Implications of Treating Social Categories as Natural Kinds

We have discussed reasons for rejecting a natural kind model for social categories, yet we suspect that social categories are often treated as if they, like natural kinds, have rich inductive potential and a fundamental essence. There are a number of interesting predictions that follow from the hypothesis that social categories are implicitly represented as having characteristics similar to natural kinds.

Surface Attributes and Underlying Attributes

As discussed earlier, it is clear that although differences in physical appearance are only surface characteristics, in the domain of natural kinds the surface characteristics are assumed to correlate with deep underlying essential features. That is, phenotypic attributes are taken as evidence for genotypic attributes. With reference to social categories, this implies that category differences in surface attributes will be assumed to reflect category differences in more basic attributes. Thus differences in social roles or physical appearance may be seen as cues to basic differences in underlying structure.

A recent study by Hoffman and Hurst (1990) provides evidence on these points.[6] Subjects were provided with information about 15 individuals from each of two hypothetical groups on another planet: the Orinthians and the Ackmians. Some members of one group functioned primarily in the role of child rearing, while some members of the other group functioned primarily as city workers. Subjects were told there were no sex differences in these categories. The information given about each individual consisted of three trait attributes, one consistent with their occupational role (that is, communal/feminine attributes for the child rearing group, and agentic/masculine attributes for the city workers), another inconsistent with their role, and a third trait irrelevant to their role. After being presented with information about the 15 individuals in each group, subjects made judgments about the traits characteristic of Orinthians and Ackmians in general, where the traits consisted of some new and some old agentic and communal attributes.

One of the manipulations in the study was whether the difference between the two groups was perceived as biological or cultural. In the biological condition the groups were described as different species, and in the non-biological condition as distinctive sub-cultures. Moreover, the stimulus materials, which included a head and shoulder line drawing for each stimulus person, depicted 'family resemblances' in the biological condition, and clothing differences in the non-biological condition.

The study revealed two findings relevant to our current argument. First, subjects inferred group differences in personality traits corresponding to the social roles of some of the group members. The child rearing group, for example, was judged as more compassionate and less individualistic, while the reverse was true for the city workers. Note that the information associated with each of the 30 exemplars showed no group differences on these dimensions. Second, this correspondent inference, between role (a surface attribute) and personality trait (a deep attribute) was stronger in the biological condition than in the non-biological condition, consistent with the premises outlined above.

The idea that deep, underlying attributes are inferred from appearance suggests that the presence of physical differences may have a somewhat special status in intergroup attitudes. Our argument is not based, of course, on the premise that gender, race, or caste categories reflect biologically based differences in behavior, nor on the argument that people have an aversion to physical attributes different from their own category, but that the imposition of natural kind structure onto our thinking about social categories gives disproportionate strength to category differences correlated with physical appearance. This prediction seems consistent with what we know about the ubiquity and power of stereotypes based on race and gender.

In addition, there is considerable evidence suggesting that people have a predilection to infer correspondent behavioral attributes from physical attributes. Strong inferences are made on the basis of physical attractiveness (Berscheid and Walster, 1978), personality traits are thought to vary as a function of body type (for example, Sheldon and Stevens, 1942; Sheldon et al., 1969), and subjects infer youthful personality attributes on the basis of facial attributes constructed to be youthful in appearance (McArthur and Apatow, 1983–84; McArthur and Berry, 1987). While it is tempting to argue that there is no basis 'in reality' for these inferences, there are behavioral differences as a function of physical attractiveness (Berscheid and Walster, 1978) and some evidence for differences as a function of body type (Walker, 1962). The problem with these findings, of course, is that we do not know whether the behavioral differences are a direct function of biology, whether the differences result from cultural expectations about morphology (for example, Lerner, 1969), or both. For this reason, experimental studies, such as those conducted by Hoffman and Hurst, are valuable because we can compare subjects' inferences with reality – at least with the reality present in the experimental materials.

Although we expect inferences about social categories based on physical differences to be particularly potent, we do not wish to overemphasize this point, because there are a number of cases in which a lack of physical identifiability is rectified by creating a visible stigma for the despised group. Jews in the Middle Ages were required to wear special hats, later yellow arm bands during the Nazi period, and the Burakamin of Japan have worn leather patches to facilitate identification (De Vos and Wetherall, 1983). As in the natural kinds model, physical appearance may be diagnostic of an underlying essence, but it is not considered to be the essence itself.

Essentialism and the Assumption of Mutual Exclusivity
As discussed earlier, one of the strong implicit beliefs regarding natural kinds is the assumption that category members possess some essential quality differentiating them from members of other categories. One clear implication of this assumption of psychological essentialism is that since an object has only a single essence, it cannot be a member of more than one category. Given that social categories may in reality be far more overlapping than natural kinds (Lingle et al., 1984) as evidenced by the earlier description of our own multiple memberships in social categories, it is a strong claim to say that social categories are treated like natural kinds in this way. However, the finding that people tend to simplify and exaggerate inter-category differences (Dawes, 1964, 1966; Taylor, 1981; Wilder, 1986), and to represent members of multiple social categories in terms of a single category (Rothbart and John, 1985; Saltz and Medow, 1971) can be interpreted as reflecting the assumption of mutual exclusivity.

Simplification and Exaggeration of Inter-category Differences
The idea that people have difficulty in representing individuals as members of more than one category implies a simplification of the relations among categories in a way that

accentuates differences between category boundaries and minimizes differences among the members within a category. There is a fairly long history of research on this problem, using non-social as well as social stimuli.

Using social categories, Dawes (1964, 1966) had subjects read a complex story about a 'Circle Island' society, consisting of *ranchers* and *farmers*, some of whom were in favor of building a canal (*pro-canal*), with others opposed (*anti-canal*), with the final decision made by elected senators. In this complex story, the set relations among categories varied, with some being nested (for example, 'all As are Bs'), some disjunctive ('no As are Bs'), but with most overlapping ('some As are Bs'). Dawes was interested in the kinds of memory errors subjects would make, particularly with respect to overlapping categories. In general, it was rare for a nested or disjunctive relation to be remembered as overlapping, but common for an overlapping relation to be remembered as either nested or disjunctive. The psychological transformation of the overlapping relation to disjunction is consistent with our argument, but the movement from overlap to nested relation may be inconsistent. The ambiguity is whether the nested relation is represented as truly nested, in which the subject perceives two distinct categories, with one subsumed under the other, or whether the subject perceives an identity relation, in which A and B are somehow represented as a single category.

Evidence for the minimization of within-category differences has been provided by Wilder (1978) and Taylor et al. (1978). Wilder videotaped four individuals who were described as an unrelated aggregate, or as a 'group.' Subjects, hearing one of the stimulus person's opinions, were asked to predict those of the other three individuals. There was greater assumed similarity in the group than in the aggregate condition. Taylor et al. found evidence of greater within-category than between-category confusions in an innovative experiment designed to examine an implication of social perception based on gender and racial categories. Subjects listened to an audiotape of eight speakers (either four males and four females, or four whites and four blacks), with each speaker associated with specific comments. Later, when observers were asked whether a given comment was associated with a speaker from a particular gender or racial category, subjects were more likely to confuse speakers within the same gender or racial category than to confuse speakers across categories. Despite the innovative procedures, there is a potential problem in interpreting the results because categorization is confounded with real differences in similarity. That is, male voices are actually more similar to one another, for example, than they are to female voices.

Taken together, these studies demonstrate a general tendency to enhance category boundaries. However, this effect has been demonstrated with non-social groupings of lines and numbers (Krueger and Rothbart, 1990; Krueger et al., 1989; Tajfel and Wilkes, 1963) as well as with social categories like race and gender. Thus, our hypothesis that boundary enhancement is related to a belief in essentialism is clearly not the whole story (for example, see Freyd, 1983). However, if a belief in essence contributes to boundary enhancement, this effect should be particularly pronounced when meaningful social categories are used as stimuli.

Mutual Exclusivity and Overlapping Social Categories: Do Some Labels 'prevent alternative . . . or even cross-classification?' The enhancement of category boundaries can be thought of as a weak or indirect implication of the mutual exclusivity assumption, in that subjects appear to have a preference for information that reduces category overlap. The stronger, more direct prediction of mutual exclusivity is that we have difficulty in seeing a single object or person as simultaneously belonging to more than one category. Powerful social categories – categories that are most similar to natural kinds in their unalterability and rich inductive potential – may dominate the psychological field in a way that inhibits multiple classification. Set relations that are in reality conjunctive may nonetheless be construed as disjunctive, just as the Nazi's definition of a Jew precluded membership in the category *German*. One of the clearest recent examples of this process occurred during a period in which terrorist activity was directed against French Jews, in opposition to Israeli policy. In 1980, a synagogue on the Rue Copernic in Paris was bombed, and the Prime Minister of France, Raymond Barre, commented that 'the criminal attack killed Jews as well as innocent Frenchmen.' The implication that Jews were considered to be in a category other than innocents or other than French did not escape the attention of his audience.

Note that mutual exclusivity has a weak and a strong form. In the weak form, it may be difficult to view a female as both a woman and a rock climber (cf. Rothbart and Lewis, 1988) because our sexist assumption is that the two categories are negatively correlated, or incompatible. The strong form predicts the same implicit exclusivity would occur even when the categories were independent – for example, when race and gender were combined. As an example, if we were exposed to information about a black woman, would it be the case that her attributes would become associated with both of her membership categories (that is, blacks and women), or would they be associated predominantly with one or the other category?

There is some developmental work on 'concept conservation' which suggests that children, at least, demonstrate the strong form of mutual exclusivity with respect to social categories. Saltz and his colleagues have shown in several studies that children tend to deny that a person can simultaneously belong to two separate categories such as *father* and *doctor* or *mother* and *teacher*. Sigel, Saltz, and Roskind (1967) found that 63% of five-year-old children reported that a father who studied until he became a doctor would no longer be a father. Children not only refuse to use the second label, they also deny that the stimulus person possesses the attributes of the original category (Saltz and Medow, 1971). For example, children reported that a good baseball player who became a liar should no longer be called a baseball player and, in fact, would no longer be able to play baseball well. When the valence of the two categories differs (for example, doctor and thief), even eight-year-olds tend to claim that a single person cannot belong to both categories (Saltz and Hamilton, 1968). Similarly, the conventionality of the co-occurrence of the two categories (sister–librarian versus sister–mechanic) affects children's judgments (Jordan, 1980).

It is worth noting that some recent attempts to understand how we isolate category members who are 'poor fits' to the category from modifying category attributes relies implicitly on the idea that exemplars associated with one category are unlikely to be associated with alternative categories (for example, Rothbart and John, 1985; Rothbart and Lewis, 1988). That is, an observer who assumes that women are unscientific will, when meeting Dr Jane Smith *nuclear physicist*, be likely to think of her as a *scientist* rather than a *woman*, even though Dr Smith is of course both a *scientist* and a *woman*.

Psychological Assessment, Expert Judgment, and Illusory Meaning

A prominent psychoanalyst, teaching a course on psychotherapy, discussed the dilemma of satisfying the bureaucratic needs of medical insurance companies without compromising the therapeutic process. This analyst was loath to classify his clients into psychiatric categories, yet insurance companies required a recognized diagnosis before authorizing payment. The analyst solved the problem by checking the category 'other' at the bottom of the long list of traditional categories, supplying the diagnosis: 'Psychoneurotic, Mixed Type.' To the analyst, this label was about as meaningful as Macbeth's phrase, 'man, of woman born,' but to the insurance company and, perhaps most observers, the category was meaningful.

One could argue that the imputed meaning was appropriate given the expert knowledge of the analyst. However, we would interpret this claim as evidence that psychiatric categories function like natural kinds, at least with respect to the role of expert knowledge. As mentioned in our previous discussion of essentialism and the 'linguistic division of labor', reliance on expert judgment may be more characteristic of natural kind than human artifacts. We would pay little attention if an expert in home furnishings informed us that the 'bean bag' is in reality a pillow and not a chair. At most, we might revise our idea about the range of variation allowed in the category of *pillow*, but we would probably continue to think of bean bags in the same way.

Our view is that if experts are deemed necessary in determining definitive category membership, the adjustment of categorization on the advice of experts would also be possible. In the domain of social categories, one might consider the implications of experts deciding that one's child was emotionally disturbed rather than mentally retarded. We suggest that the adjustment in label would be accepted and have an important impact on the way parents thought about their child. Clinical categories are a good example of social categories that are assumed (in our view, incorrectly) to have the underlying structure of natural kinds. A belief that an essence underlies one's membership in categories such as 'mentally retarded' exists despite the lip service given to the heterogeneity of symptoms, clinical histories, etiology, and prognosis for individuals given such a label. Such heterogeneity may be inconsistent with the idea of essence, but the belief in essence persists.

As stated at the outset of this chapter, it is often difficult to assess whether we give too much weight to a label, as in the clinical example above, because we have neither full knowledge of category attributes nor exemplar attributes. Rothbart and Davis-Stitt (in preparation) attempted to circumvent this problem by giving subjects two types of information about a number of stimulus persons. The first piece of information was their 'score' on a continuous scale that reflected their predicted ability to perform at a task; this information corresponds to what may be regarded as 'the underlying reality.' The second piece of information was the verbal label associated with the different regions of the continuous scale, the boundaries of which were described as arbitrary. Would the perceived similarity between stimulus persons be influenced by category membership, even though the meaningful information about each stimulus person is the continuous information, rather than the arbitrarily placed category boundaries?

Subjects were provided with information about seven women, who were all applicants for a particular class of job. Brief descriptions were given of each woman, along with a single composite score ranging from 500 to 1000, reflecting their overall qualifications. Subjects were informed that the scale could be divided into three types of candidates: *marginal, acceptable,* and *ideal,* but the placement of the category boundaries was determined by the number of jobs available and the number of applicants for these jobs – both factors that fluctuated greatly from year to year. Subjects in different conditions were given different boundary positions, allowing a comparison of the perceived similarity between a given pair of applicants when those applicants were on the same or opposite sides of the boundary. In fact, pairs were perceived as more similar when on the same side of an arbitrarily placed boundary. In this experiment the continuous numerical score represented the underlying reality, and the category boundaries reflected irrelevant factors which, nonetheless, influenced perception.

Summary

Two general ideas from Gordon Allport provided the initial motivation for this chapter. The first was that category labels have disproportionate power and discourage multiple classifications, and the second was that some social categories appear to have a mysterious essence that applies to all members. We have tried to argue that these two observations are related. The idea of essentialism, while counter to contemporary thinking about category structure, persists in people's perceptions of both natural kinds and social categories. We have argued that the characteristics of natural kinds have been implicitly used as a model for thinking about social categories, which seems to us particularly inappropriate given the degree to which a given social category can vary in its perceived alterability and centrality.

A number of interesting predictions follow from the essentialist principle, as applied to social categories. First, it suggests that stereotypes based on physical differences may be particularly pernicious, given the strong inferences that are based on surface similarities. Second, it suggests an implicit exclusivity among even independent categories, such that membership in one category appears to inhibit membership in another. Third, it helps us to understand why even arbitrary labels, based on social convention, may be imbued with deep meaning. Given the conceptual difficulty in meaningfully distinguishing among types of categories, and the empirical difficulty of separating the effects of the label from the 'thing-in-itself,' it has been challenging to try to advance beyond Allport's original insights. We hope the ideas developed in this chapter make some progress toward that goal.

Notes

Authorship is alphabetical. This research was supported by National Institutes of Mental Health Grant MH40662 to the first author. We are grateful to Doug Hintzman, Oliver John, Greg Murphy, and Mary Rothbart for their extensive, thoughtful critiques on an earlier draft of this manuscript. We also wish to thank Deborah Frisch, Tom Givon, Lew Goldberg, Shinobu Kitayama, Robert Mauro, Peter Schönbach, and Gün Semin for their helpful suggestions.

1. The function of an artifact might be hypothesized as constituting an essence; however, Malt and Johnson (1989) have shown that an artifact's function is viewed as neither necessary nor sufficient for category membership. We would add that when an artifact is broken, it retains category membership even though it no longer serves the function associated with the artifact category. For example, a car that has thrown a rod is still a car, although it cannot be driven.

2. As we shall argue soon, the reverse prediction may actually be less plausible; that is, it may be easier for small apparent differences to generate disproportionally large effects, than for large apparent differences to be inconsequential (for reasons related to the essentialist assumption that surface differences reflect deep differences).

3. A discussion of how seemingly meaningless social divisions, such as under- or over-estimating, can grow into social distinctions of fundamental importance, is beyond the scope of this chapter. To return to Swift's parody of Catholic–Protestant differences as the equivalent of the large and small end of the egg, nations could be founded on these differences, power differences could evolve between nations, wars could be fought between nations, inequality could result from the wars, and so on. However arbitrary the initial difference, that difference becomes correlated with phenomena of considerable importance to individual and collective social behavior. The developmental sequence of intergroup conflict shows rather clearly that initially arbitrary differences can, with time, crystallize into social distinctions that are anything but trivial.

4. Given the central importance to the National Socialists for distinguishing between Germans and Jews, a great deal of thought was given to the formal definition of a Jew. Although a Jew was originally defined as anyone with at least one Jewish grandparent, the consequences of this definition for a society with substantial intermarriage was to include an unacceptably large number of people who, on the surface, appeared quite German. The definition was altered to create a number of different categories. A person with two Jewish parents was clearly a Jew, but a person with one non-Jewish parent could be a Jew or German, depending on the *religious* practices of the person (Hilberg, 1961). There are two points of interest. First, there was some objection to this definition, with the argument that 'Among half-Jews, the Jewish genes are notoriously dominant' (Hilberg, 1961: 46). Second, whereas the hereditary/racial definition was clearly critical, ambiguous heredity was

resolved by a voluntary criterion, religious practice. This decision created problems for how to treat those Germans without Jewish ancestors, who embraced Judaism as a religion. The problem with this morbid exercise, of course, was that the concept of Jew was treated as a biological category, which does not really permit entry and exit by volition.

5. The current meaning of the category *Jew* is probably more ethnic than anything else. It is interesting to reflect on the ambiguity of the concept of ethnicity, which seems to have both a voluntary as well as hereditary component. That is, it would be somewhere in the middle of the alterability continuum.

6. In fairness to the authors, our preferred interpretations are not necessarily their preferred interpretations.

References

Allport, G. W. (1954) *The Nature of Prejudice*. Cambridge, MA: Addison-Wesley.

Berscheid, E. and Walster, E. H. (1978) *Interpersonal Attraction*. Reading, MA: Addison-Wesley.

Billig, M. and Tajfel, H. (1973) Social categorization and similarity in intergroup behavior. *European Journal of Social Psychology*, 3: 27–52.

Campbell, D. T. (1956) Enhancement of contrast as composite habit. *Journal of Abnormal Psychology and Social Psychology*, 53: 350–355.

Carey, S. (1985) *Conceptual Change in Childhood*. Cambridge, MA: MIT Press.

Dawes, R. M. (1964) Cognitive distortion. *Psychological Reports*, 14: 443–459.

Dawes, R. M. (1966) Memory and distortion of meaningful written material. *British Journal of Psychology*, 57: 77–86.

Dawkins, R. (1986) *The Blind Watchmaker*. Essex, England: Longman Scientific and Technical.

De Vos, G. A. and Wetherall, W. D. (1983) Japan's minorities: Burakumin, Koreans, Aina and Okinawans. London: Minority Rights Group, Report no. 3.

Freud, S. (1922/1959) *Group Psychology and the Analysis of the Ego*. New York: W. W. Norton & Co.

Freyd, J. J. (1983) Shareability: The social psychology of epistemology. *Cognitive Science*, 7, 191–210.

Gelman, S. A. (1988) The development of induction within natural kind and artifact categories. *Cognitive Psychology*, 20: 65–95.

Gelman, S. A. and Coley (1991) Language and categorization: The acquisition of natural kind terms. In S. A. Gelman and J. P. Byrnes (eds), *Perspectives on Language and Cognition: Interrelations in Development*. Cambridge: Cambridge University Press.

Gelman, S. A. and Markman, E. M. (1986) Categories and induction in young children. *Cognition*, 23: 183–208.

Gelman, S. A. and O'Reilly, A. W. (1988) Children's inductive inferences within superordinate categories: The role of language and category structure. *Child Development*, 59: 876–887.

Hilberg, R. (1961) *The Destruction of the European Jews*. New York: Harper & Row.

Hoffman, C. and Hurst, N. (1990) Gender stereotypes: Perception or rationalization? *Journal of Personality and Social Psychology*, 58: 197–208.

Jordan, V. B. (1980) Conserving kinship concepts: A developmental study in social cognition. *Child Development*, 51: 146–155.

Keil, F. C. (1989) *Concepts, Kinds, and Cognitive Development*. Cambridge, MA: MIT Press.

Kripke, S. (1972) Naming and necessity. In D. Davidson and G. Harman (eds), *Semantics of Natural Language*. Dordrecht, Holland: Reidel.

Krueger, J. and Rothbart, M. (1990) Contrast and accentuation in category learning. *Journal of Personality and Social Psychology*, 59: 651–663.

Krueger, J., Rothbart, M. and Sriram, N. (1989) Category learning and change: Differences in sensitivity to information that enhances or reduces intercategory distinctions. *Journal of Personality and Social Psychology*, 56: 866–875.

Lakoff, G. (1987) *Women, Fire and Dangerous Things: What Categories Reveal about the Mind*. Chicago: University of Chicago Press.

Lerner, R. M. (1969) The development of stereotyped expectancies of body build–behaviour relations. *Child Development*, 40: 137–141.

Lingle, J. H., Alton, M. W. and Medin, D. L. (1984) Of cabbages and kings: Assessing the intendibility of natural object concept models to social things. In R. W. Wyer and T. K. Srull (eds), *Handbook of Social Cognition*, vol. 1, pp. 71–117. Hillsdale, NJ: Erlbaum.

McArthur, L. Z. and Apatow, K. (1983–84) Impressions of babyfaced adults. *Social Cognition*, 2: 315–342.

McArthur, L. Z. and Berry, D. S. (1987) Cross-cultural agreement in perceptions of babyfaced adults. *Journal of Cross-Cultural Psychology*, 18: 165–192.

Malt, B. C. (1989) Features and beliefs in the mental representation of categories. *Journal of Memory and Language*, 29: 289–315.

Malt, B. C. and Johnson, E. C. (1989) Does function provide a core for artifact concepts? In the *Proceedings of the Eleventh Annual Conference of the Cognitive Science Society*. Hillsdale, NJ: Erlbaum.

Markman, E. M. (1977) How children constrain the possible meanings of words. In U. Weisser (ed.), *Concepts and Conceptual Development: Ecological and Intellectual Factors in Categorization*. Cambridge: Cambridge University Press.

Markman, E. M. (1987) How children constrain the possible meanings of words. In U. Neisser (ed.) *Concepts and Conceptual Development: Ecological and intellectual factors in categorization*, pp. 255–287. New York: Cambridge University Press.

Markman, E. M. (1989) *Categorization and Naming in Children*. Cambridge, MA: MIT Press.

Markman, E. M. and Wachtel, G. F. (1988) Children's use of mutual exclusivity to constrain the meanings of words. *Cognitive Psychology*, 20: 121–157.

Medin, D. L. (1989) Concepts and conceptual structure. *American Psychologist*, 44: 1469–1481.

Medin, D. and Ortony, A. (1989) Psychological essentialism. In S. Vosnaidou and A. Ortony (eds), *Similarity and Analogical Reasoning*, pp. 179–195. Cambridge: Cambridge University Press.

Murphy, G. L. and Medin, D. L. (1985) The role of theories in conceptual coherence. *Psychological Review*, 92: 289–316.

Putnam, H. (1975) The meaning of meaning. In H. Putnam (ed.), *Mind, Language and Reality*, vol. 2. London: Cambridge University Press.

Putnam, H. (1988) *Representation and Reality*. Cambridge, MA: MIT Press.

Quine, W. V. O. (1977) Natural kinds. In S. P. Schwartz (ed.), *Naming, Necessity, and Natural Kinds*. Ithaca, NY: Cornell University Press.

Rabbie, J. M. and Horwitz, M. (1969) Arousal of ingroup–outgroup bias by a chance win or loss. *Journal of Personality and Social Psychology*, 13(3): 269–277.

Rosch, E. and Mervis, C. B. (1975) Family resemblances: Studies in the internal structure of categories. *Cognitive Psychology*, 7: 573–605.

Rosch, E., Mervis, C. B., Gray, W. D., Johnson, D. M. and Boyes-Braem, P. (1976) Basic objects in natural categories. *Cognitive Psychology*, 8: 382–439.

Rothbart, M. and Davis-Stitt, C. (in preparation) Categories and continua: The effects of arbitrarily placed category boundaries.

Rothbart, M. and John, O. P. (1985) Social categorization and behavioral episodes: A cognitive analysis of the effects of intergroup contact. *Journal of Social Issues*, 41: 81–104.

Rothbart, M. and Lewis, S. (1988) Inferring category attributes from exemplar attributes: Geometric shapes and social categories. *Journal of Personality and Social Psychology*, 55: 861–872.

Saltz, E. and Hamilton, H. (1968) Concept conservation under positively and negatively evaluated transformations. *Journal of Experimental Child Psychology*, 6: 44–51.

Saltz, E. and Medow, M. L. (1971) Concept conservation in children: The dependence of belief systems on semantic representation. *Child Development* 42: 1533–1542.

Schwartz, S. P. (1978) Putnam on artifacts. *Philosophical Review*, 87: 566–574.

Schweitzer, F. M. (1971) *A History of the Jews since the First Century, AD*. New York: Macmillan.

Sheldon, W. H., Lewis, N. D. C. and Tenney, A. (1969) Psychotic patterns and physical constitution. In D. V. Siva Sanker (ed.), *Schizophrenia: Current Concepts and Research*. Hillsdale, NJ: PJD Publications.

Sheldon, W. H. and Stevens, S. S. (1942) *The Varieties of Human Temperament*. New York: Harper & Row.

Sherif, M., Harvey, O. J., White, B. J., Hood, W. R. and Sherif, C. W. (1961/1988) *The Robber's Cave Experiment: Intergroup Conflict and Cooperation*. Middletown, CT: Wesleyan University Press.

Sigel, I. E., Saltz, E. and Roskind, W. (1967) Variables determining concept conservation in children. *Journal of Experimental Psychology*, 74: 471–475.

Swift, J. (1735/1977) *Gulliver's Travels*. New York: Oxford University Press.

Tajfel, H. (1970) Experiments in intergroup discrimination. *Scientific American*, 223: 96–102.

Tajfel, H. and Wilkes, A. L. (1963) Classification and quantitative judgment. *British Journal of Social Psychology*, 54: 101–114.

Taylor, S. E. (1981) A categorization approach to stereotyping. In D. L. Hamilton (ed.), *Cognitive Approaches in Stereotyping and Intergroup Behavior*. Hillsdale, NJ: Erlbaum.

Taylor, S. E., Fiske, S. T., Etcoff, N. L. and Ruderman, A. J. (1978) Categorical and contextual bases of person memory and stereotyping. *Journal of Personality and Social Psychology*, 36: 778–793.

Walker, R. N. (1962) Body build and behavior in young children: I. Body build and nursery school teachers' ratings. *Monographs of the Society for Research in Child Development*, 27 (3, serial no. 84).

Wilder, D. A. (1978) Perceiving persons as a group: Effects on attributions of causality and beliefs. *Social Psychology*, 1: 13–23.

Wilder, D. A. (1986) Social categorization: Implications for creation and reduction of intergroup bias. In *Advances in Experimental Social Psychology*, vol. 19, pp. 291–355. New York: Academic Press.

3

Trait–Behavior Relations in Social Information Processing

Glenn D. Reeder, John B. Pryor and
Bogdan Wojciszke

According to legend, Diogenes held a lantern in hand as he roamed ancient Athens in an unsuccessful search for an honest man. Most likely, Diogenes wished to dramatize the moral decay he perceived in Athens at the time. The cynic in many of us might suggest that the trait of honesty is rare in our own era as well. But if we believe that the *trait* of honesty is rare, are we implying that honest *behavior* is uncommon? The latter belief would seem to fly in the face of everyday reality: People normally tell the truth, movie patrons usually pay at the door, and committee treasurers seldom abscond with the funds. So it is not honest behavior, *per se*, that is in short supply. Why, then, might we experience difficulty identifying an honest person? To address this apparent paradox, we need to examine the implicit meaning of the trait 'honesty'. What behavioral criteria does the layperson have in mind when labeling a person as honest? What implicit rules of inference are involved?

This chapter examines trait–behavior relations along common traits such as honesty, intelligence, and extraversion. We explore the structure of these relations, the underlying psychological principles that are involved, and the place of these relations in social cognition. Specifically, we hope to show that the precision of theory in special cognition can be increased by taking account of these relations.

What is a Trait?

Research in the area of social cognition has the goal of explaining the way naive perceivers conceptualize their social environment (Fiske and Taylor, 1991). Not surprisingly, few terms receive wider currency in this field than that of 'trait' and its synonym 'disposition' (Newman and Uleman, 1989). When people are asked to

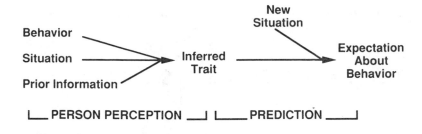

Figure 3.1 *Determinants of person perception and prediction*

describe others with whom they are acquainted, their descriptions are couched mainly in traits terms (Fiske and Cox, 1979).

Figure 3.1 outlines a very general scheme illustrating the place of trait inference in person perception. There is some agreement among researchers that perceivers infer a target person's traits based on three kinds of information: The target's behavior, the situation or context surrounding that behavior, and prior information about the target (Anderson, 1981; Jones and Davis, 1965; Kelley, 1973; Reeder and Brewer, 1979; Trope, 1986). The widely researched area of person perception is specifically concerned with documenting the processes by which each type of information is combined when trait inferences are drawn.

Less researched, but equally important from the standpoint of this chapter, are the behavioral expectations that correspond to or accompany the inference of a trait. Too often, traits have been conceptualized as categories for summarizing behavior, with insufficient attention given to the manner in which traits and situations are believed to *interact* with one another (Wright and Mischel, 1988). We hope to show that perceivers expect the nature of this interaction to vary from trait to trait. For example, a person who is very honest will be expected to behave that way, despite the varying degrees of temptation (for dishonest behavior) that are present from one situation to the next. In contrast, the implicit conception of a dishonest trait is that behavior will covary to some extent with the presence of temptation (Reeder and Brewer, 1979). For example, even a dishonest person might be expected to tell the truth under most circumstances. But when personal gain is at stake, or when temptation is too great, we would expect to see evidence of dishonesty. Thus, when explaining his spending patterns, a philandering husband might be perfectly forthright about his expenses on the golf course, but misleading when questioned about hotel bills, charges for jewelry, etc. In sum, we expect little else but honest behavior from honest persons, but we expect both honest and dishonest behavior, depending on the situation, from persons who are dishonest.

In our view, traits such as honest and dishonest can be conceptualized as occupying the extremes of a continuous dimension (Borkenau, 1986; Reeder and Brewer, 1979). Each extreme on the trait continuum implies a characteristic range of behavior (behaviors that can be categorized with regard to their honesty or dishonesty). Further, the range of implied behavior may be of unequal size at the different ends of the trait continuum. As noted in the example above, honest persons are thought to be behaviourally restricted, whereas dishonest persons are not. Reeder and Brewer (1979) chose the term *hierarchical restriction* to designate this asymmetry.

Four Principles Underlying Trait–Behavior Relations

In describing the formation of natural object categories, cognitive psychologists (Anderson, 1990; Rosch, 1978) suggest that principles of function and structure underlie the use of categories. From the standpoint of function, categories are formed so as to conserve cognitive resources. Cognitive economy is best served by drawing distinctions between objects only when such differentiation is helpful to survival. According to Rosch (1978), the use of categories is also shaped by the perceived structure of the world (feathers are thought to be characteristic of birds, but not crocodiles). To what extent does the layperson's use of trait categories obey similar principles? Although we believe there are similarities between natural object categories and trait categories, the rules governing category formation may be more complicated in the case of trait categories (Lingle et al., 1984). In particular, our social judgments are typically heavily evaluative. Our classifications of other persons are based on the hopes, pleasures, fears, and sorrows that we experience (or expect to experience) in their presence. In addition, we typically think of others as causal agents who negotiate with and manipulate aspects of their social environment. These considerations are addressed in greater detail below as we outline four principles that guide trait–behavior relations.

From the standpoint of function, two principles assume importance. First, the *principle of economy* suggests that traits are a parsimonious way of representing the observed behavioral flow. According to Heider (1958: 53), 'dispositional features serve to integrate a bewildering mass of data in the most economical of terms.' A variety of theoretical approaches suggest that trait judgments reduce complexity, restore order, and create consistency among the behaviors we have observed (Ichheiser, 1970; Asch, 1946).

A second aspect of function is concerned with pragmatic matters of adapting to a social environment. The *principle of adaptation* suggests that trait judgments are made so as to further the survival of perceivers (Anderson, 1990; Swann, 1984; Wright and Dawson, 1988). Adaptation would be best served if perceivers adopt strategies that enable them to identify persons who pose a threat. For example, a target's aggressive acts may have particularly dire implications for the survival of others. A target who is physically aggressive, even on a part time basis, can be a genuine menace. Thus, it would be adaptive for perceivers to base their judgments of a target's level of aggressiveness primarily on the occurrence of aggressive acts, rather than nonaggressive acts.

Two additional principles relate to the perception of structure in human behavior. The *base rate principle* recognizes that perceivers expect different behaviors to vary in likelihood. For instance, in most societies, honest acts are probably more common than dishonest acts. This difference may derive from the reward struc-ture of the social environment, cultural traditions, and possibly genetic factors. In any case, perceivers may hold the general expec-tation that targets will attempt to guide their behavior in socially desirable (honest) directions, rather than socially undesirable (dishonest) directions. Because dishonest behavior is judged to be infrequent, the tendency is to identify the occurrence of such behavior only with the dishonest end of the trait continuum. Implicit social comparisons may play some role here. Someone who is judged to have a higher probability of acting dishonestly than most other persons will be labeled as having a dishonest trait. This is not to say that the person is thought more likely to behave dishonestly than honestly, but only that this person is more dishonest than most other persons.

Finally, notions of cause and effect are incorporated in the lay concept of trait. According to the *principle of causality*, perceivers recognize that performance of certain behaviors requires a degree of ability or capacity on the part of the target. For example, outstanding athletic performance, scientific breakthroughs, and artistic masterpieces are accomplished only by those who are thought to possess the requisite physical coordination, intelligence, and creativity to produce or *cause* such outcomes. In contrast, persons with low ability are thought to be behaviorally restricted, unable to bring about the accomplishments listed above (Reeder and Brewer, 1979; Skowronski and Carlston, 1989).

In conclusion, we have described four principles – economy, adaptation, base rate, and causality – as underlying trait–behavior relations. The principles of economy and adaptation relate to the adaptation (or internal functioning) of the perceiver, whereas the principles of base rate and causality relate to the perceived structure of the (external) behavioral environment. Although the four principles are conceptually independent, in practice they are often confounded. For example, principles related to adaptation and base rate would both seem to be involved when perceivers make judgments based on aggressive or dishonest acts. Such behaviors are of pragmatic significance to perceivers and are also judged to occur relatively infrequently.

In the next section we offer a four-part typology of traits. Our classification of trait types is based on characteristic trait–behavior patterns and the general principles which underlie these patterns. We hope to show that the particular blend of these principles varies from one trait type to another.

A TYPOLOGY OF TRAITS

The present exposition owes much to two earlier papers. Reeder and Brewer (1979), for instance, focused on the different *structures* that may underlie trait–behavior relations. Thus, structures such as the hierarchically restrictive schema were detailed as a way of representing the asymmetrical pattern of trait–behavior relations that occur along dimensions related to honesty or morality. A subsequent paper shifted the focus to the *principles* that underlie trait–behavior relations (Reeder, 1985). The principles of cognitive economy, adaptation, base rate and causality are roughly foreshadowed by this earlier work. The present analysis tackled more difficult terrain, the identification of *trait types*. We identify four trait types: frequency-based traits, attitudes and motives, morality traits, and capacities. Table 3.1 provides a listing of these trait types and indicates the possible importance of the four general principles we discussed earlier. We now turn to our proposed typology.

Frequency-Based Traits

The trait 'talkative' provides a clear example where pure behavioral frequency determines the trait label that is inferred. A target who talks incessantly is, by definition, talkative. Thus, the correspondence between the trait inference and the act is quite

Table 3.1 *The relation of underlying principles to trait types*

Traits	Underlying principles			
	Economy	*Adaptation*	*Base rate*	*Causality*
Frequency-based	***		*	
Attitudes and motives	**		*	*
Morality traits	*	***	***	*
Capacities	*		*	***

The number of asterisks signifies the importance of a principle.

direct. If the target person is observed on multiple occasions, the target is assigned a position on the relevant dispositional continuum based on the *average level* of the target's behavior. For example, a target who talks a lot when the topic concerns football, but is mute on a variety of other subjects, would be labeled moderately talkative. The underlying principle to such inferences is one of economy.

Regardless of where we place a target along the dispositional continuum talkative–untalkative, as naive perceivers we expect only a limited range of behavior from the person. Thus, untalkative persons are not expected to give long-winded speeches. The perceiver may also hold a more precise expectation about where a target person's behavior will fall within this restricted range. This more precise expectation will be determined by the context or situation that the target is believed to be facing. In the sense of Figure 3.1, a trait label carries implicit expectations about how someone with a given trait will behave in a given *situation* (Wright and Mischel, 1988).

Related Viewpoints
The notion that implicit trait–behavior relations are grounded in frequency is hardly a controversial one in personality and social cognition. In fact, until recently, frequency appears to have been the *sole* criterion considered to govern such relations. In their influential approach to personality, Buss and Craik (1983) detail an elaborate methodology for assessing the frequency with which various dispositions give rise to particular behaviors: 'Within this approach, the fundamental measure of an individual's disposition is a multiple-act composite index, provided by frequency summary across a specified period of observation' (1983: 106). Buss and Craik's approach is purported to be a theory of personality and has not been explicitly offered as a description of the layperson's

way of thinking. Nevertheless, evidence for the theory has relied heavily on people's *perceptions* of behavior, rather than actual behavioral observation (Block, 1989). For example, in an effort to demonstrate the 'internal structure' of a disposition, under-graduates have been asked to write down behaviors that are thought to be characteristic of persons who hold a given disposition (Buss and Craik, 1980).

In the area of social cognition, a similar view is often assumed or expressed explicitly: 'the lay person often speaks with confidence of the honesty, aggressiveness, or dependency of other people – that is, the degree to which they possess a chronic disposition to behave in a particular way' (Nisbett, 1980: 109). Accordingly, traits do little more than summarize the central tendency in a target's behavior. More recently, this view of dispositions as mere summaries of behavioral acts has come under fire, and social cognition researchers have begun to distinguish between traits which do and do not imply behavioral regularity (Fletcher, 1984; Newman and Uleman, 1989; Rothbart and Park, 1986; Wright and Mischel, 1988).

Alston (1975) was perhaps the first to distinguish between traits that are based on the *frequency* with which behavior is overtly displayed and traits that are less clearly related to particular behavioral manifestations. As examples of frequency-based traits, he mentioned sociable, energetic, and methodical. Fletcher (1984) extended this view by recognizing a difference between dispositions . which are 'behavioral' versus 'mental'. Behavioral dispositions correspond to what we have called frequency-based dispositions and include traits such as untidiness and punctuality, which summarize readily observable sets of behavior. In contrast, mental traits – such as beliefs, attitudes, knowledge states, and certain abilities – are related to behavior in a looser manner. For example, one may hold an attitude that is rarely acted upon, or possess an ability (such as artistic talent) that is rarely exercised. Similarly, Rothbart and Park (1986) noted that structural aspects of the environment allow for many expressions of a frequency-based trait such as *messy*, whereas the environment allows for few expressions of a trait such as *devious*. In addition, traits such as *messy* and *devious* differ in the extent that they imply clear behavioral referents. It is quite easy to bring to mind specific instances of messy acts, but more difficult to do so in the case of devious acts. Related distinctions concern the imaginability (Rothbart and Park, 1986), abstractness (Pryor et al., 1986), and inclusiveness of traits (Hampson et al., 1986).

Although traits such as *talkative* and *devious* differ in their level of abstractness, it is worth noting that all traits are relatively abstract. For example, the linguistic category model proposed by Semin and Fiedler (1988) suggests that when actions are described concretely, at the level of the verb (Simon is *talking* to Cindy), the description is judged to be more verifiable, but less informative than a trait description (Simon is *talkative*). Indeed, there seems to be a continuum of abstraction for describing behavior which ranges from the use of simple behavioral descriptions to the use of highly abstract traits such as *devious*.

Abstract traits which describe personal preferences or the stylistic aspects of behavior are often frequency-based. For instance, traits such as reserved, trustful, lively, modest, and cheerful would fall into this category. Each of these traits is applicable to, or allows for the coding of, a broad range of behavior. Almost any instance of behavior carries some information about these dimensions. For example, if we were to interact with a person for any extended period, we would likely gather a wealth of information about how 'lively' the person is. Our impression of the person's liveliness would then be based on some computed average of these different occasions, although extreme behaviors might weight more heavily in this average (Reeder and Brewer, 1979; Skowronski and Carlston, 1987).

Implications for Social Cognition

Confirmability and Disconfirmability   The high visibility of frequency-based traits should make it easy for perceivers to verify or confirm their presence (Rothbart and Park, 1986). For example, after attending a cocktail party with a new group of acquaintances, most of us would experience little difficulty identifying those in the group who are talkative and those who are not. Research by a number of investigators suggests that some traits are inferred more or less spontaneously upon the observation of even a few behaviors (Park, 1989; Newman and Uleman, 1989). One possibility is that this tendency toward spontaneous trait inference is enhanced on dimensions that are highly visible and frequency-based.

Another possibility is that impressions that involve frequency-based traits will be highly malleable. After observing a target chatter non-stop for an hour, few of us would cling to an initial impression that the target is untalkative. In sum, the high visibility of many frequency-based traits would seem to make them relatively easy to acquire and relatively easy to lose.

Agreement   Because frequency-based traits are typically readily observable, perceivers should show high agreement when inferring their presence in a target person. Indeed, Funder and Dobroth (1987) reported that traits with high visibility such as talkative, cheerful, and assertive (which relate to extraversion) are characterized by high levels of inter-rater agreement. These conclusions are buttressed by Park and Judd (1989), who studied the acquaintance process. Ten subjects met as a group on four consecutive days and each was asked to provide ratings of the other nine participants. Trait ratings related to extraversion were once again characterized by a high level of agreement. But trait ratings of intelligence, honesty, and conscientiousness were rated with less agreement. Traits of this latter sort are best viewed as capacities or morality traits, rather than as frequency-based traits.

The Aristotle Effect   A unique characteristic of many frequency-based traits is that the most socially desirable point is found near the middle of the dimension rather than at either extreme (Peabody, 1967). In fact, pejorative terms are often reserved to describe persons with extreme styles or habits. Thus, a person at the active extreme of the *talkative* dimension might be called 'verbose' or a 'motor-mouth', while a person at the passive extreme might be designated 'taciturn'. The reader has only to imagine the prospect of spending a long train ride sitting next to a person at either extreme to obtain an intuitive understanding of why some extreme traits might be socially undesirable. Centuries ago, Aristotle anticipated the point by proposing that virtue is to be found in moderation.

From a research standpoint, the important issue is not whether trait desirability obeys a 'golden mean' rule, but rather which traits follow the rule and which do not. Reeder et al. (1982) presented subjects with traits of three different types. *Frequency-based* traits (or preferences) were represented by dimensions such as adventurous/cautious, whereas *capacities* were represented by dimensions such as physically strong / physically weak and *morality* traits by dimensions such as moral/immoral. Along each dimension, subjects rated the social desirability of the traits at each extreme, as well as at the midpoint. As expected, frequency-based traits followed the 'golden mean' rule quite well: Perceivers believed that it is more socially desirable to be moderately adventurous than to be either very adventurous or very cautious. In contrast, social desirability ratings along capacity and morality traits followed a linear rule such as 'the more of the trait the better'. For example, perceivers believed that a high level of strength was preferable to an intermediate level of strength.

Wojciszke and Pienkowski (1990) extended this work, investigating how different types of traits functioned in an evaluation-based impression task. For traits such as 'intelligence' (a capacity in our terminology), they predicted that impressions of a target person would become increasingly positive as the target was credited with greater numbers of intelligent behaviors. In contrast, for frequency-based traits, such as 'modest', they noted that it is possible to have 'too much of a good thing'. For example, although modest behavior is considered socially desirable, a person who is excessively modest (allowing competitors to take credit for his or her ideas) would be viewed in negative terms. Thus, the researchers predicted that the addition of uniformly positive modest behaviors would at first increase the level of attraction, but lead to a gradual decrease as more and more behavioral items were presented. This predicted pattern was obtained and dubbed *The Aristotle Effect*.

Attitudes and Motives

The distinguishing characteristic of attitudes and motives is that behavior relevant to the trait dimension may be expressed indirectly or, in some cases, not at all (Sabini and Silver, 1982). For example, a person may hold an attitude that is rarely acted upon. These dimensions best represent what Fletcher (1984) calls mental traits. They are states of mind which, when they are reflected in behavior, are often conceptualized as exerting a directive or *causal* influence over a target's actions. For example, we might explain a young colleague's long working hours as due to a motive to succeed. Below, we examine attitudes and motives in turn.

Attitudes

The notion that attitudes need not be directly expressed is exemplified when a person holds an unpopular or socially undesirable attitude: A person may feel negatively about a certain ethnic group, but rarely act on that prejudicial feeling. In fact, a single discriminatory remark (for example, use of a term such as 'kike' or 'nigger') may be taken as strong evidence of a negative attitude toward an ethnic or racial group. Indeed, a remark of this sort is likely to be viewed as more revealing about a person's true feelings than any number of more positive behaviors which the target may have emitted toward the same group. In this respect, the criteria for inferring a target's standing along attitudinal and motive dimensions differ from that of frequency-based traits. The inference is not based on a pure frequency count of attitudinally relevant remarks or acts. In the example above, for instance, the single negative remark is given greater weight than other more positive (socially desirable) behaviors (Jones and Davis, 1965).

The base rate principle would appear to be involved in the above example. If acts involving racial discrimination are rare in the social environment, someone who emits such behavior (even occasionally) will be viewed as having an extreme (negative) attitude. The trait–behavior relations in this example are asymmetric: persons with both positive and negative attitudes are identified with positive behaviors, but only persons with a negative attitude are identified with negative behavior. For other types of attitudes, where social desirability or normative pressure is less clear (for example, conservative versus liberal attitudes), behavioral base rate issues may be of lesser relevance. Along these dimensions, implicit trait–behavior relations are likely to resemble those of a frequency-based trait. For example, persons with a conservative (liberal) attitude will be expected to engage in conservative (liberal) behavior, or possibly middle of the road behavior, depending on the situation. Of interest is the possibility that the range of expected behavior is limited in size and that perceivers expect consistency.

Miller and his colleagues (Miller et al., 1990; Miller and Rorer, 1982) provided evidence that perceivers expect consistency between attitudes and behaviors. In their research, subjects were informed that various targets were instructed to draft an essay in favor of a particular social issue. Subjects expected an extreme essay (in favor of that issue) only when the target writer's personal attitude was in agreement with the essay assignment.

But how accurate are these expectations? Do naive perceivers expect too much consistency? Kunda and Nisbett (1986) launched an ambitious program of research to examine the accuracy of what they termed 'lay psychometrics'. They found that people systematically overestimated the extent of consistency that characterizes social behavior from one occasion to the next. This 'illusion of consistency' was especially prevalent on dimensions where the behavioral data were unfamiliar and difficult to code (or to scale along the relevant dimension). Behaviors relevant to attitudes would appear to fit this pattern. Many of our verbal statements and actions are only obliquely related to our personal opinions.

Reeder et al., (1989) investigated the accuracy of attitude–behavior expectations and sought to relate these expectations to the *correspondence bias* (Fletcher et al., 1990; Gilbert, 1989; Jones, 1979). Correspondence bias refers to the tendency for perceivers to attribute relatively correspondent attitudes (or dispositions) to a target, even when the target's behavior appears to have been constrained by situational forces. In one of Reeder et al.'s experiments, subjects were assigned to play the role of either a writer or one of several observers. In plain view of the observers, the experimenter instructed the writer to draft an essay taking a particular stand on a controversial issue. Observers were asked to make some predictions about the nature of this essay prior to hearing the writer read it aloud. In addition, observers provided further ratings after hearing the essay.

The results of this study provided strong evidence that observers overestimated the consistency of attitude–behavior relations. Although they had expected an essay of moderate extremity and quality, observers found the writer's actual essay to be quite extreme and quite convincing. In addition, these biased expectations appeared to play some role in producing correspondence bias. Observers estimated that the writer's personal attitude was more in line with her essay than was actually the case. Although the personal attitudes of the writers tended to be neutral, observers who heard what they thought was an extreme and high quality essay, attributed a rather extreme attitude to the writer. At least under some circumstances, then, perceivers fall prey to an illusion of consistency (Heider, 1958; Ichheiser, 1970; Kunda and Nisbett, 1986).

Motives

Like socially undesirable attitudes, motives are viewed as not having any necessary or direct behavioral manifestations. For instance, if we say Lacy is competitive, we are not implying any particular behavior on her part. We might have difficulty predicting whether or not she would agree to share computer software with us. Agreement on her part to share, for example, could be viewed as a 'power strategy'. Although naive perceivers do not view motives as predicting any particular pattern of behavior, motives are thought to direct or *cause* behavior in a way that attitudes do not. Thus, whereas an attitude may never find behavioral expression, a motive such as competitiveness is thought to be constantly at work, like an underlying plan (Read, 1987), shaping the target's responses. In the examples above, both Lacy's sharing of software *and* her refusal to share may be interpreted as 'caused' by her competitive nature. Sometimes a motive will be invoked to explain an extended sequence of behaviors that appear causally related. For example, the motive 'goldigger' is rarely used in reference to any single behavior by a target, but is reserved for occasions where an entire sequence of actions fit a pattern (ingratiation and favors are bestowed on a powerful person and then abruptly withdrawn).

This indirect relation between motive and behavior has a number of consequences for social cognition. Most obvious is the great latitude for different interpretations of the motive underlying any single act. Where the perceiver holds a positive impression of the target, the target's 'sharing' behavior is likely to be viewed as reflecting a positive (cooperative) motive (Regan et al., 1974). But where the perceiver holds a negative impression of the target, that same behavior may be cast in a more sinister light (as an exercise of oneupmanship or power). Fincham and Bradbury (1991) have documented this biasing potential in the context of marriage. They observed that spouses in distressed relationships tended to view their partner's negative behaviors as more selfishly motivated than did spouses in nondistressed relationships. In general, disparities in the attribution of motive may be quite common between actors and their observers. For instance, actors typically place more flattering interpretations on their own behaviors than observers do (Taylor and Brown, 1988).

Morality Traits

As noted near the beginning of this chapter, trait–behavior relations along morality dimensions tend to be asymmetric. Moral persons are commonly believed to refrain from immoral behavior, except under the rarest of circumstances: We may be shocked by allegations that moral leaders such as John F. Kennedy and Martin Luther King, Jr., had a 'weakness for women' (Abernathy, 1989). In contrast, immoral persons are believed to engage in a wider range of behavior that includes both immoral and moral behavior: We might be less surprised to learn that a mass murderer pampers his mother with flowers and frequent letters (Coovert and Reeder, 1990, Experiment 2; Reeder et al., 1982; Skowronski and Carlston, 1987).

These implicit assumptions may help to explain Diogenes' unsuccessful search for an honest man (remember Diogenes?). Suppose that Diogenes expected predominantly honest behavior both from persons who possessed the trait of honesty, as well as from those who did not. Given these assumptions, honest behavior would be viewed as relatively uninformative regarding a target person's standing on the trait of honesty. In fact, a true cynic like Diogenes might 'discount' such honest behavior in his search for an honest man – a strategy that guarantees the failure of the search.

Reeder and Coovert have viewed perceivers' representations of trait–behavior relations as cognitive schemata (Coovert and

Reeder, 1990; Reeder and Coovert, 1986). This analysis has several implications for research in social cognition. First, it provides a straightforward explanation of the *negativity effect* in impression formation (Kanouse and Hanson, 1972; Peeters and Czapinski, 1990; Skowronski and Carlston, 1989). Because only immoral persons are thought to emit immoral (negative) acts, such acts should receive great weight in final impressions. Second, the trait–behavior expectations noted above should influence response time as impressions are formed and revised. Reeder and Coovert (1986) asked perceivers to indicate a first impression of a target person based on an initial set of behaviors that were either exclusively moral or exclusively immoral. Then a final behavior was presented. The final behavior was always inconsistent with the initial set of behaviors, and perceivers were asked to revise their impression. The schematic model predicts that when an immoral behavior is added to a very positive impression, expectations should be violated (only immoral persons are thought to emit such behavior), and response time to reorganize and revise the impression should be elevated. But when a final moral behavior is added to a very negative impression, perceivers should be less surprised, and response time should be faster. Reeder and Coovert (1986) found support for these predictions.

A third prediction of the model is that a negativity effect should occur only when the target of the impression is an individual, and not when the target is a group of unrelated persons (an aggregate). The trait–behavior expectations that underlie the negativity effect represent an aspect of the unity of organization in individual behavior (Heider, 1958). Such expectations should be lacking when the target is an aggregate (whose members have little in common), and impressions of the aggregate should not follow the negativity pattern. Supporting this logic, Coovert and Reeder (1990) reported that perceivers who formed an impression of an individual placed heavier weight on immoral behavior than on moral behavior. But perceivers who formed an impression of an aggregate gave equal weight to moral and immoral behaviors.

Finally, the schematic model makes predictions about attribution – the manner in which naive perceivers balance behavioral and situational information about a target person (Heider, 1958). Because immoral behavior provides highly diagnostic information about a target person's dispositional characteristics, perceivers should be reluctant to 'discount' such behavior (Kelley, 1973). Indeed, several studies (McGraw, 1985, 1987; Reeder and Spores, 1983) indicate that target persons who commit moral transgressions (steal from a charity) are perceived as immoral, even when situational demands appear to have facilitated the transgression (an acquaintance urged the target to steal).

Principles Underlying Trait–Behavior Relations for Morality Traits

In an earlier section, we proposed that a base rate principle may underlie the asymmetrical pattern of trait–behavior relations for morality. That is, because moral behavior is relatively frequent, it is identified with both moral and immoral dispositions; whereas immoral behavior is infrequent, and anyone who emits such behavior is judged to have the corresponding trait. But the principle of adaptation may be equally relevant. Targets who demonstrate moral behavior benefit those with whom they interact, whereas targets who behave immorally do so to the detriment of other people. If we assume further that the immoral acts of others (such as theft and adultery) are more important to adaptation than the moral acts of others (help and kindness), it follows that perceivers should be concerned mainly with immoral behavior (Peeters and Czapinski, 1990; Taylor, 1991).

The trait of aggression provides an informative example. In extreme instances, our very survival may depend on our managing to avoid aggressive persons. Two forms of aggression may be distinguished. First, instrumental aggression is the use of force to secure some end: A mugger might hit a victim over the head as a means of securing the victim's wallet. The aggressive act is generally one that benefits the actor at the expense of a victim. In this respect, acts of instrumental aggression resemble other forms of immoral behavior such as thievery and adultery. Although empirical support is presently lacking, we believe that trait–behavior relations for aggression should take the following form: Nonaggressive persons should be viewed as emitting only nonaggressive behavior, whereas aggressive persons should be viewed as emitting both aggressive *and* nonaggressive behavior. Following our previous logic, perceivers should view instances of aggressive behavior as especially informative regarding a target's dispositional level of aggression.

The second type of aggression is variously referred to as expressive, reactive, or angry aggression. The prototypical case involves an actor's angry explosion in response to frustration or provocation of some sort: Johnny pulled Melissa's hair when she teased him (Shoda et al., 1989). The aggressive reaction is not designed to bring about a desired end, but is more an expression of negative affect. Nevertheless, moral considerations are involved. Regardless of provocations, actors usually have a moral obligation to refrain from violent outbursts, whether verbal or physical. Someone who fails to 'control' him or herself is guilty of a moral infraction: The offender has expressed him or herself at the expense of someone else.

The reader may discern the workings of the causality principle in the last example. Specifically, a target's violent outburst may represent an inability to produce or cause more desirable outcomes. The complexity of negativity phenomena would seem to require a recognition of multiple theoretical factors (Taylor, 1991). In conclusion, trait–behavior relations along morality dimensions are asymmetric. As a consequence, immoral behavior tends to weight relatively heavily in tasks of impression formation and dispositional attribution. In the next section we examine the last category of traits, those concerned with capacity.

Capacities

The underlying principle for capacity is that of causality: Low-ability persons are thought to lack the causal power to bring about a high level of performance. But persons with high ability are thought to be capable of high *or* low performance, depending on their level of motivation. Thus, a tennis pro could play a lethargic game or even deliberately hit into the net as a means of boosting a patron's ego. This perception – that targets with high ability can be quite flexible in their behavior – distinguishes capacities from the category of frequency-based traits. Capacities can also be distinguished from morality traits. For capacities, it is the socially undesirable end of the trait dimension (low ability) that is behaviorally restricted, whereas for morality, it is the socially desirable end (high morality) that is behaviorally restricted.

Despite the behavioral flexibility that accompanies a trait of high ability, perceivers ordinarily expect ability-related performances to be quite stable (Weiner, 1986). The reason for this expectation of consistency is that the social environment tends to encourage high performance. As a result, perceivers expect that others are motivated to do their best, and that most performances accurately reflect the performer's level of competence. The greater behavioral flexibility which is attributed to persons with high ability applies mainly in the case where high motivation is in doubt. For example, in situations where rewards are present for a low level of performance (a tennis pro who has the opportunity to ingratiate himself with a rich patron), perceivers expect that persons with high ability are both willing and able to perform at a low level (Reeder et al., 1982).

The attributional implications of these trait–behavior expectations are straightforward. A high level of performance will lead to a correspondent inference that the target possesses a high level of ability. This should occur regardless of situational demands surrounding the behavior because only persons with high ability are thought capable of such behavior. In contrast, a low level of performance will result in a less correspondent pattern of inference. This follows because (when motivation is in doubt) persons with low *and* high ability are thought capable of performing at a low level (Reeder et al., 1977; Reeder and Fulks, 1980).

Impression formation may also be affected by trait–behavior expectations for ability traits (Skowronski and Carlston, 1987; Wojciszke and Brycz, 1990). For example, Skowronski and Carlston (1987) reported that perceivers weighted intelligent behaviors more heavily than unintelligent behaviors when forming an impression of a target's intelligence. Finally, the impact of trait–behavior relations can be see when perceivers test hypotheses about a target's traits (Devine et al., 1990). Devine and her colleagues took note of research indicating that perceivers view extraverts as having more behavioral flexibility (social ability) than introverts (Reeder et al., 1977). That is, while both introverts and extraverts can behave in an introverted manner, only extraverts are thought capable of certain extraverted behaviors. Consequently, Devine et al. predicted and found support for the idea that perceivers would be especially interested in gathering information about extraverted behavior, as opposed to introverted behavior. This finding is consistent with the notion that perceivers are drawn toward highly diagnostic information when testing hypotheses about others (Trope and Bassok, 1983).

It is worth noting that the dimension of extraversion/introversion represents a particularly interesting mix of trait–behavior relations. As described above, the trait of extraversion has characteristics of a capacity. On the other hand, perceivers attain an impressive degree of agreement when estimating a target's standing on this dimension (Park and Judd, 1989), a finding that suggests the dimension is frequency-based. In general, the accuracy with which ability-related traits are perceived should depend on observability and the codability of behavior (Kunda and Nisbett, 1986). It would seem that behaviors relevant to extraversion are both highly observable and easy to code.

Conclusion

We began this chapter by noting an apparent paradox in Diogenes' unsuccessful search for an honest man. That is, although a perceiver might observe honest acts in abundance, the perceiver could still hold the view that *honest persons* are in short supply. We proposed that an appreciation of trait–behavior expectations may help to resolve this issue. More generally, our goal has been to describe four types of traits, each of which has a different pattern of trait–behavior relations. Trait–behavior relations for frequency-based traits follow a pattern which accords closely with the layperson's commonsense view of traits. That is, traits are viewed as having a direct relationship with behavior: Persons with a talkative trait are thought to talk a lot. But for the remaining three types – attitudes and motives, morality traits, and capacities – the relations between trait and behavior are more complex. Our analysis also included some speculation about the underlying principles that shape these different patterns. These include the principles of economy, adaptation, base rate, and causality.

The four-part typology of traits is just a beginning, and a number of loose ends remain. We hope the ideas and literature cited here will spur researchers to take a closer look at trait-behavior relations. There are real differences among traits, and the precision of theory in social cognition will increase when such differences are recognized. Theories that address only abstract principles tend to miss the specificity and rich content that characterize everyday thinking.

Note

The authors wish to acknowledge the helpful comments of Raymond Bergner, Garth Fletcher, and Maria Lewicka.

References

Abernathy, R. D. (1989) *And the Walls Came Tumbling Down*. New York: Harper & Row.

Alston, W. P. (1975) Traits, consistency and conceptual alternatives for personality theory. *Journal for the Theory of Social Behavior*, 5: 17–48.

Anderson, J. R. (1990) *The Adaptive Character of Thought*. Hillsdale, NJ: Erlbaum.

Anderson, N. H. (1981) *Foundations of Information Integration Theory*. New York: Academic Press.

Asch, S. E. (1946) Forming impressions of personality. *Journal of Abnormal and Social Psychology*, 41: 258–290.

Block, J. (1989) Critique of the act frequency approach to personality. *Journal of Personality and Social Psychology*, 56: 234–245.

Borkenau, P. (1986) Toward an understanding of trait interrelations: Acts as instances of several traits. *Journal of Personality and Social Psychology*, 51: 371–381.

Buss, D. M. and Craik, K. H. (1980) The frequency concept of disposition: Dominance and prototypically dominant acts. *Journal of Personality*, 48: 379–392.

Buss, D. M. and Craik, K. H. (1983) The act frequency approach to personality. *Psychological Review*, 90: 105–126.

Coovert, M. D. and Reeder, G. D. (1990) Negativity effects in impression formation: The role of unit formation and schematic expectations. *Journal of Experimental Social Psychology*, 26: 49–62.

Devine, P. G., Hirt, E. R. and Gehrke, E. M. (1990) Diagnostic and confirmation strategies in trait hypothesis testing. *Journal of Personality and Social Psychology*, 58: 952–963.

Fincham, F. D., & Bradbury, T. N. (1991) Cognition in marriage: A program of research on attributions. In D. Perlman and W. Jones (eds), *Advances in Personal Relationships*, vol. 2, pp. 159–203. London: Kingsley.

Fiske, S. T. and Cox, M. G. (1979) Person concepts: The effects of target familiarity and descriptive purpose on the process of describing others. *Journal of Personality*, 47: 136–161.

Fiske, S. T. and Taylor, S. E. (1991) *Social Cognition* (2nd edn). New York: McGraw Hill.

Fletcher, G. J. O. (1984) Psychology and common sense. *American Psychologist*, 39: 203–213.

Fletcher, G. J. O., Reeder, G. D. and Bull, V. (1990) Bias and accuracy in attitude attribution: The role of attributional complexity. *Journal of Experimental Social Psychology*, 26: 275–288.

Funder, D. C. and Dobroth, K. M. (1987) Differences between traits: Properties associated with interjudge agreement. *Journal of Personality and Social Psychology*, 52: 409–418.

Gilbert, D. T. (1989) Thinking lightly about others: Automatic components of the social inference process. In J. S. Uleman and J. A. Bargh (eds), *Unintended Thought*, pp. 189–211. New York: Guilford Press.

Hampson, S. E., John, O. P. and Goldberg, L. R. (1986) Category breadth and hierarchical structure in personality: Studies of asymmetries in judgments of trait implications. *Journal of Personality and Social Psychology*, 51: 37–54.

Heider, F. (1958) *The Psychology of Interpersonal Relations*. New York: Wiley.

Ichheiser, G. (1970) *Appearances and Realities*. San Francisco: Jossey-Bass.

Jones, E. E. (1979) The rocky road from acts to dispositions. *American Psychologist*, 34: 107–117.

Jones, E. E. and Davis, K. E. (1965) From acts to dispositions: The attribution process in person perception. In L. Berkowitz (ed.), *Advances in Experimental Social Psychology*, vol. 2, pp. 219–266. New York: Academic Press.

Kanouse, D. E. and Hanson, L. R. (1972) Negativity in evaluations. In E. E. Jones et al. (eds), *Attribution: Perceiving the Causes of Behavior*, pp. 47–62. Morristown, NJ: General Learning Press.

Kelley, H. H. (1973) The process of causal attribution. *American Psychologist*, 28: 107–128.

Kunda, Z. and Nisbett, R. E. (1986) The psychometrics of everyday life. *Cognitive Psychology*, 18: 195–224.

Lingle, J. H., Altom, M. W. and Medin, D. L. (1984) Of cabbages and kings: Assessing the extendability of natural object concept models to social things. In R. S. Wyer and T. K. Srull (eds), *Handbook of Social Cognition*, vol. 3, pp. 71–117. Hillsdale, NJ: Erlbaum.

McGraw, K. M. (1985) Subjective probabilities and moral judgments. *Journal of Experimental Social Psychology*, 21: 501–518.

McGraw, K. M. (1987) Outcome valence and base rates: The effects on moral judgments. *Social Cognition*, 5: 58–75.

Miller, A. G., Ashton, W. and Mishal, M. (1990) Beliefs concerning the features of constrained behavior: A basis for the fundamental attribution error. *Journal of Personality and Social Psychology*, 59: 635–650.

Miller, A. G. and Rorer, L. G. (1982) Toward an understanding of the fundamental attribution error: Essay diagnosticity in the attitude attribution paradigm. *Journal of Research in Personality*, 16: 41–59.

Newman, L. S. and Uleman, J. S. (1989) Spontaneous trait inference. In J. S. Uleman and J. A. Bargh (eds), *Unintended Thought*, pp. 155–188. New York: Guilford Press.

Nisbett, R. E. (1980) The trait construct in lay and professional psychology. In L. Festinger (ed.), *Retrospections on Social Psychology*, pp. 109–130. New York: Oxford University Press.

Park, B. (1989) Trait attributes as on-line organizers of person impressions. In J. N. Bassili (ed.), *On-line Cognition in Person Perception*, pp. 39–59. Hillsdale, NJ: Erlbaum.

Park, B. and Judd, C. M. (1989) Agreement on initial impressions: Differences due to perceivers, trait dimensions, and target behaviors. *Journal of Personality and Social Psychology*, 56: 493–505.

Peabody, D. (1967) Trait inferences: Evaluative and descriptive aspects. *Journal of Personality and Social Psychology Monograph*, 7 (Whole no. 644)

Peeters, G. and Czapinski, J. (1990) Positive–negative asymmetry in evaluations: The distinction between affective and informational negativity effects. In W. Stroebe and M. Hewstone (eds), *European Review of Social Psychology*, vol. 1, pp. 33–60. Chichester: Wiley.

Pryor, J. B., McDaniel, M. A. and Kott-Russo, T. (1986) The influence of level of schema abstractness upon the processing of social information. *Journal of Experimental Social Psychology*, 22: 312–327.

Read, S. J. (1987) Constructing causal scenarios: A knowledge structure approach to causal reasoning. *Journal of Personality and Social Psychology*, 52: 288–302.

Reeder, G. D. (1985) Implicit relations between dispositions and behaviors: Effects on dispositional attribution. In J. H. Harvey and G. Weary (eds), *Attribution: Basic Issues and Applications*. Orlando: Academic Press.

Reeder G. D., and Brewer, M. B. (1979) A schematic model of dispositional attribution in interpersonal perception. *Psychological Review*, 86: 61–79.

Reeder, G. D. and Coovert, M. D. (1986) Revising an impression of morality. *Social Cognition*, 4, 1–17.

Reeder, G. D., Fletcher, G. J. O. and Furman, K. (1989) The role of observers' expectations in attitude attribution. *Journal of Experimental Social Psychology*, 25: 168–188.

Reeder, G. D. and Fulks, J. L. (1980) When actions speak louder than words: Implicational schemata and the attribution of ability. *Journal of Experimental Social Psychology*, 16: 33–46.

Reeder, G. D., Henderson, D. J. and Sullivan, J. J. (1982) From dispositions to behaviors: The flip side of attribution. *Journal of Research in Personality*, 16: 355–375.

Reeder, G. D., Messick, D. M., and Van Avermaet, E. (1977) Dimensional asymmetry in attributional inference. *Journal of Experimental Social Psychology*, 13: 46–57.

Reeder, G. D. and Spores, J. M. (1983) The attribution of morality. *Journal of Personality and Social Psychology*, 44: 736–745.

Regan, D. T., Straus, E. and Fazio, R. (1974) Liking and the attribution process. *Journal of Experimental Social Psychology*, 10: 385–397.

Rosch, E. (1978) Principles of categorization. In E. Rosch and B. Lloyd (eds), *Cognition and Categorization*, pp. 27–48. Hillsdale, NJ: Erlbaum.

Rothbart, M. and Park, B. (1986) On the confirmability and disconfirmability of trait concepts. *Journal of Personality and Social Psychology*, 50: 131–142.

Sabini, J. and Silver, M. (1982) *Moralities of Everyday Life*. Oxford: Oxford University Press.

Semin, G. R. and Fiedler, K. (1988) The cognitive functions of linguistic categories in describing persons: Social cognition and language. *Journal of Personality and Social Psychology*, 54: 558–568.

Shoda, Y., Mischel, W. and Wright, J. C. (1989) Intuitive interactionism in person perception: Effects of situation–behavior relations on dispositional judgments. *Journal of Personality and Social Psychology*, 56: 41–53.

Skowronski, J. J. and Carlston, D. E. (1987) Social judgment and social memory: The role of cue diagnosticity in negativity, positivity, and extremity biases. *Journal of Personality and Social Psychology*, 52: 689–699.

Skowronski, J. J. and Carlston, D. E. (1989) Negativity and extremity biases in impression formation: A review of explanations. *Psychological Bulletin*, 105: 131–142.

Swann, W. B. (1984) Quest for accuracy in person perception: A matter of pragmatics. *Psychological Review*, 91: 457–477.

Taylor, S. E. (1991) The asymmetrical effects of positive and negative events: The mobilization–minimization hypothesis. *Psychological Bulletin*, 110: 67–85.

Taylor, S. E. and Brown, J. D. (1988) Illusion and well-being: A social psychological perspective on mental health. *Psychological Bulletin*, 103: 193–210.

Trope, Y. (1986) Identification and inferential processes in dispositional attribution. *Psychological Review*, 93: 239–257.

Trope, Y. and Bassok, M. (1983) Information-gathering strategies in hypothesis-testing. *Journal of Experimental Social Psychology*, 19: 560–576.

Weiner, B. (1986) *An Attributional Theory of Motivation and Achievement*. New York: Springer-Verlag.

Wojciszke, B. and Brycz, H. (1990) Evaluation, trait inferences and prediction along ability and morality trait dimensions. Unpublished manuscript.

Wojciszke, B. and Pienkowski, R. (1990) Decreasing an impression by adding positive information: The Aristotle effect. Unpublished manuscript.

Wright, J. C. and Dawson, V. (1988) Person perception and the bounded rationality of social judgment. *Journal of Personality and Social Psychology*, 55: 780–794.

Wright, J. C. and Mischel W. (1988) Conditional hedges and the intuitive psychology of traits. *Journal of Personality and Social Psychology*, 55: 454–469.

PART 2

PROPERTIES OF INTERPERSONAL LANGUAGE AND ATTRIBUTION

4

The Inferential Properties of Interpersonal Verbs

Gün R. Semin and Klaus Fiedler

Although interest in the social psychological implications of language can be traced back over a number of decades it is only recently that a tradition of the 'social psychology of language' is emerging (see, for example, Giles and Coupland, 1991; Giles and Robinson, 1990). This is somewhat surprising in view of the fact that much of our behaviour essentially involves communication and is manifested in language use. What is more surprising in this context is that within this emerging tradition the interplay of language and *social cognition* has occupied a relatively minor role to date.

The issue we address in this chapter consists of an examination of the differing types of information that interpersonal verbs mediate. This question enlarges upon a systematic finding in the literature. Certain interpersonal verbs (such as help, hurt, cheat, amaze) when used in simple 'subject–verb–object' (SvO) sentences lead to the inference that the interpersonal event is caused by the sentence subject (thus, the sentence 'John helps David' regularly leads to the inference that John is the causal origin – 'John is helpful'). Other interpersonal verbs (such as like, hate, respect) lead regularly to object attributions (thus, 'John likes David' leads to the inference that 'David is a likeable person'. This systematic phenomenon, which has been termed the 'causality implicit in interpersonal verbs', and the search for possible theoretical accounts for it has been one paradigmatic issue in the language and social cognition domain (see, for example, Abelson and Kanouse, 1966; Brown and Fish, 1983; DeGrada and Mannetti, 1991; Fiedler and Semin, 1988, 1990; Franco and Arcuri, 1990; Garvey and Caramazza, 1974;

Hoffman and Tschir, 1990; McArthur, 1972; Van Kleeck et al., 1988). Thus, one of the significant features of interpersonal verbs is the way in which they *mark* causal origin. The question we explore in this chapter is whether interpersonal verbs *mark* other features of interpersonal relationships in a systematic way – for example: what and how interactants feel towards each other; how they relate to each other; what the inferred duration of an event or state is, and so on.

In order to investigate the features of social interaction that are marked in interpersonal verbs it is necessary to have a conceptual framework to classify interpersonal verbs that is derived *independently* from the cognitive properties of these verbs. We should at this point briefly note that by cognitive properties we refer to the inferential processes elicited by the features of interpersonal verbs that are systematically marked, such as subject causal inferences for action verbs and object causal inferences for state verbs that we noted earlier. The requirement for criteria that are independent of cognitive properties arises for the simple logical reason that a classification of verbs based on their inferential properties alone would give rise to a circular argument. For this reason, we first of all present the independent and convergent linguistic criteria for the classification of interpersonal verbs that has led us to propose a taxonomic model of interpersonal verbs (cf. Semin and Fiedler, 1988, 1991). This taxonomic model, termed the Linguistic Category Model (LCM), provides us with a framework to explore whether features of social interaction are systematically marked by interpersonal verbs.

In the section following the taxonomic approaches to interpersonal verbs, we discuss how some of the distinctive features of these verbs are marked, such as the perceived temporal duration of actions and states, the location of affect in sentence subject and object, the number of different behaviours that these terms refer to, as well as implicit causality. In each case, we then refer to empirical work that examines whether these properties have systematic cognitive implications.

In the third section, we examine whether these distinctive markers represent independent features of social interaction or whether they reflect some general underlying or latent dimensions of interpersonal verbs. We conclude with a discussion of what these findings mean for social cognition as well as for the LCM and its applications (amplified further in Fiedler and Semin's, and Maass and Arcuri's, contributions to this volume).

Table 4.1   *The classification of linguistic terms in the interpersonal domain and their classification criteria*

Category	Examples	Characteristic Features
Descriptive Action Verbs (DAV)	call meet kick kiss	Reference to single behavioural event; reference to specific object and situation; context essential for sentence comprehension; objective description of observable events

Classification Criteria: Refer to one particular activity and to a physically invariant feature of the action; action has clear beginning and end; in general do not have positive or negative semantic valence.

Interpretive Action Verbs (IAV)	cheat imitate help inhibit	Reference to single behavioural event; reference to specific object and situation; autonomous sentence comprehension; interpretation beyond description

Classification Criteria: Refer to general class of behaviours; have defined action with a beginning and end; have positive and negative semantic valence.

State Action Verbs (SAV)	surprise amaze anger excite	As IAV, no reference to concrete action frames but to states evoked in object of sentence by unspecified action

Classification Criteria: As with IAV, except that the verb expresses emotional consequence of action rather than referring to action as such.

State Verbs (SV)	admire hate abhor like	Enduring states, abstracted from single events; reference to social object, but not situation; no context reference preserved; interpretation beyond mere description

Classification Criteria: Refer to mental and emotional states; no clear definition of beginning and end; do not readily take progressive form; not freely used in imperatives.

Adjectives (ADJ)	honest impulsive reliable helpful	Highly abstract person disposition; no object or situation reference; no context reference; highly interpretive, detached from specific behaviours

Classifications of Interpersonal Verbs and the Linguistic Category Model

The linguistic category model (Semin and Fiedler, 1988, 1991) consists of a five-level taxonomy of the terms we use as predicates in interpersonal language, namely verbs and adjectives. These constitute different types of linguistic devices. Verbs are devices that are employed to describe actions (talk, help, cheat, hurt) or psychological states (like, abhor, notice), whereas adjectives are essentially devices to describe properties of persons that are generalized across situations and persons, that is traits or dispositions (such as, friendly, extroverted, aggressive and so on). This taxonomy (see Table 4.1) derived from converging linguistic criteria makes a distinction between four different verb categories and adjectives. Since our present focus is on interpersonal verbs only we shall not further elaborate on the adjective categories (see, however, Semin and Fiedler, 1991). The first verb category is Descriptive Action Verbs (DAV – kick, kiss, push). These terms refer to an action with a clear beginning and end, and maintain a direct reference to an invariant feature of the behaviour in question. DAVs, in general, do not have positive or negative semantic valence and their interpretation is highly context bound (John pushes David – either 'to save him from an oncoming car' or 'under an oncoming car'). Diverse studies have demonstrated this contextual dependency either in tasks of causal inference (DeGrada and Mannetti, 1991) or in the context of person and situation inferences (Semin and Fiedler, 1988; Semin and Greenslade, 1985).

The next category is referred to as Interpretive Action Verbs (IAV – help, cheat, imitate). The distinctive feature of these IAVs is that they act as a frame for diverse behaviours (for example, one can help a person: by giving instructions to find a place; out of financial difficulties; by preparing them for an exam; and so on). Nevertheless, the behaviours in question have distinct beginnings and ends as well as clear positive or negative semantic valence.

The third verb category that we distinguished is State Verbs (SV) which refer to mental or emotional states (recognize, like, hate, respect). In contrast to action verbs (DAV or IAV) these do not readily take the progressive form and are not freely used in imperatives (see Brown and Fish, 1983; Miller and Johnson-Laird, 1976), and refer to subjective, non-observable properties.

The final verb category we distinguish is State Action Verbs (such as amaze, thrill, surprise, bore) (see Maass et al., 1989; Semin and Fiedler, 1991). The semantic criteria for classifying SAVs are the following. Essentially, these are action verbs with one difference: they refer to an implicit action frame by the sentence subject that leads to the experience of a state in the object of a sentence (such as surprise, bore, amaze, thrill). So, instead of referring to qualities of the action these verbs identify the affective consequences of an action in the object of the action. In contrast, SVs do not require an immediate action reference (for example, love, hate, like, despise). Furthermore, for SVs the emotion of psychological state is already existent, whereas for SAVs the emotion is evoked by an action of the subject of an SvO sentence. Johnson-Laird and Oatley (1989), in a different context, make a distinction between *caused emotions* and *emotional relations*. The verbs falling in the former category are SAVs and these 'signify a feeling that has a cause known to the individual experiencing it' (Johnson-Laird and Oatley, 1989: 99). The latter refer to SVs in our terminology and these authors argue that 'one can love, hate or fear without knowing the reason why' (1989: 99). They introduce a variant of the 'but' test (Bendix, 1966) to illustrate the difference. Whereas it is possible to say 'I like Mary, but I don't know why', this is more difficult in the case of SAVs which refer to caused emotions (such as 'John amazed me, but I don't know why'). This distinction converges with the argument that for SAVs the causal origin of the action is clearly identified in the logical sentence subject, namely the originator of the action. Thus we make a distinction between four verbs classes, DAV, IAV, SAV and SV.

The approach developed by Brown and Fish (1983) on the causality implicit in interpersonal verbs makes a distinction between two types of state verbs distinguished by two 'causal schema': *stimulus–experiencer* and *experiencer–stimulus*.[1] It appears to us that the distinction between these two schemata is not based on clear semantic criteria. Furthermore, it is difficult to distinguish by the criteria advanced by Brown and Fish between Action Verbs and those state verbs which elicit the 'stimulus-experiencer' schema. We refer to verbs eliciting the 'experiencer-stimulus' schema within our terminology as SV. However, the former is what we term State Action Verbs (SAV). The similarities and differences between the Brown and Fish (1983) and our classification are illustrated in Table 4.2. We now turn to an examination of the features of interpersonal terms.

Features of Social Interaction Marked in Interpersonal Verbs

The Marking of Affect and Causality in Interpersonal Verbs

Affect is an explicit feature of SVs and SAVs. In the former case, affect is marked in the logical subject of SvO sentences (John likes Mary; John is the person who is marked with the state of liking) and in the latter in the logical object of active sentences (John surprises Mary; Mary is the person who is marked with the state

Table 4.2   *Classificatory systems of interpersonal verbs*

Brown and Fish categories	Examples	Semin and Fiedler Categories
Action Verbs	help, cheat, imitate	Interpretive Action Verbs
Agent–patient	phone, kick, kiss	Descriptive Action Verbs
State Verbs		
Stimulus–experiencer	amaze, surprise, bore	State Action Verbs
Experiencer–stimulus	like, hate, abhor	State Verbs

of surprise). In the case of DAV and IAV there is no such obvious marking. A question that can be raised with reference to IAV and DAV is whether affect is systematically marked across these four verb categories.

A relevant set of findings to this problem can be found in our earlier studies (Fiedler and Semin, 1988; Fiedler et al., 1991) on the contextual embeddedness of causal inferences. In these studies we regarded SvO sentences with the different verb categories as part of a string in a minimum discourse sequence of three sentences depicting a simple interpersonal event. That is, we asked subjects to tell us what they thought happened prior to a focal sentence and following the focal sentence. The objective of these studies was to find a contextual explanation of causal inference which goes beyond the sentence level (Fiedler and Semin, 1988; Fiedler et al., 1992). However tentative and incidental to the original design of these studies, some of the results are indicative of how affective inferences may be marked.

As can be seen from Table 4.3, one finds the following patterns with focal S-IAV-O sentences. When asked to retrodict what preceded an interpersonal event the participants use the logical subject of the focal sentence as the logical subject of the antecedent sentences in more than 56 per cent of the cases. More importantly, the majority of these sentences are constructed with an SV. The majority of the consequent sentences use the object of the focal sentence as sentence subject (81 per cent), but predominantly with an action verb (52 per cent) (SVs are used in 23 per cent of the cases). In contrast, if the focal sentence is constructed with an SV and participants are given the predictive task of constructing what happened next, then we find that the subject of focal and consequent sentence remain identical in most of the responses (87 per cent of cases). Additionally, the most likely verb to be used in consequent sentences is an IAV.

Table 4.3   *Percentages of antecedent and consequent implications of interpersonal verbs*

Antecedent sentence forms			Focal sentence		Consequent sentence forms	
S Action	6.15				S Action	20.66
S-State	13.68	(22.88)		(38.47)	S State	10.76
S-Trait	3.05				S Trait	1.05
			SV			
O Action	29.86				O Action	21.87
O-State	9.89	(70.59)		(43.91)	O State	15.66
O-Trait	30.84				O Trait	6.38
S Action	14.85				S Action	8.82
S-State	31.33	(56.30)		(12.67)	S State	2.84
S-Trait	10.12				S Trait	1.01
			IAV			
O Action	25.08				O Action	52.25
O-State	4.89	(38.35)		(81.18)	O State	23.27
O-Trait	8.38				O Trait	5.66

Source: Fiedler et al., 1992

The implications of these incidental findings from a study designed with a completely different objective suggest, however tentatively, the following. A feature of SVs is that they 'refer to the relation between someone who experiences an emotion and its object' (Johnson-Laird and Oatley, 1989: 98) as in the case of 'David likes Mary'. From the findings sketched above one could argue that the affect marked in SVs functions as a motive or motivational account for action. 'John helps Jim', but why? It is clear that John is the 'agent', but his motives for this action are only understandable with some preceding relational 'motivation' for the action. We regard this as a potential function of sentences, such as 'John likes Jim'. While describing a relation between the person who experiences an emotion and its object, this affective marking also functions as a motivational explanation for action. Thus, it is perhaps not surprising that when asking for the antecedents of an action we find that SV sentences are relatively prominent. Moreover, when we ask for the consequences of an SV focal sentence ('John likes David'), then we find that the most prominent response is one which involves an action originating in the sentence subject of the focal sentence ('John helps David'). Thus, what is seen as a pattern in preceding an action verb sentence becomes even more prominent in the pattern found for the consequences of state verb sentences.

In the case of SAVs, as we noted earlier, the reference is to an implicit action frame by the sentence subject that leads to the experience of a state in the object of a sentence. Affect or emotion is clearly marked in the sentence object. Finally, with DAVs which merely describe the concrete features of social interaction we would not expect differential affective inferences for sentence subject or sentence object. To summarize: In the case of action verbs we expect an affective marking of sentence objects for action verbs relative to sentence subjects, particularly for IAVs and SAVs. In the case of SVs, affect is clearly marked for sentence subject over sentence object.

It is noteworthy that the pattern of affect marking is precisely the reverse of how causal inference is marked in studies examining the causality implicit in verbs. But this suggests a further rationale based on a reciprocal relation between motive and action, affect marking the motivational features of action and cause marking the action origins. This reciprocal relation is one of the most fundamental properties of meaningful action. Thus a sequential interpretation of the features of social interaction marked in interpersonal verbs leads to this hypothesis.

In a study with 96 Sussex University undergraduates, we examined how affective and causal information are marked in SvO sentences as a function of four verb categories (DAV, IAV, SAV, SV).

To measure how affect was marked we used the following procedure. Each focal sentence was followed by the statement 'The amount of emotion experienced by "subject" (or "object") is'. This was then followed by a nine-point scale, the ends of which were anchored with 'Negligible' (1) and 'Considerable (9). After judging the amount of emotion, participants also had to answer how *confident* they felt about their judgement on a nine-point scale, the ends of which were anchored with 'Not Confident' (1) and 'Very Confident' (9).

To examine causal inferences, we employed the methodology that Brown and Fish (1983) adopted from Cunningham et al. (1979). After each SvO sentence, subjects had three questions to answer (for example, sentence: David impresses John. (1) David is the kind of person who impresses people. (2) Jim is the kind of person who is impressed by people; and (3) Some other reason. In each case the subjects had to respond on a nine-point scale indicating the likelihood of the cause).

Two independent samples of 48 subjects were used for each study and they received a booklet with ten focal sentences which were randomly selected from a total of 40 sentences. These ten

Table 4.4 *Affective inferences in interpersonal words*

		$\bar{X}_{SE}$	$\bar{X}_{OE}$	SOdiff	t-value	sig.	S Conf.	O Conf.
DAV	call	2.54	2.54	0.00	0.00	n.s.	4.85	5.31
	dance	2.64	2.36	0.27	0.71	n.s.	4.91	4.91
	drive	1.71	2.57	−0.86	−1.11	n.s.	5.93	5.64
	hug	6.38	5.23	1.15	3.64	0.01	6.23	4.77
	phone	2.81	1.91	0.91	1.84	0.05	5.18	5.09
	shout at	4.86	3.57	1.29	4.22	0.01	5.14	4.71
	talk to	2.79	2.57	0.21	0.90	n.s.	5.71	5.93
	touch	4.07	3.79	0.29	0.65	n.s.	4.79	4.71
	visit	3.79	3.29	0.50	0.86	n.s.	4.93	4.86
	wave at	4.08	3.84	0.23	0.43	n.s.	5.15	5.00
	$\bar{X}$	*3.57*	*3.17*	*0.40*			*5.28*	*5.09*
IAV	betray	4.27	5.91	−1.64	−1.96	0.05	5.91	5.27
	defy	6.23	5.46	0.77	2.25	0.03	5.77	5.23
	deceive	3.64	5.21	−1.57	−1.53	0.08	5.14	5.21
	dominate	5.08	5.46	−0.38	−0.69	n.s.	5.62	5.15
	flirt	4.21	2.78	1.42	1.88	0.05	5.07	4.50
	harm	4.36	5.86	−1.50	−1.88	0.05	4.79	6.07
	help	4.50	4.29	0.21	0.52	n.s.	5.00	5.00
	persuade	5.50	5.21	0.29	0.45	n.s.	5.14	5.29
	protect	5.45	3.45	2.00	2.08	0.05	6.09	5.81
	support	4.76	5.62	−0.85	−2.67	0.01	5.07	5.54
	$\bar{X}$	*4.80*	*4.93*	*−0.13*			*5.86*	*5.31*
SAV	amaze	2.77	6.08	−3.30	−5.06	0.01	5.69	5.92
	amuse	3.63	5.36	−1.73	−2.56	0.02	5.09	5.18
	attract	3.09	5.82	−2.74	−4.04	0.01	4.91	5.45
	excite	3.00	6.55	−3.55	−4.85	0.01	5.82	6.37
	impress	2.57	6.07	−3.50	−4.28	0.01	5.43	5.79
	oppress	1.85	5.50	−3.64	−6.18	0.01	5.57	6.14
	repulse	3.79	6.86	−3.07	−4.55	0.01	5.64	6.50
	surprise	3.92	5.69	−1.77	−3.12	0.01	4.85	5.38
	tire	2.57	6.21	−3.64	−8.53	0.01	5.36	5.93
	trouble	2.78	6.07	−3.29	−8.55	0.01	4.86	5.79
	$\bar{X}$	*3.00*	*6.02*	*−3.02*			*5.32*	*5.85*
SV	admire	5.92	2.85	3.07	4.44	0.01	6.23	5.38
	detest	7.00	2.09	4.91	8.47	0.01	7.00	5.91
	dread	6.27	2.64	3.64	5.59	0.01	6.45	6.09
	envy	6.45	2.36	4.09	8.60	0.01	6.09	5.64
	esteem	5.93	2.93	3.00	4.98	0.01	6.00	5.07
	like	5.71	2.50	3.21	5.32	0.01	6.07	5.29
	love	6.93	3.93	3.00	6.08	0.01	6.77	5.46
	loath	6.92	3.29	3.64	6.87	0.01	6.92	5.20
	trust	5.78	3.07	2.71	3.25	0.01	5.85	5.57
	pity	6.00	3.93	2.07	3.92	0.01	6.07	5.07
	$\bar{X}$	*6.91*	*3.17*	*3.33*			*6.34*	*5.47*

sentences were presented in both cases in a fixed random order. The ten verbs for each of the four verb categories of DAV, IAV, SAV and SV were selected from a corpus of over 3000 interpersonal verbs avoiding obscure or unusual terms (see Table 4.4 for the verbs used in the two studies).

Affective Inference   The average emotion ascribed to the subject and the object of the sentences as a function of verb category can be seen in Table 4.4 above. The subject–object differences for DAVs are mostly negligible and in three cases reach significance but in the reverse direction. In the case of IAVs the pattern is erratic with 4 of the 10 verbs showing the expected relationship (object ascribed more emotion than subject); 3 in the reverse direction and 3 non-significant differences. However, in the case of SAVs and SVs the predicted differences are very systematic and strong for all 10 verbs. In the case of all SAV sentences, the object of the sentence is ascribed significantly higher emotion and the reverse is observed for SV.

Causal Inference   Table 4.5 depicts the average causality ascribed to the subject and object of sentences as a function of verb category. The expectation for all action verbs was a stronger ascription of causality to sentence subject relative to sentence object and the reverse for SV sentences, namely relatively stronger ascription of causality to sentence object. Indeed, as can be seen from Table 4.5, these expectations were, by and large, confirmed within each verb category. For DAVs, all mean differences were in the expected direction, with 2 of the mean differences showing a trend and 5 significant by conventional standards. For IAVs, all mean differences were in the expected direction, with 2 non-significant differences, 2 showing a trend and 6 significant by conventional standards. In the case of SAVs, all mean differences are significant bar 4, which are also in the expected direction. With SVs, 7 mean differences are in the expected direction and 3 show a reverse relationship to the expected one. This is basically a replication of previous findings in the literature.

Correlational Analyses   A property of DAVs in contrast to the other verb categories is the interactional symmetry between sentence object and subject. This is in part reflected by the absence of systematic differences between subject and object in affective marking, but also by the relatively weak causal inference difference between subject and object. These causal and affective differences are more distinctly marked for the remaining verb categories,

Table 4.5 *Causality implicit in verb categories*

		Ascribed causality Subj.	Obj.	Xdiff.	t-value	sig. (df = 12)
DAV	call	3.85	3.54	0.31	1.48	0.09
	dance	4.69	4.15	0.54	1.72	0.06
	drive	4.77	3.15	1.62	2.19	0.05
	hug	4.69	3.30	1.39	2.25	0.03
	phone	3.92	3.07	0.84	2.01	0.05
	shout at	4.08	2.62	1.46	3.08	0.01
	talk to	5.38	5.00	0.38	0.79	n.s.
	touch	5.07	3.54	1.54	2.59	0.02
	visit	4.69	4.30	0.38	0.51	n.s.
	wave at	3.23	2.77	0.46	0.74	n.s.
	$\bar{X}$	*4.44*	*3.55*	*0.89*	*4.76*	*0.01*
IAV	betray	5.23	3.30	1.92	3.95	0.01
	defy	4.77	2.69	2.08	4.39	0.01
	deceive	4.77	4.00	0.77	1.64	0.07
	dominate	4.92	4.08	0.84	1.02	n.s.
	flirt	4.77	3.92	0.84	1.37	0.10
	harm	4.69	2.62	2.07	4.39	0.01
	help	4.69	3.69	1.00	1.56	0.08
	persuade	5.07	4.77	0.31	0.74	n.s.
	protect	4.77	3.15	1.62	3.07	0.01
	support	5.23	3.23	2.00	3.85	0.01
	$\bar{X}$	*4.89*	*3.55*	*1.35*	*5.16*	*0.01*
SAV	amaze	4.08	2.69	1.38	3.45	0.01
	amuse	5.69	2.77	2.92	7.98	0.01
	attract	4.85	3.23	1.62	3.15	0.01
	excite	3.69	3.54	0.15	0.20	n.s.
	impress	4.23	4.77	− 0.54	− 1.13	n.s.
	oppress	4.69	3.38	1.31	1.94	0.05
	repulse	3.77	3.69	0.08	0.20	n.s.
	surprise	4.38	3.69	0.69	1.82	n.s.
	tire	4.62	3.62	1.00	1.84	0.05
	trouble	4.69	3.69	1.00	1.70	0.06
	$\bar{X}$	*4.47*	*3.51*	*0.96*	*4.51*	*0.01*
SV	admire	3.33	5.15	− 1.77	− 2.38	0.02
	detest	2.92	4.77	− 1.84	− 1.80	0.05
	dread	3.54	5.00	− 1.46	− 2.30	0.03
	envy	4.77	4.23	0.54	0.86	n.s.
	esteem	4.69	4.46	0.23	0.38	n.s.
	like	3.92	4.07	− 0.15	− 0.43	n.s.
	love	3.84	4.38	− 0.54	− 0.99	n.s.
	loath	3.77	3.46	0.31	0.53	n.s.
	trust	4.07	4.62	− 0.54	− 1.29	n.s.
	pity	3.38	4.69	− 1.31	− 2.06	0.03
	$\bar{X}$	*3.83*	*4.48*	*− 0.65*	*− 3.09*	*0.01*

particularly SAV and SV. One possible way of elucidating this symmetry–asymmetry is by examining the relationship between subject affect and object affect within each verb category. In the case of DAV this is 0.91, whereas in the remaining three this correlation is negligible (IAV: $r = 0.04$; SAV: $r = 0.15$; SV: $r = 0.03$). In the case of ascribed subject and object causality the same pattern holds, namely DAVs show a strong correlation ($r = 0.70$), while for the remaining categories this relationship is comparatively weak and negative for SAV and SV (IAV: $r = 0.20$; SAV: $r = -0.37$; SV: $r = -0.41$).

Another feature that can be examined is the postulated relationship between subject cause and object affect for action verbs and in particular IAV and SAV. In our analysis we suggested that for IAV the action of the subject gives rise to an implicit affect for the sentence object, which is found in the positive correlation ($r = 0.45$) between sentence subject cause and object affect, which increases to 0.81 in the case of SAV. For DAV and SV there is no relationship indicated ($r = 0.01$ and $r = -0.03$ respectively).

These results suggest that for DAVs affective and causal inference is marked nearly symmetrically for sentence subject and object. We find that this symmetry does not hold for the remaining three verb classes. In the case of IAVs the idea that each action has some affective consequences upon the object of action finds some support in that the stronger the causal inference to the subject of a sentence, the stronger the ascribed affect to the object of the same sentence, and this effect increases for SAVs. For SAVs and SVs the expected affective marking for sentence object and subject respectively is supported.

The Temporal Properties of Interpersonal Verbs

The idea for this study was also derived by considering the features of social interaction that are preserved in interpersonal verbs. Although time is of central importance in understanding and examining the unfolding of social interaction it has remained a relatively neglected variable. One of the central aspects of social interaction is that each type of interaction and the type of state expressed towards or experienced about a person have different temporal implications. This time element can be seen as informative about social interaction and the persons involved in at least two different ways. The first is simply the temporal duration of the event. The second is the *stability* of the quality that can be ascribed to a person on the basis of the action or state expressed in an SvO sentence (see Semin and Fiedler, 1988, Studies 1 and 2), a property we termed 'endurability'.

If one considers these two properties as a function of verb category, then in the case of endurability we know from earlier studies (Semin and Fiedler, 1988) that sentences with DAVs do not suggest an inference of any stable characteristics or qualities about a person. We had argued and found that IAVs refer to characteristics that are manifested in an action and to that extent refer to relatively enduring properties of persons. SVs refer to states of longer duration and therefore are more likely to yield stable information about the person. Finally, with SAVs we have no information about the person eliciting the state, and the state that is evoked is temporary. Consequently, we would expect less stable inferences from this verb class than IAVs and SVs.

With respect to the first question, namely the temporal duration of the interpersonal event, we can make the following observations. For most DAVs the temporal reference of action is of very limited duration (such as, push, kiss, kick, and so on), though in other cases (such as phone, talk) the temporal duration of the event may be prolonged. In comparison, however, the temporal duration of events with IAVs is longer. Our expectation with regard to SAVs was unspecific (see above). Nevertheless, most SAVs refer to unspecified activities which have a longer duration than DAVs (such as amuse, oppress, tire, and so on). Obviously, with SVs the main reference is to a state which extends beyond a specific situation and to that extent we would expect the information about time implied by SVs to have the longest temporal duration of all four verb classes.

With a further 48 Sussex University undergraduates we examined the way in which time is marked in interpersonal verbs by simply asking them the temporal reference for the 40 sentences we used earlier. They had to indicate how long the event or state lasted on a seven-point scale, the needs of which were marked by 'Extremely Short' (1) and 'Very Prolonged' (7). The 40 SvO sentences were presented in a fixed random order in a booklet with some general instructions and examples preceding the task. A second group of 48 subjects took part in the 'Endurability Study'. The question that these subjects had to answer for the same sentences was 'How enduring a quality does the action or state described in this sentence express about the subject?'

To examine (1) the endurability of the quality expressed in the sentences, and (2) the temporal duration of the interpersonal event as a function of verb category, we first of all calculated the average value for each verb within category and subjected these averages to two one-way ANOVAs with verb category as the within-subjects factor with four levels.

Table 4.6   *Temporal properties of interpersonal verbs*

Verb class	DAV	IAV	SAV	SV
Duration of interpersonal event	2.15	3.77_a	4.13_a	5.52
Endurability of quality	3.04	4.96_a	4.10	4.69_a

Means sharing the same subscript do not differ from each other significantly at $p<0.05$ (SNK).

As can be seen from Table 4.6, we had a significant main effect in both cases (Endurability $F(3,39) = 17.07$; $p<0.01$). A closer inspection of the means reveals that there is a monotonic trend for the *temporal duration* as a function of verb class; however, the means for IAV and SAV are not significantly different from each other at the 5% level. In the case of *endurability* we find that IAV and SV do not differ from each other significantly at the 5% level, and that DAVs display the lowest degree of endurability. SAVs show an intermediary level of endurability between DAV and SV/IAV and are significantly different from all three categories.

Verifiability and Imaginability of Actions and States

The final set of features that we examined concerned an extension of what we originally termed 'verifiability', namely the ease or difficulty with which the actions and states that are referred to by interpersonal verbs can be objectively verified (Semin and Fiedler, 1988). Related to this variable is the issue of *disputability*, namely the contentiousness of propositions with these verb categories. The earlier argument that we advanced was that the more concrete a verb class the easier it is to verify the proposition and the less disagreement such statements will generate. This issue is also related to a contribution made by Rothbart and Park (1986) on the degree to which 'traits' are visible. These authors examined properties of traits that mark their 'visibility' by investigating a number of differential properties that they manifest. Chief among these was the ease of *imagining* behaviours that could *confirm* and *disconfirm* a trait. The confirmability/disconfirmability of interpersonal verbs is essentially related to the degree to which the referents of the verbs refer to concrete particularistic or abstract generalizing properties of social interaction. One can make specific predictions from the LCM about the operationalization of confirmability/disconfirmability, along the lines of the argument developed for the verifiability/disputability hypothesis (Semin and Fiedler, 1988, 1991). The more concrete the verb class in question, the more unambiguous the behavioural reference and the easier to imagine confirming or disconfirming instances. Furthermore, we would expect a complete symmetry between the confirmability and disconfirmability. That is, the easier it is to confirm a behaviour or state the easier it is to disconfirm it and, vice versa, the more difficult it is to disconfirm a behaviour or state the more difficult it is to confirm it. This contradicts Rothbart and Park's (1986) expectations and findings in the trait domain, but is in line with Funder and Dobroth's (1987) findings.

Finally, we also considered the possibility of examining an additional variable, which had to do with the number of different behaviours that people can imagine for each verb class. The prediction here was simply that the more abstract the verb category, the more alternative types of behaviours could be visualized. This is an alternative way of conceptualizing inclusiveness (see, among others, Hampson et al., 1986; John et al., 1991). That is, the more abstract verb classes refer to a greater number of behaviours that are distinct and are therefore more inclusive in terms of the general number of distinctive behaviours they can potentially refer to. The distinctive element in this approach, in contrast to category structure based arguments as espoused by Hampson and her colleagues (for example, Hampson et al., 1986; John et al., 1991), is that in this case a prediction about class inclusiveness is made: (1) with reference to a category system (or taxonomy) based on criteria independent from the dependent variables by which class inclusiveness is assessed; and (2) without employing any implicit or explicit semantic overlap criteria (that is, the category exemplars do not have any a priori semantic overlap).

Sixty University of Sussex undergraduates participated in these studies. We used the same 40 sentences as in the previous studies reported here (fixed random order presentation). Each of the 5 independent groups of 12 subjects were asked to answer the following questions respectively: (1) 'to which extent the statement can be objectively verified' [VERIFY]; (2) 'If the above statement were mentioned by someone, how likely is it that it could potentially lead to disagreement?' [DISAGREE]; (3) 'How easy is it to imagine specific, observable behaviours that would provide confirmation of this statement?' [CONFIR]; (4) 'How easy is it to imagine specific, observable behaviours that would provide disconfirmation of this statement?' [DISCON]; and finally (5) 'How many alternative behaviours can you visualize for the statement?' [BEHAV]. These variables were preceded with detailed instructions and the answers were provided on nine-point scales, with correspondent anchors for both scale and ends.

Table 4.7 provides the means for the five respective variables

Table 4.7 *Mean differences on verifiability measures as a
function of verb category*

Verb category	DAV	IAV	SAV	SV	F(1,3)	p
Verifiability	7.14$_a$	5.25$_b$	5.00$_b$	3.72$_c$	38.73	<0.001
Disagreement	2.80$_a$	5.28$_b$	4.91$_b$	5.12$_b$	20.38	<0.001
Confirmability ease	6.32$_a$	3.76$_b$	3.70$_b$	3.18$_b$	34.37	<0.001
Disconfirmability ease	5.71$_a$	3.87$_b$	3.86$_b$	3.56$_b$	18.02	<0.001
N of behaviours	2.48$_a$	4.73$_b$	5.20$_b$	4.24$_b$	15.75	<0.001

Means sharing the same subscript do not differ from each other significantly at
p<0.005 (SNK).
High values: on Verifiability mean easy to verify; on Disagreement, high
disagreement; on Confirmability and Disconfirmability, easy to confirm or
disconfirm; on N of behaviours, high number of alternative behaviours.

broken down by verb class and the planned mean comparisons. As
can be seen, with the exception of the number of behaviours
subjects can visualize, all the variables proceed in the expected
direction. DAVs are the easiest to verify, the easiest category to
imagine instances of confirming and disconfirming behaviours, and
present the lowest level of disagreement; SVs occupy the other end
on all these four continua. The main exception is the number of
different behaviours that subjects are able to visualize for SVs.
This category is lower, but not significantly, than the IAV and
SAV categories. This is not surprising to the extent that SVs refer
to unobservable states. Table 4.8 displays the correlations between
the 5 measures, showing that they are all interrelated in the
expected direction. Indeed, the relationship between confirmability
and disconfirmability is very strong and positive (0.91). These
results contradict Rothbart and Park's findings. There are two
possible accounts for this: (1) in the case of interpersonal verbs, it
may be the case that there is symmetry with respect to the number
of behaviours required to confirm and disconfirm an interpersonal
event or state; but (2) it may also be the case that Rothbart and
Park's findings are exceptional. The latter view is strengthened by
findings in the trait domain that contradict their research findings
(such as Funder and Dobroth, 1987; Semin and Fiedler, 1991).
   Essentially, these findings converge with our earlier findings, and
suggest that the categorization of interpersonal verbs proposed by
the LCM marks properties of verbs to do with their imaginability,
verifiability and related dimensions such as behavioural inclusiveness
along a dimension of concreteness–abstractness that moves from
DAV to SV. However, in order to examine if there is one or more
latent dimensions that underlie interpersonal verbs, we turned to an

Table 4.8   *Overall correlations between verifiability measures*

	BEHAV	VERIFY	DISAGREE	CONFIR	DISCON
VERIFY	−0.4250**				
DISAGREE	0.4450**	−0.6929**			
CONFIR	−0.5902**	0.7212**	−0.6932**		
DISCON	−0.4978**	0.6353**	−0.7081**	0.9139**	

** Signif. LE 0.01 (2-tailed)

overall analysis of interpersonal verbs, discussed in the final section below.

Discussion and Conclusions: Dimensions underlying Interpersonal Verbs

We have attempted to identify different features of social inter-action that are marked in interpersonal verbs. In doing so we utilized a classification that is derived *independently* from the cognitive properties of these verbs. In the studies reported above, our aim was to investigate types of systematic cognitive inferences these features mediate. The question that arises in this context is whether the diverse features that have been identified here can be simplified in terms of some underlying general dimensions that are characteristics of interpersonal verbs in general. Our previous research (Semin and Fiedler, 1988) suggested a dimension of concreteness–abstractness underlying the LCM on the basis of five inferential tasks; that is, with DAV as the most concrete category and SV as the most abstract verb category with IAV in between these two. The present research indicates that there are similar rela-tions operating at least for some of the marked properties of interpersonal verbs. These included *endurability, temporal duration* of an interpersonal event or state, questions related to *verifiability* and ease of *imaginability* of confirming and disconfirming instances. Evidently, the questions of how affect and causality are marked do not follow this pattern. In order to examine dimensions that underlie the marked properties of interpersonal verbs, we turned to a factor analysis of the above variables. This involved a principle components factor analysis with a varimax rotation. As can be seen from Table 4.9, the emerging solution is a two-factorial one with the first factor explaining 46.6% of the variance (eigen-value 5.59) and on which the following variables load highly: ease of imagining confirming instances, and disconfirming instances; temporal duration of the event; disagreement; verifiability of

Table 4.9 *Factor solution to the cognitive implications of interpersonal verbs*

	Factor I Abstractness–Concreteness	Factor II Inductive Inference
Confirmability	−0.91	−0.04
Disconfirmability	−0.86	−0.10
Temporal Duration	0.83	−0.30
Disagreement	0.83	0.10
Verifiability	−0.82	0.31
Endurability	0.81	0.13
Informativeness	0.71	0.19
Number of Behaviors	0.63	0.43
Affect/Object	0.31	0.78
Causality/Subject	−0.04	0.67
Causality/Object	0.29	−0.66
Affect/Subject	0.47	−0.53

statement; endurability of the quality in question, and how much it reveals about the person; and the number of different behaviours that can be visualized for the verb in question. This factor appears to be distinctly related to the concreteness–abstraction factor we identified in previous research (Semin and Fiedler, 1988, 1991).

The second factor, which accounts for 18.6% of the variance (eigenvalue of 2.23) is essentially characterized by the affective and causal inferential properties. Thus, the ends of this dimension are distinctively identified by Subject Causation / Object Affect versus Object Causation / Subject Affect.

An analysis of variance using the concreteness–abstractness factor score as dependent variable and Verb Category as a four-level factor yields a significant mean effect. As can be seen from Table 4.10, this supports the ordering of the four-level classification of interpersonal verbs in the expected direction with DAVs occupying the most concrete position and SVs the most abstract. IAVs and SAVs do not differ from each other significantly, and occupy an intermediary level of abstractness.

Table 4.10 *The Abstraction–Concreteness dimension as a function of verb category*

Verb category	DAV	IAV	SAV	SV	$F(1,3)$	p
Mean Abstraction score Factor I	−1.56$_a$	0.50$_b$	0.22$_b$	0.84$_c$	89.45	<0.001

Means not sharing the same subscripts significantly differ from each other at $p<0.05$ (SNK).

With respect to the second factor, a similar ANOVA of the factor scores by verb class also yields a significant main effect, as can be seen in Table 4.11. This suggests that SAVs and IAVs load positively and significantly differently from the remaining two classes, namely on the subject cause and object affect end of this inferential dimension. In contrast, SVs load on the subject affect and object cause end of the dimension and are significantly different from the remaining three categories. DAVs, not surprisingly, occupy an intermediary position, near the midpoint of this dimension, since they barely mediate any systematic affective or causal inference.

Table 4.11 *The Inference dimension as a function of verb category*

Verb category	DAV	IAV	SAV	SV	$F(1,3)$	p
Mean S/O Inference score						
Factor I	-0.23_a	0.70_b	0.86_b	-1.33_c	42.94	<0.001

Means not sharing the same subscripts significantly differ from each other at p<0.05 (SNK).

These final analyses suggest two fundamental aspects of the use of interpersonal terms. The first one is the level of abstraction that is used and the second one is about the position that affect/cause inferences occupy. Thus, it would seem that interpersonal terms code two general propensities. The first one relates to the diverse properties of the interaction (such as duration, the different types of behaviours that verbs can refer to, and so on), as well as the information that is revealed about the person (how enduring a quality the person manifests in interpersonal situations, and so on). At the same time, this dimension also subsumes information about the ease and difficulty with which the behaviours or states that these verbs refer to are identified, verified and the like. All this information is contributory to the abstraction–concreteness dimension; that is, information conveyed about qualities of the interaction. The inferential properties about who is doing what, why and what affective implications this doing has, are coded in the second dimension. These dimensions, however, are central in terms of understanding how discourse about social psychological matters are conveyed. These two dimensions thus provide an anchor, both conceptually and methodologically, about how people structure their communications. Where and how do they locate the origin of actions, how abstract is the communication and what does it convey about the personal properties of the interactants? The direct implications of these propensities are elaborated in the next chapter, as well as the chapters by Arcuri and Maass and by Hamilton et al.

Note

1. See Chapter 5 by Fiedler and Semin for a discussion of the use of the term *schema*.

References

Abelson, R. P. and Kanouse, D. E. (1966) Subjective acceptance of verbal generalizations. In S. Feldman (ed.), *Cognitive Consistency: Motivational Antecedents and Behavioral Consequents*, pp. 171–197. New York: Academic Press.

Bendix, E. H. (1966) *Componential Analysis of General Vocabulary: The Semantic Structure of a Set of Verbs in English, Hindu and Japanese*. The Hague: Mouton.

Brown, R. and Fish, D. (1983) The psychological causality implicit in language. *Cognition*, 14: 233–274.

Cunningham, J. D., Starr, P. A., and Kanouse, D. E. (1979) Self as actor, active observer and passive observer: Implications for causal attribution. *Journal of Personality and Social Psychology* 37: 1146–1152.

DeGrada, E. and Mannetti, L. (1991) Interpersonal verbs: implicit causality of action verbs and contextual factors. *European Journal of Social Psychology* 21: 429–444.

Fiedler, K. and Semin, G. R. (1988) On the causal information conveyed by different interpersonal verbs: The role of implicit sentence context. *Social Cognition*, 6: 12–39.

Fiedler, K. and Semin, G. R. (1990) Further semantic studies on the external validity of the Linguistic Category Model. Unpublished research, University of Giessen.

Fiedler, K., Semin, G. R., Ritter A., Bode, P. and Medenbach, M. (1991) A discourse grammar approach to understanding the causal impact of interpersonal verbs. MS under editorial consideration.

Fiedler, K., Semin, G. R. and Bolten, S. (1989) Language use and reification of social information: Top-down and bottom-up processing in person cognition. *European Journal of Social Psychology*, 19: 271–295.

Fiedler, K., Semin, G. R. and Koppetsch, C. (1990) Language use and attributional biases in close personal relationships. *Personality and Social Psychology Bulletin*, 17: 147–154.

Franco, F. and Arcuri, L. (1990) Effect of semantic valence on implicit causality of verbs. *British Journal of Social Psychology*, 29: 161–170.

Funder, D. C. and Dobroth, K. M. (1987) Differences between traits: Properties associated with interjudge agreements. *Journal of Personality and Social Psychology* 52: 408–418.

Garvey, C. and Caramazza, A. (1974) Implicit causality in verbs. *Linguistic Inquiry*, 5: 459–464.

Giles, H. and Coupland, N. (1991) *Language: Contexts and Consequences*. Oxford: Oxford University Press.

Giles, H. and Robinson, P. W. (eds) (1990) *Handbook of Language and Social Psychology*. Chichester: Wiley.

Hampson, S. E., John, O. and Goldberg, L. R. (1986) Category breadth and hierarchical structure in personality: Studies of asymmetries in judgments of trait implications. *Journal of Personality and Social Psychology*, 51: 37–54.

Heider, F. (1958) *The Psychology of Interpersonal Relations*. New York: Wiley.

Hoffman, C., Lau, I. and Johnson, D. R. (1986) The linguistic relativity of person cognition: An English–Chinese comparison. *Journal of Personality and Social Psychology*, 51: 1097–1105.

Hoffman, C. and Tschir, M. A. (1990) Interpersonal verbs and dispositional adjectives: The psychology of causality embodied in language. *Journal of Personality and Social Psychology*, 58: 765–778.

John, O. P., Hampson, S. E. and Goldberg, L. R. (1991) The basic level in personality-trait hierarchies: Studies of trait use and accessibility in different contexts. *Journal of Personality and Social Psychology*, 60: 348–361.

Johnson-Laird, P. N. and Oatley, K. (1989) The language of emotions: An analysis of a semantic field. *Cognition and Emotion*, 3: 81–123.

Maass, A., Salvi, D., Arcuri, L. and Semin, G. R. (1989) Language use in intergroup contexts. *Journal of Personality and Social Psychology*, 57: 981–993.

McArthur, L. (1972) The how and what of why: Some determinants and consequences of causal attribution. *Journal of Personality and Social Psychology*, 22: 171–193.

Miller, G. and Johnson-Laird, P. N. (1976) *Language and Perception*. Cambridge: CUP.

Rothbart, M. and Park, B. (1986) On the confirmability and disconfirmability of trait concepts. *Journal of Personality and Social Psychology*, 50: 131–142.

Semin, G. R. (1989). The contribution of linguistic factors to attribute inferences and semantic similarity judgments. *European Journal of Social Psychology*, 19: 85–100.

Semin, G. R. and Fielder, K. (1988). The cognitive functions of linguistic categories in describing persons: Social cognition and language. *Journal of Personality and Social Psychology*, 54: 558–567.

Semin, G. R. and Fielder, K. (1989). Relocating attributional phenomena within a language–cognition interface: the case of actors' and observers' perspectives. *European Journal of Social Psychology*, 19: 491–508.

Semin, G. R. and Fielder, K. (1991). The linguistic category model, its bases, applications and range. In W. Stroebe and M. Heartstone (eds), *European Review of Social Psychology*, vol. 2. Chichester: Wiley.

Semin, G. R. and Greenslade, L. (1985). Differential contributions of linguistic factors to memory based ratings: Systematizing the systematic distortion hypothesis. *Journal of Personality and Social Psychology*, 49: 1713–1723.

Van Kleeck, M. H., Hilliger, L. A. and Brown, R. (1988) Pitting verbal schemas against information variables in attribution. *Social Cognition*, 6: 89–106.

5

Attribution and Language as a Socio-cognitive Environment

Klaus Fiedler and Gün R. Semin

The basic assumption underlying the present chapter is that many psychological phenomena which are usually conceived as cognitive, motivational or emotional processes within the minds and brains of individual people are permanently installed in language as an autonomous system above and beyond the individual. Language not only provides a connected network of crystallized world knowledge but also a sophisticated system of rules and communication norms that restrict the kind of information which is likely to be conveyed and maintained in social encounters. Thus, encyclopaedic knowledge is reflected in verbal taxonomies, conceptual similarities, or goal structures (Borkenau, 1990; Hoffman et al., 1981; Rosch and Mervis, 1975); empirical correlations are represented, although sometimes misrepresented, in semantic similarities between attributes (Fiedler, 1985; Semin and Greenslade, 1985; Shweder, 1977); the potential range of variability and quantitative or qualitative distinctions in certain content domains relies on the availability of appropriate terms and quantifiers (Brown, 1986; Whorf, 1956); and even the experience of emotions seems to be moderated by linguistic labels (Schachter, 1964; Weiner, 1986). Moreover, the human need to be understood, to appear credible and attractive, and to be cooperative in communication (Grice, 1975) imposes marked constraints on the selection and format of information that is actually conveyed, comprehended, and socialized in language acquisition. Language provides, as it were, a crucial ecology for the informational and behavioural exchange between people.

Highlighting the autonomy of language as an external complement to human memory does of course not imply a simple unicausal relation from language to cognition. As with many other complex, dialectic systems (such as traffic systems in big capitals, economic markets, or the world climate), the concept of (local) causality is rather worthless when it comes to understanding the language–cognition interface which reflects a long cultural and phylogenetical development. Over hundreds of human generations, linguistic terms have been coined to express finer and finer cognitive distinctions, but language has been used to socialize the communicable part of human intelligence. And so does the dialectic interplay of the thinkable and the expressible continue to develop with cultural need. From such a perspective, it is evident that general assumptions on the causal primacy of either language or cognition cannot be derived from, say, reaction time analyses of arbitrarily selected experimental tasks. Let us therefore avoid the chicken–egg problem and try to tolerate the premise that we are not concerned here with causal direction.

However, it is nevertheless reasonable and theoretically important to separate cognition as an intrapersonal process and language as a complementary ecological factor at any given time in the cultural or ontogenetic development. This is important for theories in social cognition, for instance, to point out that the ecology of language provides alternatives to many cognitivist explanations in much the same way as Garner (1986) or Gibson (1979) have emphasized neglected ecological factors deliminiting the range of internal information processing. It is interesting to note that nobody would come to doubt the theoretical autonomy of the ecological factors alluded to in the Gibsonian approach, although these external factors are clearly not independent of internal processes. Rather, the impact of any ecological forces depends on the availability of appropriate receptors and neural mechanisms to respond to these forces. Thus, with some reflection we see that the language approach to social cognition has the same theoretical relevance and justification as the ecological approach in general. It *is* in fact, one such approach.

It makes sense to pretend that many social-cognitive phenomena are already inherent in language in that (1) purely linguistic analyses of text corpora or of the lexicon may 'simulate' cognitive phenomena (for example, Semin, 1989); (2) cognitive phenomena may turn out to be special cases of more general or inclusive linguistic habits (Fiedler, Semin, Ritter, Bode and Medenbach, 1992; Semin and Fiedler, 1989); (3) language rules may override predictions from cognitive theories (Fiedler, Semin and Koppetsch, 1991); or (4) rational decisions and behaviours may depend on the linguistic framing of logically equivalent problem situations (Fiedler, 1988; Tversky and Kahneman, 1981). In all these respects, the explicit consideration of language as a complement to intrapersonal, cognitive factors can improve and enrich our theorizing in the cognitive and social-cognitive domain.

Attribution Theories and Language

In the remainder of this chapter, we attempt to illustrate the neglected role of language with reference to the one discipline of social psychology that is most representative of the 'cognitive revolution' (Dember, 1974) and that has prompted the greatest number of published articles, namely, theories of attribution. Attribution research is concerned with subjective explanations of social behaviour, and such explanations usually involve an inference from observable data (actions, events, speech acts) to non-observable, generic attributes (causes, reasons, dispositions). Because of the resemblance of this task to scientific inference tasks, attribution theorists have modelled attribution processes as causal or dispositional inferences based on either empirical data arrays (Jones and Davis, 1965; Kelley, 1967) or cognitively represented theories or causal schemata (Kelley, 1972; Reeder and Brewer, 1979). Even when these data-driven or theory-driven explanations are occasionally subject to motivational or self-serving biases (Hewstone, 1989; Zuckerman, 1979), such biases are still described as deviations from normative models of scientific explanations. However, reviews and textbook treatments of attribution theories virtually never mention the potential role of language and the possibility that some causal schemata and attributional biases may be located in language as a collective store outside the memories of individual people (see Hewstone, 1983; Kelley and Michela, 1980; Watson, 1982).

If attribution involves an inference from observable information to non-observable explanatory constructs, or speaking loosely, from behaviours to dispositions, this process can be paraphrased in linguistic terms as a shift from a more specific level of language use (typically verbs) to a more abstract level (typically adjectives). As a methodological tool for the content-free assessment and analysis of such variation in the domain of interpersonal language, we have proposed the Linguistic Category Model (LCM; Semin and Fiedler, 1988, 1991) which entails a four-level hierarchy of predicates to be used in interpersonal language.[1] As summarized and illustrated in Table 5.1, the four linguistic categories are, ordered from the least to most abstract level: Descriptive Action Verbs (DAV), Interpretive Action Verbs (IAV), State Verbs (SV), and Adjectives (ADJ). This classification or coding system is termed a 'model' because it can not only be used for the coding of free behaviour descriptions (at an objectivity of about 90 per cent) but is also charged with theoretical implications regarding the cognitive-semantical implication of different word classes. With increasing

Table 5.1 *Four-level distinction of interpersonal terms according to the Linguistic Category Model (Semin and Fiedler, 1988)*

Level	Category	Examples	Characteristic features
I	Descriptive Action Verbs (DAV)	call meet hit visit	Reference to single behavioural event; reference to specific context or situation; objective description of observable events; at least one physically invariant feature.
II	Interpretive Action Verbs (IAV)	cheat imitate help inhibit	Reference to single behavioural event; reference to context or situation; interpretation beyond mere description; no physically invariant feature; typically evaluatively charged.
III	State Verbs (SV)	admire hate like abhor	Enduring states, abstracted from single events; reference to social object, but not situation; no context reference preserved; interpretation and evaluation.
IV	Adjectives (ADJ)	honest reliable helpful hostile	Highly abstract person disposition; no object reference or situation reference; no context reference; highly interpretive, detached from specific behaviours.

abstraction, from DAVs to ADJs, behaviour descriptions become increasingly informative regarding the sentence subject, more temporally stable, more disputable and dependent on subjective interpretations, more detached from the situational context, but less verifiable, and abstract sentences imply less voluntary control. When stimulus sentences with DAVs, IAVs, SVs, and ADJs as predicate are rated with respect to these semantic implications, discriminant analyses on the covariance matrix of these ratings typically result in at least 90 per cent correct identifications of predicates as DAV, IAV, SV, or ADJ (Semin and Fiedler, 1988, 1991). Therefore, using the LCM for attributional analyses of free behaviour descriptions is not only practicable but promises to reveal new insights into semantic implications confounded with attribution-like shifts in language level (that is, from less to more abstract statements).

The pervasive 'explanatory need' (Schachter, 1964) or the ubiquitous tendency to provide attributions to maintain control over the social and physical world is likewise reflected in a similarly pervasive tendency toward abstract levels of language use, at least in descriptions of *other* people's behaviour. Since language users are committed to Grice's (1975) principle of cooperation, it is part of their communication task to be informative and interesting in addition to being accurate, and this forces them to provide interpretations and (affective) evaluations beyond pure descriptions. Talking about people in terms of DAVs is certainly most objective and verifiable, but would soon cause a breakdown of communication because purely descriptive speech is extremely monotonous and circumstantial and undermines people's motivation to communicate. We demonstrated this phenomenon in a recent study (see Fiedler et al., 1989) employing the following retelling game. Subjects were provided with descriptions of social characters which were constructed to represent persons on certain levels of the LCM. Their task was to identify the characters (for example, porter, manager, nurse, designer) belonging to the descriptions and then to retell the descriptions in their own words. Subsequent subjects then received the second version and were again asked to retell the texts for even other subjects. Analyses of such successive communications showed that the prevalence of abstract terms, especially adjectives, increased rapidly in free communications (Fiedler et al., 1989).

However, this tendency towards abstract, interpretive language use is not invariant across people and situations but is obviously moderated by social factors. Of most interest to attribution theory is the variation between self-related and other-related speech. In general, people are much more reluctant to describe themselves in the same abstract, trait-like attributes that they use when describing other persons. It is obviously not our own role and task to bestow personality traits or dispositions to ourselves because such self-related testimonies are ambiguous and less than credible. Claiming to be *honest* would mean to be one's own witness. Likewise, one can hardly convincingly claim to be *intelligent* or *attractive* for such attributions require independent and unbiased referees. Self-attribution of negative traits is no less problematic because the speech act underlying self-derogation is seldom clear. If someone speaks of himself or herself as *wicked*, this is seldom understood (and meant) literally but often ironically or tactically. Thus, for various reasons, self-attributions appear blatant and suspect, and the very act of abstraction involved in the attribution process requires the participation of other, less prejudiced and biased people than the self.

There are further reasons for the assumed difference between self- and other-related language that we shall readdress in the final discussion. For the moment, let us take it for granted, as a general rule, that self-descriptions tend to be less abstract than descriptions of other people. We then arrive at an alternative account of the familiar actor–observer discrepancy in attribution (Jones and Nisbett, 1972; Watson, 1982) which may simply reflect differential language styles underlying actors' self-attributions as opposed to observers' other-attributions. That is, actors' reluctance to explain their own behaviour in terms of internal dispositions or traits and their preference for external attributions to situational circumstances may reflect their avoidance of abstract self-related terms. By contrast, observers' preference for internal, dispositional attributions may originate in their generalized abstractness tendency. Recall that specific terms (DAVs and IAVs) entail references to the situational context while abstract terms (ADJs and SVs) are most revealing about the personality.

Linguistic Simulation of the Actor–Observer Effect

The hypothesized language-differences between actors and observers and the potential of these differences to account for attributional biases were tested in a 'simulation' of the well-known results by Nisbett et al. (1973, Study 2). These authors asked their subjects to rate possible causes of why they had chosen their subject major and why they liked their boyfriend/girlfriend (actor perspective) as well as why their best friend had chosen his/her major or liked his/her boyfriend/girlfriend (observer perspective). The perspective bias was manifested in higher ratings of internal causes in observers' attributions about their best friends but relatively higher ratings of external causes for their own behaviour. Exactly the same tasks were employed by Semin and Fiedler (1989) except that free verbalizations of actors' and observers' explanations were assessed using the LCM as a coding scheme. All statements were coded at the sentence level using abstractness weights 1, 2, 3, and 4, to represent DAVs, IAVs, SVs, and ADJs, respectively. Moreover, these weights were multiplied by a positive or negative sign ($+1$ or -1) depending on whether a sentence referred to external (positive sign) or internal factors (negative sign). The resulting coefficients can vary between -4 (most abstract internal attribution) to $+4$ (highest level of external attribution). In these coding decisions, the well-documented fact was considered that SVs, as opposed to DAVs, IAVs, and ADJs, point to a cause within the sentence object rather the subject (for example, the sentence 'Mary admires Joan' implies a cause within Joan; see Abelson and Kanouse, 1966; Brown and Fish, 1983; Fiedler and Semin, 1988). The sign of SV coefficients was therefore inverted.

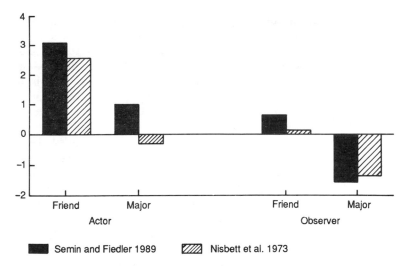

Figure 5.1 *Simulation of actor–observer discrepancy according to Nisbett et al. (1973) using linguistic analyses of free data*

A composite score was computed that aggregates these scores across all sentences produced by each individual in a given task (subject versus friend) × perspective (actor versus observer) condition. The pertinent means are shown in Figure 5.1 along with a comparable score constructed from the Nisbett et al. data. The similarity of both patterns of results is compelling, suggesting that typical findings in the actor–observer domain can be 'simulated' successfully in a linguistic analysis of free verbalizations. In this respect, it is important to note that the coding is based on formal criteria and never involves any 'silent' attributions. Furthermore, the language approach is independent of meaningful decisions as to what constitutes an internal or an external attribution and thereby evades a serious problem associated with free response attributions

Language Styles Extending to Non-causal Descriptions
However, the methodological issue of free response data aside, the assumption can be upheld that language styles may provide an alternative account of the actor–observer bias. On the other hand, the evidence presented thus far is merely correlational, showing that biased attribution judgments from actors' and observers' perspectives are accompanied by corresponding differences in linguistic abstractness. Thus, while a neglected factor is certainly identified, we have not yet gained any new evidence. The differential language styles may simply reflect different judgments which

may be expressed at an appropriate level of linguistic abstractness, rather than a genuinely linguistic phenomenon in its own right. That is, the less abstract statements by actors than observers may occur *because* actors reach different causal attributions than observers in the first place. Thus, an important next step is to demonstrate the independence of language styles from causal reasoning. For this purpose, we extended the analysis of actors' and observers' language to cover non-causal person descriptions that do not involve any *why* questions (Semin and Fiedler, 1989, Study 1). If the abstractness effect is still obtained, it can hardly be dismissed as an artificial consequence of intermediate causal judgments. Rather, the perspective influence on language styles may turn out to be a more universal phenomenon than the actor–observer bias in causal attribution.

Subjects were simply asked to recall and describe behaviour episodes prompted by ten thematic cues pertaining to five positive topics (such as pleasant acquaintance, an altruistic act) and five negative topics (such as great fear, failure at school). They were instructed to remember one particular experience in response to each cue and then to describe that experience in one or two sentences. In the actor condition, the subject himself/herself was the protagonist of the reported episode; in the observer condition, the protagonist had to be some other person. Causal explanations were not called for, and the reported descriptions virtually never included causal references (for example, 'because' phrases, reasons, intentions, explicit explanations) but protocol-like statements. Sentences were coded for the abstractness of the predicate (using LCM) as well as the inclusion of references to the spatial, temporal, instrumental, and social context of the reported episode.

Of major interest are the proportions of sentence predicates produced by actors and observers at different levels of linguistic abstractness, as summarized in Figure 5.2. To control for the unequal base rates of linguistic categories, we present the *ratios* of actor proportions divided by observer proportions for each predicate level. Ratios greater than 1 indicate a predominance of actor attributions at the particular language level. The central prediction of higher abstractness from the observer than the actor perspective is clearly borne out in that the ratios decrease sharply and monotonically from left (No Predicate) to right (ADJ). ADJ attributions were most likely to stem from observers while DAV sentences were mainly produced from the actor perspective. Equally typical of the actor perspective are statements with no explicit predicate, consisting of nothing but adverbial references to situational circumstances.

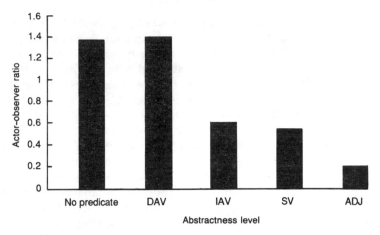

Figure 5.2 *Actor–observer ratio of attributions at different linguistic levels (Semin and Fiedler, 1989)*

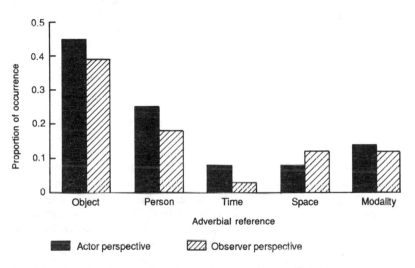

Figure 5.3 *Prevalence of context references for attributions from different perspectives* (Semin and Fiedler, 1989)

Our contention that actors' and observers' opposite attribution tendencies are correlated with differential language habits is further supported by the analysis of situational references (Figure 5.3). Here we find consistently higher proportions of references to object persons and third persons and temporal adverb phrases in actors' as compared to observer's descriptions. Although this trend does not hold for spatial and modality adverbs, the perspective main effect is statistically significant and highlights the linguistic 'preparedness' of actors to provide situation attributions.

No doubt, language habits change markedly with the perspective even when verbal reports are non-causal in nature. This precludes the most artificial interpretation of the language differences obtained in the first study, but does of course not represent a strict proof of *causal independence* of language from causal thinking. Even when it could be assured by clever experimentation or cognitive process analyses that free verbalizations in this experiment were never mediated by causal thinking, the language habits may nevertheless reflect a long learning history of causal judgments. As already noted, this argument is impossible to refute experimentally, just as the argument cannot be denied that the cognitive learning of causal knowledge is influenced by the language of socialization agents and by the linguistic ecology. In any case, it would be worthless to create an artificial distinction between language and cognition or to make the point that one has causal primacy over the other.

Actor–Observer Bias versus Egocentric Bias

We therefore followed a more promising research strategy in our attempt to substantiate the important role of language in attributions. Instead of separating language and cognition artificially, we tried to establish the *theoretical* autonomy of the language approach showing that it may solve theoretical conflicts and improve on existing attribution theories. For instance, contradictory predictions can be derived from the actor–observer bias and the so-called egocentric bias (Ross and Sicoly, 1979; Thompson and Kelley, 1981) when it comes to attributions in close personal relationships. Applying the actor–observer bias to dyadic relations, internal attributions to the partner should be more likely than internal self-attributions. On the other hand, the notion of an egocentric bias says that people living in intimate relationships attribute more responsibility for dyadic behaviours to themselves rather than their partners.

Since the theories underlying the two biases are not explicitly restricted to specific kinds of attribution, the theoretical conflict can hardly be denied. Thus, aside from motivational factors, the actor–observer discrepancy is theoretically explained in terms of perceptual perspectives or the asymmetry of knowledge about the self and others (see Watson, 1982). An observer perceives the actor as a figure against the ground of the environment, whereas the actor's own perception is directed at environmental factors. Likewise, the actor has knowledge of many external factors forcing him or her to act in a certain way while the observer does not share that background knowledge. Theories such as these do not in and of themselves impose constraints on the kind of perspective-contingent attributions; the figure–ground principle should lead observers to highlight observable actions as well as latent traits in the actor.

With regard to the commonly accepted availability explanation of the egocentric bias (see Ross and Sicoly, 1979; Tversky and Kahneman, 1973), there is also no reason to doubt that the easier recall of one's own behaviours as compared to one's partner's behaviours implies a similar bias at all levels of attribution. Thus, there is no cogent way of inferring from the availability theory different predictions for attributions at different levels of abstraction. This should be stated in advance to prevent an 'I knew it all along effect' (Fischhoff, 1975) reaction to the language-based solution of the theoretical conflict.

If language habits generalize to intimate relationships, we would expect partner-related verbalizations to be more abstract than self-related statements. Is is therefore possible that both tendencies, the actor–observer bias as well as the egocentric bias, occur simultaneously although at different language levels. This is actually what a closer look at the relevant literature reveals. Experiments in the actor–observer domain are typically concerned with trait attributions at the ADJ level. By contrast, the empirical evidence for the egocentric bias refers to attributions of actions and accomplishments that are usually expressed at the IAV level. Thus, the LCM was again employed by Fiedler, Semin and Koppetsch (1991) to elucidate the systematic tendencies underlying attributions in close relationships.

Participants were student couples that could be classified as intimate relationships; most of them had been living together for several years. Both members of each pair were received separately and their data were analysed independently. Their task was simply to provide written descriptions of their relationship pertaining either to themselves or their partners. No further restrictions were mentioned in the instruction; their verbal reports might refer to traits, activities, feelings, or habits. In addition to the free verbalization task, all participants were presented with a traditional egocentric-bias questionnaire (translated from Thompson and Kelley, 1981) and answered several questions about the relationship. Free descriptions were coded at the sentence level with regard to the subject (self, partner, unclear), the predicate (DAV, IAV, SV, ADJ, No Predicate) and the evaluative tone (positive, negative, neutral).

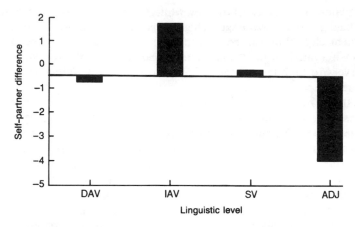

Figure 5.4   *Prevalence of self and partner attributions at different linguistic levels (Fiedler, Semin and Koppetsch, 1991)*

First of all, the usual egocentric bias in the questionnaire responses could be replicated for the present sample. Of greater interest, however, are the analyses of the free descriptions. As is evident from Figure 5.4, we find strong and reliable differences between self-related and partner-related descriptions in terms of the level of linguistic abstraction. In particular, there is a predominance of partner attributions at the ADJ level (that is, an actor–observer bias) but at the same time a predominance of self-attributions at the IAV level (that is, an egocentric bias). Further analyses showed that this pattern of results is independent of subject sex and not mainly due to a self-serving bias. Moreover, ratings of satisfaction with the relationship could be predicted from the proportions of positive terms used to describe the dyad (with IAVs receiving the highest regression weight).

Several conclusions from these findings seem justified. First, the usefulness of the LCM as a methodological tool is demonstrated in another study. Second, we have another piece of evidence for the lower abstractness of self-related as compared to other-related language, and this simple principle of language use can account in a parsimonious fashion for various phenomena. Third, the language approach is shown to predict and explain new phenomena that cannot be derived from the established cognitivist theories. And finally, an increase in theoretical precision is gained by the inclusion of language levels as a moderator of attributions in interpersonal contexts.

Thus, regardless of the causal relation between language and cognition, the linguistic approach may be of heuristical value and may help to improve existing theories. Again one might argue that language styles are but a reflection of the cognitive origins assumed to underlie the egocentric bias or the perspective bias. But one may respond, with the same justification, that those biases are unlikely to develop independently of the linguistic ecology. What is more important, however, is that the systematic reversal in partner attribution would be difficult to understand if the moderating influence of language levels were not taken into account.

Let us carry the analysis of attributional biases one more step further and raise the social platform from interpersonal to *intergroup* attribution. Neither the perceptual perspective deemed to explain the actor–observer bias nor the availability account of the egocentric bias can be readily applied to ingroup–outgroup differences in attribution (see Hewstone, 1988). Members of the outgroup as well as the ingroup (except the self) are perceived from an observer perspective. And to the extent that group-serving biases occur in *ad hoc* groups and minimal group situations (see Brewer, 1979; Tajfel, 1970), ingroup-related information cannot be assumed to be more familiar or more available in memory. However, the difference between self- and other-related language may well extend to group situations, suggesting an analogous difference between ingroup- and outgroup-related language. Thus, intergroup studies afford a new opportunity to demonstrate the autonomy of the language approach.

Language and Intergroup Biases

As a matter of fact, again, research and theorizing on intergroup processes has largely ignored the role of language. Theories originating in the cognitive tradition (Hamilton and Trolier, 1986; Rothbart and John, 1985) or in the sociological tradition (Tajfel and Turner, 1979) have emphasized either the greater sophistication of ingroup than outgroup concepts or the dynamics of group identity to account for intergroup biases. Social identity theory (Tajfel and Turner, 1979) states that people who identify with their social group try to achieve positive identity in a kind of social comparison process at the group level, attributing more favourable characteristics to the ingroup than the outgroup. Therefore, the basic attributional bias derived from social identity theory as well as real conflict theories (Sherif, 1967) is *ingroup favouritism* and *relative outgroup devaluation*. On the other hand, the basic domain of cognitive approaches is the phenomenon of relative *outgroup homogeneity*; that is, the tendency to judge an outgroup in a more undifferentiated and global fashion than the ingroup

(Park and Rothbart, 1982), generalizing outgroup attributions uncritically over many individual group members. While the abstractness of language use is obviously related to the latter phenomenon, its relevance to the former phenomenon of outgroup devaluation is not apparent at first sight.

A recent investigation by Maass et al. (1989), using the LCM to analyse attributions among Italian *palio* teams (*palio* is a competitive horse-racing game), suggests a common linguistic factor involved in the two basic intergroup phenomena. Attributions that confirm the group-serving bias were found to be expressed at a higher level of abstractness. That is, negative attributes of the outgroup and positive attributes of the ingroup were likely to be expressed in more abstract terms than attributions which counteract a group-serving bias. Thus, a process of differential abstraction may contribute to outgroup devaluation and ingroup favouritism. Moreover, since negative outgroup attributes were especially likely to be expressed in abstract, simplifying terms, the pattern of language use also simulates a relative outgroup homogeneity effect and suggests a possible link between outgroup devaluation and homogeneity. The following study by Fiedler, Semin and Finkenauer (1992) provides an attempt to replicate and extend these findings and sheds further light on the role of language in attributions at the group level.

The design of the study was a conceptual analogue of the partner study by Fiedler, Semin and Koppetsch (1991) reported above. Instead of having male and female individuals describe themselves and their partners, however, we now asked male and female people to provide free verbalizations about male and female people in general – that is, about their gender ingroup and outgroup. Free descriptions were prompted by ten cue words representing typical topics of the 'battle of words' between gender groups. These topics are listed in Table 5.2 along with mean ratings (from independent judges) on several scales that are most relevant to common intergroup theories: conflict proneness, degree of intergroup experience or familiarity with the opposite gender group in relation to each topic, emotional involvement, and the symbolic value of each topic for identification with one's gender group. The resulting verbal data were quite comparable to the free verbalizations from the partner study. All statements were again coded for subject reference (ingroup, outgroup, unclear), predicate level (DAV, IAV, SV, ADJ, rest category) and valence (positive, neutral, negative).

The percentages of positive, negative and neutral sentences with either the self or one's partner as a subject and a predicate at the

Table 5.2 *Outgroup derogation and relative outgroup homogeneity in language descriptions of gender ingroup and outgroup, as a function of topics*

Topic	Relative outgroup devaluation	Relative outgroup homogeneity	Conflict proneness of topic	Intergroup experience per topic	Emotional involvement	Identification value
Driving	27.83	1.53	3.90	3.78	3.85	4.58
Pregnancy prevention	22.72	2.29	4.49	4.54	2.15	5.26
Work competition	22.26	2.37	3.88	2.76	2.91	5.56
Housework	11.91	1.72	4.52	3.56	3.24	5.35
Initiative in dating	11.56	1.11	3.18	4.89	3.44	4.49
Fidelity	10.45	0.45	5.21	5.41	2.35	3.30
Affect	9.88	0.50	4.81	6.02	3.85	4.80
Education	5.25	1.39	3.61	1.38	3.03	4.19
Sexuality	5.28	0.34	5.15	5.34	3.65	5.04
Outfit	5.22	1.08	3.17	4.37	3.38	4.50

Relative devaluation is defined as the prevalence of positive ingroup and negative outgroup statements minus negative ingroup and positive outgroup statements, when statements at different levels of abstractness are weighted 1 (DAV), 2 (IAV), 3 (SV), and 4 (ADJ), respectively. Relative outgroup homogeneity is defined in terms of loadings on the first principal component of a language use similarity matrix, as explained in the text.

DAV, IAV, SV, or ADJ level were calculated for each participant (aggregating across topics). More specifically, three different scores were derived from these basic percentages, separately for positive versus negative statements and for ingroup- versus outgroup-related statements: (1) a PERC score which indicates the summed percentage (across topics and predicate levels) and which is sensitive to relative *frequency* of all positive and negative statements about the ingroup and outgroup; (2) an ABST score for mean *abstractness* of all statements (giving abstractness values 1, 2, 3, or 4 to statements at levels DAV, IAV, SV, and ADJ, respectively); and (3) an integral score INT defined as a weighted sum (weighting percentages of DAVs, IAVs, SVs, and ADJs by the abstractness values 1, 2, 3, and 4, respectively) such that $INT = PERC \times ABST$. Note that separate PERC, ABST, and INT scores can be computed for descriptions of positive ingroup behaviour $(I+)$, positive outgroup behaviour $(O+)$, negative ingroup behaviour $(I-)$ and negative outgroup behaviour $(O-)$. Note further that PERC, ABST, and INT can be computed per subject (aggregating across topics) as well as per topic (aggregating across subjects).

The first result to be reported is the replication of the familiar perspective (ingroup versus outgroup) by language use (DAV, IAV, SV, ADJ) interaction even at the intergroup level. Ingroup descriptions were more likely at lower levels of abstraction whereas a reversal was obtained for ADJ statements which were more likely in outgroup descriptions. Thus, we have further evidence for a perspective bias in language use, and this bias is more universal than the domain of the actor–observer bias or the egocentric bias at the individual level. Adjectives or simplifying trait terms seem to be more adequate or 'permissible' in descriptions of others than in self-descriptions, according to some quite general communication rule.

At the same time, however, the group results diverge markedly from the partner results. While there was no sign of a self-serving bias or derogation of the loved partner, the basic phenomenon of outgroup derogation is clearly evident at the group level (although largely confined to female respondents). Thus, the tendency to use more abstract ADJs in outgroup than ingroup descriptions is moderated and overridden by a much stronger tendency to give more favourable ingroup than outgroup descriptions. While this difference is not surprising, it is worth noting, incidentally, that an LCM count of free response data can also be profitably used in intergroup research.

The central phenomenon of ingroup-favouritism and relative outgroup derogation is clearly evident in an analysis of the integral

INT score that is sensitive to *how many and how abstract* terms are used to ascribe positive or negative attributes to the ingroup and the outgroup. The inequality $(INT_{I+} + INT_{O-}) > (INT_{I-} + INT_{O+})$ is highly significant, indicating a strong group-serving bias.

However, when INT is decomposed into its multiplicative components, ABST and PERC, we find only partial support for the Maass et al. (1989) finding that outgroup devaluation is due to differential abstraction. Although the ordinal condition $(ABST_{I+} + ABST_{O-}) > (ABST_{I-} + ABST_{O+})$ is met for all but one topic, a quantitative analysis shows that the greatest part of the group-serving bias is due to PERC rather than ABST. That is, ingroup favouritism and relative outgroup derogation, in the present context, are more due to frequent repetition of group-serving statements, $(PERC_{I+} + PERC_{O-}) > (PERC_{I-} + PERC_{O+})$, than to differential abstraction.

We did *not* find any support for either real conflict theories (Sherif, 1967) or cognitive conceptions (Hamilton and Trolier, 1986) because the degree of relative outgroup derogation per topic (see Table 5.2) was unrelated to conflict proneness, inter-sex experience, and affective involvement. The only topic-specific characteristic with which the bias was correlated was the rated importance of topics for identification with one's gender group. This lends some support to a social identity account (Tajfel and Turner, 1979) of the topic-specific variance.

What can be said about the other basic group phenomenon, outgroup homogeneity? If 'homogeneity' is operationalized in terms of *generality* (that is, generalization of statements to many individual group members, as assessed in subsequent ratings) or in terms of *diversity* (that is, number of different attributes ascribed to the gender ingroup and outgroup), then we find no homogeneity effect. However, there is a marked outgroup homogeneity effect which again highlights the contention that language about others is more undifferentiated than language about oneself, where 'undifferentiated' has a broader meaning than 'abstractness' alone. This kind of outgroup homogeneity is manifested in the *consistency* or *stereotypicality* of language use over topics in ingroup and outgroup descriptions.

Speech act profiles, defined as the summed percentage of DAV_+, IAV_+, SV_+, ADJ_+, DAV_-, IAV_-, SV_-, and ADJ_- used by all subjects in response to each topic, were constructed separately for ingroup and outgroup descriptions. These topics provide a content-free measure of the language use based on LCM coding. For all pairs of topics, profile similarities (that is, covariations) were then computed, yielding a 10×10 similarity matrix for the ingroup and for the outgroup. Regardless of the specific similarity measure (covariances, or alternatively, correlations or Euclidic similarities), the overall similarity of speech act profiles for the outgroup was markedly and significantly higher than for the ingroup. That is, the language used to characterize the outgroup is much more uniform and stereotypical over topics than the language of ingroup descriptions.

When the two similarity matrices are factorized, a remarkable finding emerges. There is a strong first factor in both solutions representing, as it were, the prototypical or stereotypical language profile. This overwhelming first factor is especially pronounced for the outgroup matrix, due to the greater uniformity of outgroup than ingroup descriptions. Most interestingly, however, the loadings of the topics on that first factor (reflecting the closeness of each topic to the stereotypical profile) bear a strong relation to outgroup discrimination. The four topics which contribute most to outgroup devaluation (that is, the uppermost four topics in Table 5.2) also contribute most to outgroup homogeneity, as assessed by their loadings on the first factor of the outgroup similarity matrix. Thus, while group-serving biases can hardly be described in terms of the abstractness principle alone, the broader notion of undifferentiated, stereotypical language use is related to homogeneity *and* discrimination and suggests a common language factor underlying both phenomena.

Conclusions

At this point, it is time to summarize the reported results on the role of language in attribution and then to return to the question of where the differences in self- and other-related language originate that have been emphasized and taken for granted throughout this chapter.

To begin with, we have introduced the LCM classification of interpersonal terms as a content-free research instrument for the analysis of format-free attributions embedded in natural discourse. Starting from the assumption that attribution can be conceptualized as inferences from situated behaviour to abstract dispositions, it was expected that the LCM distinction of specific terms (such as DAV or IAV) and more abstract dispositional terms (especially ADJ) would successfully catch the attribution process in free verbalizations. Apart from the methodological issue of assessing format-free attributions, however, our main intention was to establish the theoretical importance of language as an ecological complement to the intracognitive processes usually deemed to govern social attribution.

To make this point, we have presented a series of experiments on perspective biases in attribution that we have interpreted with reference to a habitual principle of language use, namely, the principle to speak about other people in more abstract and undifferentiated terms than about ourselves. In the first study reported, we employed this principle in a 'language simulation' of classical research on the actor–observer bias, showing that the abstractness of observers' descriptions of other people 'mimic' the attribution of dispositional attributes. By contrast, actors' less abstract self-descriptions provide the linguistic basis for their tendency toward non-dispositional, situational attributions. In a second experiment, these differential language styles have been shown to hold even for non-causal reports, suggesting a broader domain for the language bias than the familiar attribution bias. We have then pointed out the theoretical heuristic of the language approach, showing that the theoretical conflict between the actor–observer bias and the so-called egocentric bias in close relationships can be reconciled when the linguistic level of attributions is taken into consideration. And finally, the language approach to attribution was raised from the inter-personal level to the inter-group level where completely new cognitive and social theories are advocated to account for attribution biases. Yet the differential abstraction of self- and other-related language was still obtained. In addition, the linguistic analysis of ingroup and outgroup descriptions helped to bridge the theoretical gap between the phenomena of outgroup discrimination and outgroup homogeneity. Both effects turned out to be correlated with undifferentiated, simplified and abstract language use.

What may be the reason for and the functional value of the language habits that we have presupposed and confirmed theoretically, but not explained up to now? We actually lack a complete answer, and it may in fact be impossible to answer functionalist questions of this kind empirically. Since language habits cannot be manipulated experimentally, we cannot ultimately test their necessary and sufficient conditions. However, we do suggest some reasonable assumptions which lend some psychological meaning and significance to the differential abstractness of self-descriptions and descriptions of other people.

In the introduction, we have already pointed out the social psychological inappropriateness of abstract self-attributions. Just as a person cannot be his or her own witness in the courtroom, it is less than credible to ascribe adjectives like *honest* or *intelligent* to oneself. By extrapolation of this social rule, other persons who are less involved than the self are more justified and more likely to take the role of 'social referees' who have the right, as it were, to categorize people in terms of adjective classes. In a similar vein, it might be argued that people are most accountable and responsible for their own pretensions and behaviours, and accountability conditions have been shown to lead speakers to stick to the facts and provide less abstract verbalizations (Fiedler et al., 1989, Study 3). Thus, people may avoid the weight of abstract statements in self-descriptions because such verbal behaviour entails too much commitment and makes the descriptions vulnerable to be disconfirmed and become incredible (Semin and Fiedler, 1988).

However, we do not believe that such considerations of tactical language use alone can account for the abstractness effect. Rather, we believe that abstractness of language is no less dependent on the cognitive representation of knowledge about the self and others. The very richness and multitude of self-knowledge may prevent a commitment to specific simplifying adjectives. Another person is clearly an introvert, but our self-knowledge is sufficiently rich and intimate to infer that oneself is both introvert and extravert. We are quick to say that others are dishonest, but although we can remember many instances of our own dishonesty, we remember even more instances of the self engaging in honest behaviours. Thus, the very richness of self-knowledge may prevent simplistic adjective attributions. In terms of Tversky's (1977) feature model of similarity, the self is a highly inclusive feature set: it includes many features of almost all traits; however, it is likely to also include many features of the opposite traits. In this respect, Sande et al. (1988) found that the summed self-attributions of antonymous ADJ pairs are higher than ratings of other persons when both judgments are made on separate unipolar scales. That is, they claim to be, say, both extravert and introvert, whereas other people are seen as possessing only one of the two attributes. However, when antonymous traits are rated on the same bipolar scale, people avoid decided or extreme self-ratings and provide more pronounced ratings for other people. Generalizing from this intriguing research, it is conceivable – and we are currently testing this hypothesis – that our reluctance to ascribe meaningful attributes to the self may reflect the paradoxical fact that we attribute so many different, partly overlapping and sometimes contrary attributes to the self, which is the most multi-faceted knowledge structure we have.

Note

1. This finding is not an evaluation artifact, due to the possible fact that the negative components of outgroup profiles are elevated, thereby increasing the

profile variance and, indirectly, the covariation among all outgroup profiles. When the means for positive and negative profile components are partialled out, the main findings remain unchanged. Thus, the uniformity of outgroup-related language is independent of a superficial evaluation effect, and is mainly due to variation between linguistic categories.

References

Abelson, R. P. and Kanouse, D. E. (1966) Subjective acceptance of verbal generalizations. In S. Feldman (ed.), *Cognitive Consistency: Motivational Antecedents and Behavioral Consequences*, pp. 171-197. New York: Academic Press.

Allport, G. W. (1954) *The Nature of Prejudice*. Cambridge, MA: Addison-Wesley.

Borkenau, P. (1990) Traits as ideal-based and goal-derived social categories. *Journal of Personality and Social Psychology*, 58: 381-396.

Brewer, M. B. (1979) Ingroup bias in the minimal intergroup situation: A cognitive-motivational analysis. *Psychological Bulletin*, 86: 307-324.

Brown, R. (1986) Linguistic relativity. In S. H. Hulse and B. F. Green, Jr. (eds), *One Hundred Years of Psychological Research in America: G. Stanley Hall and the Johns Hopkins Tradition*, pp. 241-276. Baltimore: Johns Hopkins Press.

Brown, R. and Fish, D. (1983) The psychological causality implicit in language. *Cognition*, 14: 233-274.

Dember, W. N. (1974) Motivation and the cognitive revolution. *American Psychologist*, 29: 161-168.

Fiedler, K. (1985) *Kognitive Strukturierung der sozialen Umwelt*. Göttingen: Hogrefe.

Fiedler, K. (1988) The dependence of the conjunction fallacy on subtle linguistic factors. *Psychological Research*, 50: 123-129.

Fiedler, K. and Semin, G. R. (1988) On the causal information conveyed by different interpersonal verbs: The role of implicit sentence context. *Social Cognition*, 6: 21-39.

Fiedler, K., Semin, G. R. and Bolten, S. (1989) Language use and reification of social information: Top-down and bottom-up processing in person cognition. *European Journal of Social Psychology*, 19: 271-295.

Fiedler, K., Semin, G. R. and Finkenauer, C. (1992) The battle of words between gender groups: A language based approach to intergroup processes. Paper submitted for publication.

Fiedler, K., Semin, G. R. and Koppetsch, C. (1991) Language use and attributional biases in close personal relationships. *Personality and Social Psychology Bulletin*, 17: 147-155.

Fiedler, K., Semin, G. R., Ritter, A., Bode, P. and Medenbach, M. (1992) A discourse grammar approach to understanding the causal impact of interpersonal verbs. Paper submitted for publication.

Fischhoff, B. (1975) Hindsight = foresight: The effect of outcome knowledge on judgment under uncertainty. *Journal of Experimental Psychology: Human Perception and Performance*, 1: 288-299.

Garner, W. (1986) Interactions of stimulus and organism in perception. In S. H. Hulse and B. F. Green, Jr. (eds), *One Hundred Years of Psychological Research in America: G. Stanley Hall and the Johns Hopkins Tradition*, pp. 199-240. Baltimore: Johns Hopkins Press.

Gibson, J. J. (1979) *The Ecological Approach to Visual Perception.* Boston: Houghton Mifflin.

Grice, H. P. (1975) Published in part as 'Logic and conversation'. In P. Cole and J. L. Morgan (eds), *Syntax and Semantics, vol. 3: Speech Acts,* pp. 365–372. New York: Seminar Press.

Hamilton, D. L. and Trolier, T. K. (1986) Stereotypes and stereotyping: An overview of the cognitive approach. In J. Dovidio and S. L. Gaertner (eds), *Prejudice, Discrimination, and Racism,* pp. 127–163. New York: Academic Press.

Hewstone, M. (1983) (ed.) *Attribution Theory: Social and Functional Extensions.* Oxford: Basil Blackwell.

Hewstone, M. (1988) Attributional bases of intergroup conflict. In W. Stroebe, A. W. Kruglanski, D. Bar-Tal and M. Hewstone (eds), *The Social Psychology of Intergroup Conflict: Theory, Research and Applications.* New York: Springer.

Hewstone, M. (1989) *Causal Attribution: From Cognitive Processes to Collective Beliefs.* Oxford: Basil Blackwell.

Hoffman, C., Mischel, W. and Mazze, K. (1981) The role of purpose in the organization of information about behavior: Trait-based versus goal-based categories in person cognition. *Journal of Personality and Social Psychology,* 40: 211–225.

Jones, E. E. and Davis, K. E. (1965) From acts to dispositions: The attribution process in person perception. In L. Berkowitz (ed.), *Advances of Experimental Social Psychology,* vol. 2, pp. 220–266. New York: Academic Press.

Jones, E. E. and Nisbett, R. E. (1972) The actor and the observer: Divergent perceptions of the causes of behavior. In E. E. Jones et al. (eds), *Attribution: Perceiving the Causes of Behavior,* pp. 121–136. Morristown, NJ: General Learning Press.

Kelley, H. H. (1967) Attribution theory in social psychology. In D. Levine (ed.), *Nebraska Symposium on Motivation,* vol. 15, pp. 192–238. Lincoln, NE: University of Nebraska Press.

Kelley, H. H. (1972) Causal schemata and the attribution process. In E. E. Jones et al. (eds), *Attribution: Perceiving the Causes of Behavior,* pp. 151–174. Morristown, NJ: General Learning Press.

Kelley, H. H. and Michela, J. L. (1980) Attribution theory and research. *Annual Review of Psychology,* 31: 457–503.

Maass, A., Salvi, D., Arcuri, L. and Semin, G. R. (1989) Language use in intergroup contexts: The linguistic intergroup bias. *Journal of Personality and Social Psychology,* 57: 981–994.

Nisbett, R. E., Caputo, C., Legrant, P. and Maracek, J. (1973) Behavior as seen by the actor and as seen by the observer. *Journal of Personality and Social Psychology,* 27: 154–165.

Park, B. and Rothbart, M. (1982) Perception of outgroup homogeneity and levels of social categorization: Memory for the subordinate attributes of ingroup and outgroup members. *Journal of Personality and Social Psychology,* 42: 1051–1068.

Reeder, G. D. and Brewer, M. B. (1979) A schematic model of dispositional attribution in interpersonal perception. *Psychological Review,* 86: 61–79.

Rosch, E. and Mervis, C. B. (1975) Family resemblances: Studies in internal structure of categories. *Cognitive Psychology,* 7: 573–605.

Ross, M. and Sicoly, F. (1979) Egocentric biases in availability and attribution.

Journal of Personality and Social Psychology, 37: 322–336.

Rothbart, M. and John, O. P. (1985) Social categorization and behavioral episodes: A cognitive analysis of the effects of intergroup contact. *Journal of Social Issues*, 41: 81–104.

Sande, G. N., Goethals, G. R. and Radloff, C. E. (1988) Perceiving one's own traits and others': The multifaceted self. *Journal of Personality and Social Psychology*, 54: 13–20.

Schachter, S. (1964) The interaction of cognitive and physiological determinants of emotional state. In L. Berkowitz (ed.), *Advances of Experimental Social Psychology*, vol. 1, pp. 49–80. New York: Academic Press.

Semin, G. R. (1989) The contribution of linguistic factors to attribute inferences and semantic similarity judgments. *European Journal of Social Psychology*, 19: 85–100.

Semin, G. R. and Fiedler, K. (1988) The cognitive functions of linguistic categories in describing persons: Social cognition and language. *Journal of Personality and Social Psychology*, 54: 558–568.

Semin, G. R. and Fiedler, K. (1989) Relocating attributional phenomena within a language–cognition interface: The case of actors' and observers' perspectives. *European Journal of Social Psychology*, 19: 491–508.

Semin, G. R. and Fiedler, K. (1991) The linguistic category model, its bases, applications and range. *European Review of Social Psychology*, 2: 1–30.

Semin, G. R. and Greenslade, L. (1985) Different contributions of linguistic factors to memory based ratings: Systematizing the systematic distortion hypothesis. *Journal of Personality and Social Psychology*, 49: 1713–1723.

Sherif, M. (1967) *Social Interaction Process and Products*, Chicago: IL: Aldine.

Shweder, R. A. (1977) Likeness and likelihood in everyday thought: Magical thinking in judgment about personality. *Current Anthropolgy*, 18: 637–648.

Tajfel, H. (1970) Experiments in intergroup discrimination. *Scientific American*, 223: 96–102.

Tajfel, H. and Turner, J. C. (1979) An integrative theory of intergroup conflict. In W. G. Austin and S. Worchel (eds), *The Social Psychology of Intergroup Relations*, pp. 33–47. Monterey, CA: Brooks/Cole.

Thompson, S. C. and Kelley, H. H. (1981) Judgments of responsibility for activities in close relationships. *Journal of Personality and Social Psychology*, 41: 469–477.

Tversky, A. (1977) Features of similarity. *Psychological Review*, 84: 327–352.

Tversky, A. and Kahneman, D. (1973) Availability: A heuristic for judging frequency and probability. *Cognitive Psychology*, 5: 207–232.

Tversky, A. and Kahneman, D. (1981) The framing of decisions and the psychology of choice. *Science*, 211: 453–458.

Watson, D. (1982) The actor and the observer: How are their perceptions of causality divergent? *Psychological Bulletin*, 92: 682–700.

Weiner, B. (1986) *An Attributional Theory of Motivation and Emotion*. New York: Springer.

Whorf, B. L. (1956) Science and linguistics. In J. B. Carroll (ed.), *Language, Thought, and Reality: Selected Writings of Benjamin Lee Whorf*, pp. 207–219. Cambridge, MA: MIT Press.

Zuckerman, M. (1979) Attribution of success and failure revisited, or: The motivational bias is alive and well in attribution theory. *Journal of Personality*, 47: 245–287.

PART 3

LANGUAGE, INTERGROUP RELATIONS AND STEREOTYPES

6

Stereotypes and Language Use

*David L. Hamilton, Pamela A. Gibbons,
Steven J. Stroessner and Jeffrey W. Sherman*

Language is a primary vehicle for communication. It is an important element in the social processes by which we adjust to, interact with, and perhaps even influence others in our interpersonal world. A prominent feature of many of those social interactions concerns the group memberships of the interactants. We are often cognizant of whether another person belongs to the same or a different group than we do. And we have well-developed stereotypes about numerous groups, based on race, gender, age, nationality, religion, and other features. These group concepts can influence our use of language in both our comprehension of and communication in those social interactions.

This chapter is concerned with the relationship between stereotypes and language in the context of communication. Stereotypes based on a person's group membership can be particularly influential in social perception, guiding not only the processing and use of information but also the course of one's actions based on that information. Stereotypes can influence our attention to stereotype-relevant aspects of the information and the inferences we make based on a target person's group membership; our evaluations of and causal attributions for a target person's behaviors; what aspects of that information we are most likely to retain and how it is stored in memory; and what information is retrieved and how overt responses are generated. This approach to understanding how stereotypes function within an information processing system has generated an impressive research literature (for reviews, see Hamilton et al., 1990; Hamilton and Trolier, 1986; Stephan, 1985). The question we address in this chapter is: Where does language fit into this system? How can the relationship between stereotypes and language be conceptualized in this framework?

The interface between stereotypes and language use has been investigated in a variety of ways, spawning research on a number of specific topics. We briefly review several of these approaches, highlighting their implications for intergroup perception. We then report the findings of our own research investigating manifestations of stereotypic thinking in perceivers' spontaneous language use. Finally, we offer some speculations on a system for thinking about intergroup descriptions and how preexisting stereotypes might influence language use in this context.

Varieties of Research on Stereotypes and Language

In this section we briefly discuss several lines of research that have explored various aspects of the interface between stereotypes and language use.

Language as the Content of Stereotypes

From its beginning, social science research has defined the content of stereotypes in the language of traits. The implicit assumption has been that trait terminology effectively captures the fundamental aspects of perceivers' stereotypic conceptions. This emphasis on trait language can be traced back to the first empirical study of stereotypes, in which Katz and Braly (1933) presented subjects with a list of trait words and asked them to indicate which terms characterized members of various national and racial groups. Ever since then, the reliance on trait terms to assess stereotypes is clearly evident in the literature on the measurement of racial, national, and ethnic stereotypes (for reviews, see Brigham, 1971; McCauley and Stitt, 1978; Miller, 1982).

Although the richness of our trait terminology affords considerable diversity for a language of stereotypes, we do not believe that the content of stereotypes is adequately captured solely in terms of trait-descriptive adjectives. It seems likely that these cognitive structures also include mental representations of specific instances of experiences with group members (Smith, 1990) as well as of other general, nontrait features, such as physical features, occupational and socioeconomic characteristics, and likely behavior patterns (Hamilton and Trolier, 1986). The content of stereotypes, then, is more diverse than is represented in trait terminology.

It follows that analyses of the effects of stereotypes on language use should not be limited exclusively to the study of subjects' use of trait terms. Analyses of linguistic forms other than adjectives may shed useful light both on the content of stereotypes and on the rules governing perceivers' use of language in their characterizations of and interactions with group members.

Language as Stimulus Information

There is a long tradition of research examining ways in which language influences impressions of a speaker. Various properties of language can serve as important stimulus cues that activate group stereotypes and thereby influence intergroup perceptions.

Research has shown that both men and women hold a number of stereotypic *beliefs about gender differences* in speech (Kramer, 1977). These beliefs can affect how people evaluate male and female speakers. Specifically, subjects consistently rate women's speech as more aesthetically pleasing and men's speech as more dynamic, a gender-linked language effect (Mulac and Lundell, 1980). Moreover, sex-role stereotypes and this gender-linked language effect have independent effects on naive raters' evaluations of speech transcripts. Mere identification of a speaker as male or female can influence a perceiver's evaluations of a message. Additionally, however, even when the transcripts provide no information about speaker sex, subjects differentially evaluate men's and women's transcripts in the systematic ways noted above (Mulac et al., 1985).

It is important to note that these subtle linguistic features produce positive evaluations of women's speech as aesthetically pleasing rather than the negative evaluations of 'weakness' suggested by earlier work (Lakoff, 1975). Thus, language features can function to influence perceptions of the speaker.

Several other properties of language have also been shown to affect evaluations of communicators. For example, there is strong evidence that there are differences in speech style as a function of social power. *'Powerful'* and *'powerless' speech* have been associated with communicators ostensibly high or low in social power, regardless of gender (Bradac and Mulac, 1984; O'Barr, 1982). Speakers using the powerless style are rated as less attractive and less competent that speakers using a powerful style in a number of communication contexts (Gibbons et al., 1991).

Lexical diversity (sometimes referred to by its opposite, verbal redundancy) refers to the richness of a communicator's manifest vocabulary, and this variable also has evaluative consequences for how a speaker is perceived. High diversity messages typically yield higher ratings of speaker competence, dynamism and effectiveness than low diversity (redundant) messages (Bradac and Wisegraver, 1984).

Linguistic intensity reflects the strength of a communicator's feelings about a particular target or group, indicating a move away from neutrality (Bowers, 1964). The effects of linguistic intensity are importantly influenced by aspects of context, especially the listener's perception of who the speaker is and the role that he or she plays. For example, studies on persuasion have shown that females are judged to be more predictable, more persuasive, and are more positively perceived when they use low intensity language, whereas the opposite is true for men (Burgoon et al., 1975).

In addition to the language variables we have briefly discussed, research has also examined the effects of other linguistic variables on impression formation, including linguistic immediacy (the positivity or negativity of a speaker's feelings about a particular topic as manifested in language), good and bad grammar, silences and interruptions, and other paralinguistic cues such as pitch, speech rate and volume. In sum, a large variety of linguistic features provide stimulus cues that can make group memberships salient and activate stereotypes, which in turn can guide the listener's inferences and evaluations about the communicator.

Group Influence on Language Effects in Encoding

Behaviors that we observe others perform are often ambiguous and open to interpretation. Therefore those behaviors take on meaning only when the perceiver has imposed some interpretation on them. Recently Semin and Fiedler (1988; Fiedler and Semin, 1988) demonstrated the potential importance of linguistic factors in this process. The Semin–Fiedler model posits a four-category system of linguistic choices that reflect increasingly abstract levels of encoding of behavioral events: descriptive action verbs (DAVs), which describe specific, observable actions; interpretive action verbs (IAVs), which also refer to a single behavioral episode but in addition summarize and give interpretation to the action; state verbs (SVs), which refer to an actor's psychological state and not to any specific action or episode; and, at the highest level of abstraction, the use of adjectives that describe an actor's disposition. Semin and Fiedler (1988) have argued that more abstract descriptions of behavior are considered to be more revealing about the actor, imply greater persistence over time, are less verifiable, and provide less information about circumstance, and thus arguably, perpetuate stereotypes.

Research by Maass et al. (1989) demonstrated that group membership can influence the language used to describe intergroup behavior. In one study they asked members of a particular social group to evaluate both ingroup and outgroup members performing either socially desirable or undesirable behaviors. Subjects had well developed conceptions of their own and the other group, the result of a long-standing rivalry based on historic and geographic divisions between the two groups. For each stimulus behavior, respondents were given four linguistic choices varying in degree of abstractness, based on the Semin and Fiedler model, and their task was to indicate which option best described the stimulus event. The results showed that subjects described ingroup members performing desirable behaviors in more abstract terms than when the same behavior was performed by outgroup members. In contrast, undesirable behaviors performed by outgroup members were characterized in more abstract terms than were the same behaviors when performed by ingroup members. These findings indicate that beliefs about ingroup and outgroup members produced differential interpretations and evaluations of the same behavior, and consequently influenced the linguistic label applied to it as it was encoded. Subsequent studies have replicated and extended these results (see Maass and Arcuri, this volume). This research provides evidence for the influence of a linguistic encoding effect on differential mental representations of ingroups and outgroups.

Group Influence on Language Production

The attentional and encoding effects we have discussed so far influence what aspects of the available stimulus information are processed, how they are interpreted, and therefore the nature of one's cognitive representation of that information. We have seen evidence for the role of both linguistic factors and stereotypic beliefs in the way this representation is formed. However, the primary function of language is communication, and hence involves a process in which knowledge and thoughts are retrieved from memory and translated into speech. Numerous factors can influence the process of communication in conversational discourse (see Kraut and Higgins, 1984). One potential influence on this language production process is the speaker's cognizance of group memberships, both his or her own and that of the recipient of the communication.

Speech Accommodation Theory (Giles, 1980) is a cognitively based theory focusing on how interactants' speech behavior may converge or diverge from that of their partners, particularly when an encounter is construed in intergroup rather than interpersonal terms. The motivation for speech adjustments is derived from the values, attitudes and intentions of the interactants toward their own and other social groups. Convergence adjustments (minimizing differences in speech pattern between interactants by adopting similar speech characteristics) reflect the speaker's desire for social approval. Convergence is most likely to occur when there is minimal social cost for adopting such a strategy, when doing so is not in opposition to social norms, or in some cases, for efficiency's sake. Divergence (emphasizing the speech patterns that distinguish one's own social group from that of one's interactant) reflects a focus on the positive self-identity of one's own group (Street and Giles, 1982). If an intergroup encounter is perceived as threatening, or when the motivation is to differentiate one's own group from the other group, speech divergence is likely to occur.

Convergence and divergence moves are based on an interactant's perceptions of message characteristics rather than on the objective features of the message (Bourhis et al., 1979). This suggests that cognitive structures, such as stereotypes, may influence these perceptions. That is, the speech patterns of an outgroup communicator can activate a stereotype and thereby influence the likelihood of convergence or divergence.

In Speech Accommodation Theory, speech convergence and divergence are part of the speaker's response to the perceived intergroup relationship with his or her partner. These effects, then, are defined in terms of the differentiation between ingroup and outgroup and hence are not specific to the stereotype of any particular group. Other research, however, has shown that a communicator's linguistic choices in speech production may be influenced by the stereotype activated by the partner's group membership. For example, Caporael (1981; Caporael et al., 1983) studied the communication styles of caregivers when interacting with residents of a nursing home for the elderly. She found that caregivers used a high degree of 'babytalk' with care receivers. Presumably, stereotypic beliefs about the dependency of the elderly guided the type of speech style caregivers used when conversing with these patients.

Summary

Our discussion of past research on language and stereotypes illustrates the important point that there is no single relationship between language and stereotyping. Even our brief review reveals several ways in which language and stereotypes can influence each other. On the one hand, linguistic features can be important stimulus cues provided by a speaker, and these cues can activate a stereotype that will affect subsequent perceptions of the speaker. Conversely, a stereotype activated by a stimulus person's group membership can influence the linguistic terms used in interpreting and encoding that person's behavior, and can also guide the perceiver's own language productions in the communication process.

Effects of Stereotypes on Spontaneous Language Use

Our research has focused on how stereotypes influence people's use of language in their free, unconstrained characterizations of members of significant ethnic groups. Specifically, we investigated the effects of stereotypes on the production of language describing group members.

Stereotypes are cognitive structures that contain one's beliefs about groups and their members. Perception of or interaction with a member of a stereotyped group activates that stereotype such that subsequent processing is colored by the content and evaluative tone of those beliefs. If one's thought processes are influenced in this way, then we might expect one's language use to reflect those effects. Such influences might occur in a variety of ways. Some of these effects would be obvious manifestations of stereotyping, such as characterizing members of disliked groups in negative terms and using stereotypic content to describe group members. Other influences of stereotypes might be more subtle. The complexities of language afford remarkable versatility in the way people and events are characterized. Stereotypes, through their effects on thought processes, might guide language use such that seemingly minor differences in word selection and usage can create important differences in the meaning of what is communicated. Our research sought to investigate some of these distinctions.

We do not presume, of course, that language will reflect the effects of stereotypes on thought processes in every circumstance. Language is a tool of communication and hence is an inherently social process. The nature of any communication will reflect many aspects of that process, including the speaker's relationship to his or her audience, his or her goals for this particular communication, and the social context in which the communication occurs. As speakers we are quite facile in managing our language presentations to fit our immediate purposes, and an issue as sensitive as stereotypes of ethnic groups is certainly a sufficient cause for monitoring and controlling the nature of our verbal expression. However, in situations where such concerns are minimized, one's spontaneous language use may reveal the influence of stereotypic conceptions.

A major problem, of course, in studying spontaneous free descriptions is how one can assure that subjects' responses are indeed spontaneous. Our approach to dealing with this problem was to create a context in which free, spontaneous description was encouraged; in fact, our subjects were told that the purpose of our experiment was to investigate people's ability to generate such thought.[1] The task presented for our subjects involved spontaneously generating stories about people they would see. Subjects (67 white UCSB students) were shown a slide providing a head-and-shoulders photograph of a person, and simultaneously the experimenter identified a situational context in which the person is seen. The subjects' task was then to generate a story about this person in that setting.

Subjects completed this task for four male stimulus persons. Two of the photos were of whites and two were of blacks, and within each race one photo showed a smiling face, the other a nonsmiling face. Thus race and facial expression were manipulated within subjects. In addition, two different stimulus sets were used such that the age of the stimulus persons was manipulated between subjects. One set consisted of photos of college-aged men, the other set portrayed middle-aged men. For each photo the experimenter indicated the setting by indicating, for example, 'You see this person at a bank.' The four settings used – a bank, a basketball game, a hospital, and a shopping mall – were counterbalanced with the independent variables so that across subjects every photo was paired with every setting.

The descriptive stories generated by the subjects were tape recorded and later transcribed. The stories were then coded for a number of variables that constitute the basis for our analyses. In all cases the design of our analyses was a 2 (age) × 2 (race) × 2 (facial expression) analysis of variance.[2] The following subsections summarize the results of several such analyses.

Favorability of Descriptions

Our first analysis examined the overall favorability with which the target person was described, as assessed by judges' ratings.[3] This analysis produced a significant main effect due to race as well as an interaction of race with age, the means for which are shown in Figure 6.1 Overall, black target persons elicited more favorable descriptive stories than did white target persons. However, the interaction indicates that this difference was actually true only for older black target persons, who where described more favorably than the other three categories of target persons. Favorability ratings of the descriptions of the younger black and the two white target persons did not differ significantly.

The fact that subjects generated more favorable descriptions of black than of white target persons may suggest that subjects were

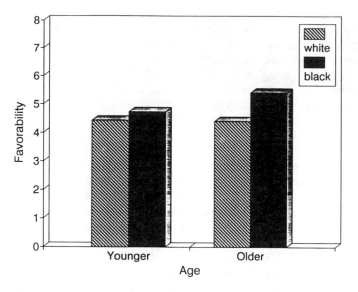

Figure 6.1 *Mean favorability of descriptions of target persons*

in fact being cautious in their characterizations of blacks due to their sensitivity to racial stereotypes. This would imply that subjects were quite controlled in the stories they generated, carefully avoiding the appearance of being prejudiced. If so, then our assumption that the descriptions reflect spontaneous thought would be questionable at best. Although this interpretation cannot be definitively refuted, it does encounter difficulties that make it less plausible. One immediate problem it faces is the significant interaction of this race effect with age. That is, it isn't clear why a desire to appear unbiased would affect stories about middle-aged black men, but not stories about younger black men. Beyond this specific problem, the results of several other analyses, reported below, make it difficult to maintain that subjects were responding to the black target persons in a socially desirable manner.

Length of Descriptions
We next analyzed the length of the descriptions that subjects generated, coded as the number of words in each story. This analysis again produced a significant race-by-age interaction (the means for which are shown in Figure 6.2) which reveals the same pattern observed in the favorability ratings. Specifically, subjects generated shorter stories about middle-aged black target persons than for any of the other three cases.

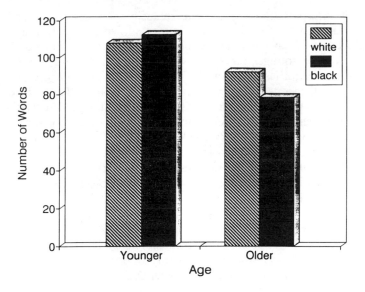

Figure 6.2 *Mean number of words in subjects' stories*

How should this finding be interpreted? Some past research (Siegman and Pope, 1972) indicates that the length of verbal productions often reflects the speaker's affective state, such that longer productions reflect positive affect whereas more constrained output is indicative of anxiety, discomfort, or other negative affects. In the present case, however, this is not a viable interpretation in that the shortest stories, on average, occurred in the same condition that had the highest mean favorability ratings. In fact, the correlation (across all stories) between length and favorability was -0.12.

Alternatively, a cognitive processing approach suggests that, given the impoverished stimulus cues they were presented with, subjects generated their stories largely on the basis of knowledge representations stored in memory. The race and age of the target person, as well as the specified setting, would activate relevant cognitive categories, and subjects' knowledge and beliefs about those categories would provide the basis for the descriptions they generated. The richer and more differentiated the knowledge representation, the greater would be the basis for developing detailed descriptions, which in turn would generate greater length of story. Differences in cognitive differentiation presumably are a function of experience with members of the relevant category – the more experience one has with category members, the more differentiated one's representation of that category becomes.

This interpretation seems quite plausible in understanding the differences in the lengths of the stories shown in Figure 6.2. Our subjects would have had more experience with people in the same age group as the younger target persons (the main effect for age was marginally significant), and the white middle-aged target person represents the same category as the subjects' fathers. Thus, the only category of target person with whom they would have had relatively little experience is the older black male, and it is here that they generated the shorter, less developed stories. It seems plausible, then, that in the present case the length of the descriptions is at least partially a function of the richness, differentiation and complexity of the cognitive structures that subjects would have used in generating them.[4]

Verb Phrases

We analyzed subjects' use of verb categories by adapting Semin and Fiedler's (1988) classification system to our materials. In their system, the same act can be characterized by using a descriptive action verb (Jack carries Jill's pail of water), an interpretive action verb (Jack helps Jill), a subjective state verb (Jack likes Jill), or with an adjective (Jack is helpful). Their research has demonstrated the importance of these distinctions for both the way behavior is encoded and understood and the way its meaning is communicated. Our interest was in determining whether group stereotypes would have an influence on the use of these alternative levels of abstractness in the descriptions our subjects generated.

Our analysis differed in one important respect from the typical studies reported by Semin, Fiedler, and others. In their analyses the focus has been on specific verbs used in sentences describing interpersonal actions. To use a frequently cited example, their analysis would examine what difference it makes to encode an action as A hit B, A hurt B, or A hates B. In our study, however, subjects generated stories that were wide ranging in both form and content, yet were rich in the scenarios they created. For our purposes, then, a focus on specific verbs pertaining only to interpersonal actions was deemed too constraining. Therefore, we analyzed verb phrases instead of verbs, adapting the distinctions specified in Semin and Fiedler's system. To preserve the distinction between the original coding system of Semin and Fiedler and our adaptation of it, we will use the terms descriptive action phrase (DAP), interpretive action phrase (IAP), and state descriptive phrase (SDP) for the categories used in our analyses. Examples of each of these categories are shown in Table 6.1.

It is also important to note that the task we presented to our

Table 6.1   *Examples of Descriptive Action Phrases,
Interpretive Action Phrases, and State Descriptive Phrases
coded from subjects' stories*

Descriptive Action Phrases	Interpretive Action Phrases	State Descriptive Phrases
'walks up to the teller'	'does well in school'	'hopes his wife is OK'
'was talking to a friend'	'is hanging out (in the mall)'	'feels lost in this environment'
'went to the hospital'	'helps patients'	'expects everyone to like him'
'is shopping for an engagement ring'	'tries to save as much as he can'	'wants to make everyone laugh'
	'was driving a little too fast'	'wishes he could play'

subjects required them to generate descriptions of episodes in particular settings. This task naturally induced a rather concrete level of description, with relatively little abstract characterization. Because of these task constraints, DAPs were used most frequently in each target person condition, adjectives were used least frequently in each condition, and neither measure differed significantly as a function of any of the target person variables. These general patterns were a consequence of the fact that the task did not encourage character development in the stories.

There were, however, meaningful differences associated with the subjects' use of both IAPs and SDPs. Subjects used significantly more IAPs in their stories about white target persons ($M = 2.92$) than about black target persons ($M = 2.39$). In contrast, the analysis of SDPs produced a significant race by age interaction which, as can be seen in Figure 6.3, was similar in form to comparable interactions observed already in previous measures. Specifically, SDPs were used more frequently in stories about the middle-aged black than in those about the other three target persons.

We can consider these results in terms of the relationship between IAPs and SDPs. IAPs provide relatively concrete and specific descriptions of action which, combined with the high rate of DAPs, suggests that subjects generated fairly rich and detailed stories. IAPs include modest interpretive character, for example, an inference as to the actor's motivations underlying a given behavior. This pattern, which presumably would reflect a fairly well developed cognitive structure, was more prevalent in subjects' stories about white target persons. SDPs, on the other hand, provide more abstract characterizations of the target person's wants, fears, and the like that are less tied to detailed aspects of the specific situation at hand. These more generalized descriptions may reflect a more impoverished, but stereotyped, knowledge base from which the stories were derived. It is interesting, then, that these SDPs were most prevalent in that category of target person with which, according to our earlier

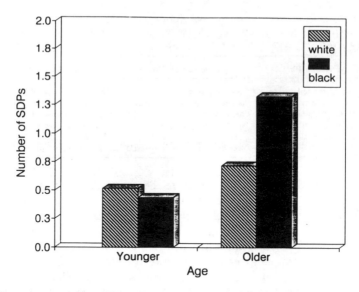

Figure 6.3   *Mean number of state descriptive phrases (SDPs) in subjects' stories (adjusted for story length)*

argument, subjects would have had the least experience and familiarity.

This relative lack of complexity in subjects' thinking about middle-aged blacks is thus reflected both in their comparatively short descriptions and in their greater use of abstract verb phrases. These differences may have consequences for both the producer and the recipient of such messages. Abstract verbs, such as state verbs, remove the focus from the specifics of the situation in which the action occurred. Instead, they refer to properties of the person(s) involved, often locate causality in those persons, and hence can be difficult to disconfirm. Such verbs can subsume a large number of diverse behaviors, and consequently a large amount of disconfirming information would be necessary to change beliefs stated in such terms. By characterizing behaviors in more abstract terms, then, existing expectancies can seemingly be reinforced. Moreover, these effects can be manifested in the minds of both the perceiver and the recipients of messages from the perceiver. That is, stereotypes might affect the representation formed by the perceiver as information is initially encoded, and this representation in turn might generate a more generalized, abstract level of language that is communicated to others.

Trait Ratings

After subjects had completed generating their spontaneous descriptions of each of the target persons, the experimenter projected their photos again, one at a time, and for each one the subject was asked to rate him on a series of trait-descriptive rating scales. For purposes of analysis we grouped the attributes into three categories or clusters that intuitively seemed pertinent to the issues of interest to us, which we refer to as (a) a traditional black stereotype cluster, (b) an ability–achievement cluster, and (c) a sociability cluster. In each case a measure was derived by averaging subjects' ratings on several scales and the resulting measure was analyzed in a 2 (age) × 2 (race) × 2 (facial expression) analysis of variance.

Traditional Black Stereotype Cluster   Ratings on seven attributes reflecting the predominant stereotype of blacks were combined to define this cluster index. These attributes were aggressive, musical, lazy, powerless, flashy, athletic, and religious. This analysis produced a significant main effect for race, with blacks being rated higher than whites on this composite measure. In making their trait ratings, then, our subjects conveyed a rather traditional view of blacks compared to whites. We view this result as another indication that our subjects were not responding even on these rather transparent ratings, in a manner that would convey a favorable impression or avoid the appearance of racial bias.

Ability–Achievement Cluster   The six attributes comprising this measure were intelligent, competent, cultured, educated, successful, and wealthy. Neither race nor age main effects, nor their interaction, were significant in this analysis. The fact that black and white target persons were *not* differentially rated on this dimension, which is loaded heavily with evaluation (albeit in a specific domain), indicates that the differences observed above on the stereotype measure were not simply due to generalized differences in intergroup evaluation but rather were specific to the stereotypic attributes.

Sociability Cluster   Four scales all seemed to pertain to a generally happy, amiable nature and were combined into a single measure. These attributes were happy, friendly, exciting, and sociable. Obviously this dimension is most relevant to the manipulation of smiling versus nonsmiling faces, and indeed the main effect for this manipulation was highly significant. Beyond this obvious outcome, however, there was one additional finding of considerable interest, namely, a significant interaction of race and age. Means for this interaction are shown in Figure 6.4. It is apparent that the form of this interaction parallels earlier results, with the older black target

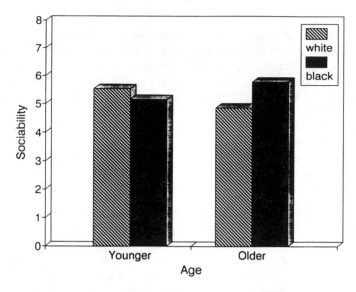

Figure 6.4   *Mean ratings of target persons on sociability traits*

persons being rated happier, friendlier, and so on, than the other three target persons. It is noteworthy that this interaction is not moderated by, but generalizes across, the distinction between smiling and nonsmiling faces. These differences, then, appear to reflect subjects' differential beliefs associated with the stimulus categories represented by this interaction.

Issues of Interpretation

These findings from the trait rating data, when considered in conjunction with the results from our other analyses, raise a number of interesting interpretive issues. One possibility, always a potentially important influence on ratings of significant social groups, is that subjects were sensitive to social norms and/or were defensive about appearing prejudiced, and hence they rated the black target persons in a socially desirable manner. As a general explanation for our findings, however, this interpretation encounters several serious difficulties. First, these motivational biases would lead to significant main effects due to race, with blacks being portrayed more favorably than whites. However, although some race main effects were obtained, they were relatively infrequent. More typical were race-by-age interactions. Second, the tendency to evaluate blacks more favorably than whites, or even older blacks more favorably than the other target persons, was not impressively consistent across dependent measures. For example, blacks were not rated higher on the ability-related cluster, even though these are certainly evaluation-laden attributes. Third, and most importantly, if subjects were strongly influenced by these motivational and self-presentation concerns, they clearly would not have rated blacks so stereotypically on the stereotype-related traits.

Alternatively, our preferred interpretation is that subjects were basing both their descriptions and their ratings on stereotypic conceptions that varied somewhat for the different categories of target person. That is, subjects have a general stereotype of blacks that is defined primarily by the traits traditionally considered stereotypic of blacks, and this stereotype produced the race main effects in several of our analyses. In addition, however, subjects have a more specific, if less well developed, stereotype of older black males than of younger black males. As we suggested earlier, most of our white undergraduate students have probably had relatively little direct interaction with adult black males, but rather have formed their conceptions of this group primarily through media exposure.

Historically, in film and other media, black males have often been portrayed in 'happy servant' roles ranging from the hotel doorman to a worker in the cotton fields. Though in clearly subservient positions, these characters were often portrayed as good-natured and as spreading happiness to those with whom they interact. The prevalence of this kind of portrayal raises the interesting possibility that our subjects, having only a poorly developed conception of this group from personal experience, relied on this stereotypic conception in generating their stories and in making their trait ratings. It is also clear that younger blacks are not portrayed in these roles, and hence were differentiated from their older counterparts in a number of the analyses.

Although this interpretation must remain quite speculative at this point, it does raise some interesting possibilities. Specifically, it suggests not only that our subjects' stories and ratings reflect a reliance on broad stereotypes of racial groups but also that *different* stereotypes were used for different target conditions, revealing the existence of subtypes in subjects' conceptions of blacks (Brewer et al., 1981; Taylor, 1981).

Language and the Use of Traits in Intergroup Perceptions

Semin and Fiedler's (1988) classification system has proven to be a valuable tool in understanding a number of properties of language use, as evidenced in the productivity of their research program (see chapters by Semin and Fiedler in this volume). The results reported above indicate that our own adaptation of their verb classification system was useful in revealing some aspects of our subjects' spontaneous descriptions of members of stereotyped groups.

The highest or most abstract level in Semin and Fielder's system is the use of adjectives to encode or characterize behavior. Certainly the use of adjectives is a more abstract, generalized level of comprehension and description than is captured by any of the verb types, as the adjective removes the characterization from a focus on the specific action to a more pervasive property of either the actor who performed the behavior or the situational entity that elicited it. There is, however, similar variability within the realm of trait-descriptive adjectives themselves. In fact, such variability is the focus of a research program conducted by Hampson, John, and Goldberg (1986; Hampson, Goldberg and John, 1987) investigating what they call breadth versus narrowness in the trait domain. This distinction refers to differences in the extent to which the trait encompasses a broad range of behaviors versus being specific to a narrow subset of behaviors. To cite one of their examples, the trait 'responsible' encompasses a broad range of behaviors that can occur in a variety of situations and can be manifested in a variety of ways. In contrast, the trait 'punctual' refers to a more specific domain of behavior, having to do with promptness, being on time for appointments, and the like. Thus 'responsible' would be considered a broad trait, whereas 'punctual' would be a narrow one.

Note that both traits refer to the same behavioral domain. Behaviors that would be characterized as responsible include, but are not limited to, those that would be characterized by the term 'punctual.' Put another way, being punctual is one way, but not the only way, of being responsible. In fact, Hampson et al. (1986) argue that traits exist in hierarchical structures with broad traits subsuming narrow traits that refer to the same behavioral domain.

Consider, then, a graduate student who is never late for class, who always shows up for research meetings on time, and who has a well-planned schedule and is generally successful in carrying it out. One might characterize this student as being punctual, a trait that certainly captures this behaviour pattern. Alternatively, one might describe her as responsible, which also seems like an apt characterization. By using a broad trait, however, one is conveying much more about her in the latter description than in the former, for it implies that she will manifest her responsibility not only in being on time for appointments but also in completing tasks thoroughly, remembering to carry out a promised favor, exercising discretion in social and work relationships, and in other ways of being a responsible person.

Given that we have this flexibility in the way we characterize persons and the behaviors they perform, what determines whether we will use a narrow, domain-specific adjective or a broad, more generalized attribute? One factor that can influence this process is the perceiver's liking for the person. John et al. (1991) have shown that perceivers described a liked person by using broad desirable and narrow undesirable traits, whereas for a disliked person the opposite pattern was observed – broad undesirable traits and narrow desirable traits.

The narrow–broad dimension underlying this research is similar in some important respects to the concrete–abstract dimension underlying the Semin–Fiedler verb classification. In both cases the authors propose a continuum moving from the specific (narrow, concrete) level of description to more general, inclusive (broad, abstract) characterization. In both cases the more general level is more removed from specific behavioral data, involves greater inference, implies more about the person so described, and is more immune from disconfirmation. Although one could focus instead on differences between these conceptual dimensions, we suggest that it may be useful to explore their similarities. If the similarities are meaningful, then we might expect to find parallels in the functions of these dimensions across linguistic forms. It is noteworthy, then, that John et al.'s (1991) results in the trait adjective domain essentially parallel the results of Maass et al. (1989) for verbs. In both cases differential evaluations of targets (liked versus disliked other; ingroup versus outgroup) were systematically related to the use of general (broad, abstract) versus specific (narrow, concrete) terminology in characterizations of others. To extend this analysis of similar patterns of results across domains, we tested the hypothesis that characterizations of groups would differ in terms of the breadth or narrowness of the traits ascribed, as a function of the perceiver's evaluation of the group.

A Study of National Stereotypes
As noted earlier, historically traits have been the language of stereotypes, at least as studied by social scientists, and this is certainly true of research on national stereotypes. Therefore, to examine our hypothesis, we analyzed the use of trait terms in perceptions of various nationalities. To do so, we made use of results reported by Eagly and Kite (1987).[5] In their study, American college students rated each of 28 nationalities on 41 rating scales, indicating in each case the percentage of members of a given nationality that possessed that attribute. To test our hypothesis, we first identified the seven most liked and the seven least liked nationalities, based on subjects' ratings of the groups on a likeability

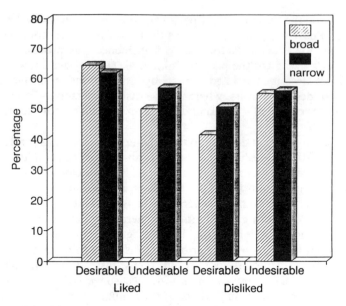

Figure 6.5   *Mean judgments of liked and disliked nationalities*

scale. We then ranked the attributes in terms of desirability and breadth, based on norms reported by Hampson et al. (1987). From these criteria, we selected desirable and undesirable broad traits as well as desirable and undesirable narrow traits from those used in the Eagly and Kite (1987) research.[6] Mean ratings of the liked and disliked nationalities on these attributes are shown in Figure 6.5.

Several findings from an analysis of variance of these data were informative. First, and not surprisingly, subjects made higher ratings of liked nationalities on the desirable traits ($M = 63.09$) than on the undesirable traits ($M = 53.53$). Similarly, mean ratings of disliked nationalities were higher on the undesirable than on the desirable traits ($M = 55.56$ and 46.05, respectively). Thus, we have evidence of both a favorability bias for liked groups and an unfavorability bias for disliked groups.

Of greatest relevance to our predictions, however, was the significant predicted three-way interaction. Separate analyses for liked and disliked nationalities both yielded significant two-way interactions. Liked nationalities were believed to exhibit significantly more broad than narrow *desirable* traits and significantly fewer broad than narrow *undesirable* traits. In contrast, disliked nationalities were believed to exhibit fewer broad than narrow *desirable* traits. Ratings of disliked nationalities on undesirable traits did not differ by breadth.

These statistical results can be best interpreted by examining the pairs of bars in Figure 6.5. The pairs of bars on the extreme left and extreme right indicate ratings on traits that are evaluatively consistent with group expectancies. Liked groups were described with desirable traits while disliked groups were described with unfavorable traits, and these ratings were relatively unaffected by trait breadth. In contrast, trait breadth had a substantial impact on judgments on traits that were evaluatively inconsistent with group stereotypes. Specifically, liked groups were seen as exhibiting more narrow than broad undesirable traits. Disliked groups, on the other hand, were seen as exhibiting more narrow than broad desirable traits.

These results provide further evidence of the differential use of broad and narrow trait descriptors in judgments of liked and disliked targets. To the extent that undesirable traits are ascribed to liked groups, and desirable traits to disliked groups, they are likely to be narrow attributes with a limited range of application. These narrow traits acknowledge that groups may be characterized by stereotype-inconsistent attributes, but do so in a way that constrains their implications for the overall evaluations of the groups. These findings also have implications for understanding a well-known property of stereotypes, namely, their resistance to change. Broad traits not only imply greater stability and generality but are also more difficult to disconfirm. Therefore, the greater assignment of broad desirable and narrow undesirable traits to liked groups and of narrow desirable traits to disliked groups may contribute to the preservation of perceived intergroup differences. Finally, it is noteworthy that the basic pattern of these results parallels Maass et al.'s (1989) findings for verb usage in describing the behaviors of ingroup and outgroup members.

Groups as Noun Categories

Whereas verbs convey properties of action and adjectives describe features of an entity, it is important to recognize that our stereotypes are belief systems about the entities themselves. Therefore, when thinking and communicating about groups our thought and speech often pertain to *categories* rather than to features of categories, and this suggests that important linguistic effects of stereotyping may be captured in nouns rather than in verbs or adjectives. Assigning a person to a noun category – 'jock,' 'German,' 'lesbian,' 'nigger,' 'Jew,' 'nerd' – invokes an abstract concept that immediately and simultaneously conveys an entire organized cluster of descriptive features. It invokes a structure that can subsume an enormous variety of features and specific behaviors, and one that often activates a strong affective component as well. Describing a person with a noun category in communication thus conveys a rich characterization.

In accordance with this view, recent research by Andersen and Klatzky (1987; Andersen et al., 1990; Klatzky and Andersen, 1988) has shown that the concepts we use in thinking about types of people are stereotypes (for example, politicians, 'jocks', and housewives), rather than trait-based categories (for example, extraverted, athletic, and feminine types). An important distinction between these two kinds of categories is that stereotypes are identified by nouns, whereas trait-based categories are identified by adjectives. The Andersen–Klatzky studies have shown that, compared to trait-based categories, these noun categories (1) are richer, having more features that afford a wider variety of inferences about category members; (2) are more imaginable, due to the fact that their features include not only traits but also physical characteristics, typical behaviors, and demographic characteristics; (3) are more distinctive in that they have idiosyncratic features not shared with other categories; and (4) function more efficiently in information processing tasks.

Other research indicates that these group concepts have a structure similar to those we have considered in previous sections on verbs and adjectives. Our cognitive structures about types of persons are organized hierarchically, such that some categories are superordinate in the structure, with several subordinate subtypes organized under them (Cantor and Mischel, 1979). Thus our concepts of significant stereotyped groups may include a variety of subtypes, and these subtypes can be important in processing information about group members (Brewer et al., 1981; Mackie and Worth, 1989; Park and Rothbart, 1982; Rothbart and John, 1985) and in whether disconfirming information affects change in those concepts (Hewstone, 1989; Weber and Crocker, 1983).

Although we know some of the structural properties of these noun categories and their relationships, a lot more remains to be learned. The issues raised in this chapter suggest some interesting directions for further work. For example, do the different levels of a hierarchical structure function in ways similar to the broad and narrow traits (which are also hierarchically organized; Hampson et al., 1986), and to the levels of abstractness in the verb domain? ·
Are we more likely to use broad (superordinate?) than narrow desirable nouns in describing liked groups, but more broad than narrow undesirable nouns in describing a disliked group? How do the various factors influencing the communication context affect the choice of noun categories used in conversation with others? How does the intergroup relationship between speaker and

audience affect these linguistic choices, and with what consequence?

A Language Hierarchy in Communicating about Groups

We have discussed verbs, adjectives and nouns and how their use might be influenced by the intergroup context in which perception and communication occurs. We have seen the usefulness of Semin and Fiedler's (1988) differentiation among three verb types – descriptive action, interpretive action, and state verbs – that vary along a continuum from concrete descriptions of action to more abstract, inferred characterizations of the internal states of the actor. A given action can be characterized by any of these verb types, yet the meaning of that action can differ substantially depending on the verb level used in its characterization. Research by Maass and her colleagues (Maass et al., 1989; Maass and Arcuri, this volume), applying this verb system to the intergroup context, has demonstrated differences in the interpretation and encoding of behaviors of ingroup and outgroup members; and our own work has revealed the influence of stereotypes on the differential use of these verb types in spontaneously generated descriptions of group members in various settings. Hence the use of these differing levels of abstractness can be influenced by group concepts and has the potential to shape not only our own conception of events we have witnessed but also the conception of those events that we convey to others in speech.

Trait adjectives, rather than being tied to action, portray features of an actor and hence move the characterization to a more abstract level (Semin and Fiedler, 1988). We have seen, however, that as with verbs, there is considerable variation in abstractness within the domain of trait adjectives. Building on the work of Hampson, John, and Goldberg (Hampson et al., 1986; John et al., 1991), we have shown differences in the extent to which traits are ascribed to stereotyped groups as a function of the breadth or narrowness of those traits.

Although breadth and abstractness are not equivalent concepts, they do share some important properties. Abstract terms are broad in that they are inclusive; that is, there are many ways of instantiating the concept. Similarly, broad terms are abstract in that they are removed from the specific behaviors from which they are inferred. And because of these features, both abstract and broad terms are more immune to disconfirmation than their lower-level counterparts.

Finally, we have considered the potential importance of noun categories in thinking about the relationship between language and stereotypes. Although stereotypes are often defined as consisting of the attributes believed to characterize a group, they nevertheless refer to groups that are identified by nouns. These noun categories themselves exist in hierarchical representations whose levels differ in breadth and abstractness, suggesting parallels with the findings and conceptualizations discussed earlier for verbs and adjectives.

These considerations lead us to propose the following framework for thinking about the relationship between language and stereotyping for both construing and communicating about interpersonal behaviors. The framework consists of three major linguistic categories – verbs, adjectives, and nouns – each of which can vary in concreteness or abstractness. We begin with verbs, basically adopting the Semin and Fiedler (1988) differentiation of three verb types. Using their common example, an action might be described as 'Bob hit Tom,' 'Bob hurt Tom,' or 'Bob hates Tom' – three alternative construals that convey different meanings of the action.

The most abstract level in the Semin–Fiedler system is the adjectival description – 'Bob is aggressive.' Rather than regarding adjectives as the most abstract level of a verb classification system, we regard them as a distinct category, the terms of which themselves vary in specificity or generality, much as the verbs do. Thus it makes considerable difference whether the perceiver construes Bob as 'temperamental' or as 'aggressive,' the latter presumably being much broader than (and perhaps superordinate to) the former. John et al. (1991) showed the importance of these differences, and our own results have extended this work to the perceptions of stereotyped groups.

Finally, our thinking about stereotypes in this framework has led us to question whether adjectives should be considered the most abstract level for construing interpersonal behavior. Rather than interpreting Bob's behavior as implying that he is aggressive, the perceiver might simply conclude that 'Bob is a fascist,' which would carry with it a whole new set of meanings. Thus we would further extend the analysis of language effects by including noun categories as a linguistic form that might be used in construing behavior. Although there is little existing work investigating the social psychological implications of noun use as a linguistic option, we believe such research is potentially important, particularly when group concepts are involved.

We have presented this framework in the context of a perceiver construing interpersonal behavior as that information is processed. The linguistic alternatives we have discussed would seem to be important determinants affecting the perceiver's processing of this behavioral information – the interpretation initially imposed, the evaluations and inferences based on that interpretation, and hence the representation of the event in memory. As we have seen, both the nature of stereotypes activated by the target person's group membership and the intergroup relationship between the perceiver and the target person can affect the outcome of this construal process.

It is important to note, however, that these language alternatives are influential not only for the perceiver's construal but also for the communication process. In communicating this information to another person, the perceiver's description would be based on his or her representation of the relevant information in memory. In conveying that information to another person, the communicator has available the diversity of linguistic options that we have discussed. Again, the salience of relevant stereotypes and/or intergroup contexts can strongly influence the communicator's choice of terminology, and the language choices made in this communication process can shape the audience's conception in meaningful ways.

Notes

Preparation of this chapter was supported by National Institute of Mental Health Grant MH 40058 to David L. Hamilton. Steven J. Stroessner was supported by a Jacob K. Javits National Graduate Fellowship. Jeffrey W. Sherman was supported by a National Science Foundation Graduate Fellowship. This chapter is based on a paper presented at a conference on 'Language and Social Cognition' held at Castle of Rauischholzhausen, Federal Republic of Germany, in May 1990.

1. Specifically, our instructions stated that, based on past research, we know a great deal about some kinds of abilities (such as, verbal, quantitative) but that much less is known about other abilities on which people differ, and that our study investigates one of them – the ability to think quickly and spontaneously, to generate new ideas 'on the spot,' etc. To further establish this scenario, the first tasks given to subjects asked them to generate, as quickly as possible, as many uses as they could think of for certain common everyday objects (such as a rubberband). They were given 30 seconds to do this for each of three objects by speaking out loud as a tape recorder recorded their responses. This initial exercise was intended to accomplish three goals: first, to bolster our cover story that we were studying an ability that can be manifested in various ways; second, to give subjects experience in spontaneous generation of thoughts; and third, to accustom them to producing these thoughts orally as they were recorded on tape.

2. Not surprisingly, for many of the dependent measures the target person's facial expression (smiling or not smiling) produced a highly significant main effect. Usually these effects fit well with intuitive expectations and, by themselves, are fairly uninteresting. What was particularly noteworthy, however, was that this variable rarely interacted significantly with either of the group membership factors, age and race. Because this chapter is primarily concerned with group-based stereotypes, these general effects of facial expression will not be reported. Our presentation focuses instead on age and race effects and their interaction. Thus, unless otherwise noted, the analyses to be reported collapse across (and generalize across) whether the target person was or was not smiling.

3. Two judges read each of the stories subjects had generated, and rated the overall favorability with which the target person was described. Their ratings were moderately correlated (r was between 0.65 and 0.75 for various conditions) so the two ratings of each target person were averaged for purposes of analysis.

4. Because of these differences in length, the frequency of various linguistic forms would be confounded with the number of words in the story as a whole. Therefore analyses of these other variables were corrected for overall length by dividing raw frequencies by the total number of words, and then multiplying that value by 100 (which was approximately the average length of the stories).

5. We are indebted to Alice Eagly for providing us with these data.

6. Because trait breadth is typically correlated with desirability, we employed breadth ratings that were residualized to remove the influence of desirability (Hampson et al., 1987). The desirability and residualized breadth ratings of the traits were split into thirds, and traits representing either middling breadth or desirability were excluded. Consequently, analyses were based on four traits each that were broad desirable, broad undesirable, and narrow desirable, and five traits that were narrow and undesirable.

References

Anderson, S. M. and Klatzky, R. L. (1987) Traits and social stereotypes: Levels of categorization in person perception. *Journal of Personality and Social Psychology*, 53: 235–246.

Anderson, S. M., Klatzky, R. L. and Murray, J. (1990) Traits and social stereotypes: Efficiency differences in social information processing. *Journal of Personality and Social Psychology*, 59: 192–201.

Bourhis, R. Y., Giles, H., Levens, J. P. and Tajfel, H. (1979) Psycholinguistic distinctiveness: Language divergence in Belgium. In H. Giles and R. St. Clair (eds), *Language and Social Psychology*, pp. 158–185. Oxford: Basil Blackwell.

Bowers, J. W. (1964) Some correlates of language intensity. *Quarterly Journal of Speech*, 50: 415–420.

Bradac, J. J. and Mulac, A. (1984) A molecular view of powerful and powerless speech styles: Attributional consequences of specific language features and communicator intentions. *Communication Monographs*, 51: 307–319.

Bradac, J. J. and Wisegraver, R. (1984) Ascribed status, lexical diversity, and accent: Determinants of perceived status, solidarity, and control of speech style. *Journal of Language and Social Psychology*, 3: 230–255.

Brewer, M. B., Dull, V. and Lui, L. (1981) Perceptions of the elderly: Stereotypes as prototypes. *Journal of Personality and Social Psychology*, 41: 656–670.

Brigham, J. C. (1971) Ethnic stereotypes. *Psychological Bulletin*, 76: 15–33.

Burgoon, M., Jones, S. B. and Stewart, D. (1975) Towards a message-centered theory of persuasion: Three empirical investigations of language intensity. *Human Communication Research*, 1: 240–256.

Cantor, N. and Mischel, W. (1979) Prototypes in person perception. In L. Berkowitz (ed.), *Advances in Experimental Social Psychology*, vol. 12, pp. 3–52. New York: Academic Press.

Caporael, L. R. (1981) The paralanguage of caregiving: Baby talk to the institutionalized aged. *Journal of Personality and Social Psychology*, 40: 876–884.

Caporael, L. R., Lukaszewski, M. P. and Culbertson, G. H. (1983) Secondary baby talk: Judgments by institutionalized elderly and their caregivers. *Journal of*

Personality and Social Psychology, 44: 746–754.

Eagly, A. H. and Kite, M. E. (1987) Are stereotypes of nationalities applied to both women and men? *Journal of Personality and Social Psychology*, 53: 451–462.

Fiedler, K. and Semin, G. R. (1988) On the causal information conveyed by different interpersonal verbs: The role of implicit sentence context. *Social Cognition*, 6: 21–39.

Gibbons, P., Busch, J. and Bradac, J. J. (1991) Powerful and powerless language: Consequences for persuasion, impression formation, and cognition response. *Journal of Language and Social Psychology*, 10: 115–133.

Giles, H. (1980) Accommodation theory: Some new directions. In S. de Silva (ed.), *Aspects of Linguistic Behavior*, pp. 253–278. York: University of York Press.

Hamilton, D. L., Sherman, S. J., Ruvolo, C. M. (1990) Stereotype-based expectancies: Effects on information processing and social behavior. *Journal of Social Issues*, 46(2): 35–60.

Hamilton, D. L. and Trolier, T. K. (1986) Stereotypes and stereotyping: An overview of the cognitive approach. In J. F. Dovidio and S. L. Gaertner (eds), *Prejudice, Discrimination, and Racisim*, pp. 127–163. Orlando, FL: Academic Press.

Hampson, S. E., Goldberg, L. R. and John, O. P. (1987) Category-breadth and social-desirability values for 573 personality terms. *European Journal of Personality*, 1: 241–258.

Hampson, S. E., John, O. P. and Goldberg, L. R. (1986) Category breadth and hierarchical structure in personality: Studies of asymmetries in judgments of trait implications. *Journal of Personality and Social Psychology*, 51: 37–54.

Hewstone, M. (1989) Changing stereotypes with disconfirming information. In D. Bar-Tal, C. F. Graumann, A. W. Kruglanski and W. Stroebe (eds), *Stereotyping and Prejudice: Changing Conceptions*, pp. 207–224. New York: Springer-Verlag.

John, O. P., Hampson, S. E. and Goldberg, L. R. (1991) The basic level in personality-trait hierarchies: Studies of trait use and accessibility in different contexts. *Journal of Personality and Social Psychology*, 60: 348–361.

Katz, D. and Braly, K. (1933) Racial stereotypes in one hundred college students. *Journal of Abnormal and Social Psychology*, 28: 280–290.

Klatzky, R. L. and Andersen, S. M. (1988) Category specificity effects in social typing and personalization. In T. K. Srull and R. S. Wyer, Jr. (eds), *Advances in Social Cognition*, vol. 1, pp. 91–101. Hillsdale, NJ: Erlbaum.

Kramer, C. (1977) Perceptions of female and male speech. *Language and Speech*, 20: 151–161.

Kraut, R. E. and Higgins, E. T. (1984) Communication and social cognition. In R. S. Wyer, Jr. and T. K. Srull (eds), *Handbook of Social Cognition*, vol. 3, pp. 87–128. Hillsdale, NJ: Erlbaum.

Lakoff, R. (1975) *Language and Women's Place*. New York: Harper & Row.

Maass, A., Salvi, D., Arcuri, L. and Semin, G. (1989) Language use in intergroup contexts: The linguistic intergroup bias. *Journal of Personality and Social Psychology*, 57: 981–993.

McCauley, C. and Stitt, C. L. (1978) An individual and quantitative measure of stereotypes. *Journal of Personality and Social Psychology*, 39: 615–624.

Mackie, D. M. and Worth, L. T. (1989) Differential recall of subcategory information about in-group and out-group members. *Personality and Social Psychology Bulletin*, 15: 401–413.

Miller, A. G. (ed.) (1982) *In the Eye of the Beholder*. New York: Praeger Publishers.

Mulac, A., Incontro, C. R. and James, M. R. (1985) Comparison of the gender-linked language effect and sex role stereotypes. *Journal of Personality and Social Psychology*, 49: 1098–1109.

Mulac, A. and Lundell, T. L. (1980) Differences in perceptions created by syntactic-semantic productions of male and female speakers. *Communication Monographs*, 47: 111–118.

O'Barr, W. M. (1982) *Linguistic Evidence: Language, Power and Strategy in the Courtroom*. New York: Academic Press.

Park, B. and Rothbart, M. (1982) Perception of out-group homogeneity and levels of social categorization: Memory for the subordinate attributes of in-group and out-group members. *Journal of Personality and Social Psychology*, 42: 1051–1068.

Rothbart, M. and John, O. P. (1985) Social categorization and behavioral episodes: A cognitive analysis of the effects of intergroup contact. *Journal of Social Issues*, 41(3): 81–103.

Semin, G. R. and Fiedler, K. (1988) The cognitive functions of linguistic categories in describing persons: Social cognition and language. *Journal of Personality and Social Psychology*, 54: 558–568.

Siegman, A. W. and Pope, B. (1972) The effects of ambiguity and anxiety on interview verbal behavior. In A. P. Goldstein and L. Kramer (eds), *Studies in Dyadic Communication*, pp. 29–89. Elmsford, NY: Pergamon Press.

Smith, E. R. (1990) Content and process specificity in the effects of prior experiences. In T. K. Srull and R. S. Wyer, Jr. (eds), *Advances in Social Cognition*, vol. 3, pp. 1–59. Hillsdale, NJ: Erlbaum.

Stephan, W. G. (1985) Intergroup relations. In G. Lindzey and E. Aronson (eds), *The Handbook of Social Psychology*, vol. 2, pp. 599–658. New York: Random House.

Street, R. L. and Giles, H. (1982) Speech accommodation theory: A social cognitive approach to language and speech behavior. In M. E. Roloff and C. R. Berger (eds), *Social Cognition and Communication*, pp. 193–226. Beverly Hills, CA: Sage.

Taylor, S. E. (1981) A categorization approach to stereotyping. In D. L. Hamilton (ed.), *Cognitive Processes in Stereotyping and Intergroup Behavior*, pp. 83–114. Hillsdale, NJ: Erlbaum.

Weber, R. and Crocker, J. (1983) Cognitive processes in the revision of stereotypic beliefs. *Journal of Personality and Social Psychology*, 45: 961–977.

7

The Role of Language in the Persistence of Stereotypes

Anne Maass and Luciano Arcuri

Since the very beginning of social psychology, the study of prejudice and stereotyping have been at the center of the field. One of the most striking aspects, noted early on, is the persistence of stereotypes in the face of contradicting behavioral evidence. Apparently, people are reluctant to revise their stereotypic beliefs even when confronted with evidence that disconfirms their expectations. We will argue in this chapter that biased language use contributes in predictable ways to the remarkable resistance of social stereotypes to change. Using Semin and Fielder's (1988) Linguistic Category Model as a conceptual framework and methodological tool, we will advance the thesis that stereotype-congruent episodes tend to be described in abstract linguistic terms such as adjectives (for example, Levine is stingy) whereas stereotype-incongruent behavioral episodes tend to be described in concrete linguistic terms · that do not generalize beyond the specific event (for example, Levine donated five hundred dollars to the National Heart Association). In particular, we will argue that desirable in-group and undesirable out-group behaviors tend to be communicated in abstract terms, whereas undesirable in-group and desirable out-group behaviors are communicated in concrete language – referred to as the linguistic intergroup bias (LIB) throughout this paper. Considering that information encoded at an abstract level is relatively resistant to disconfirmation and implies high stability over time (Semin and Fiedler, 1988), we will also argue that this language bias contributes to the persistence of preexisting ideas about social groups. Thus, we propose a model in which existing stereotypes produce a biased language use which in turn contributes to the maintenance of existing biases. We will briefly outline Semin and Fiedler's model and subsequently describe our own research program in which we attempted to (1) demonstrate biased language use in intergroup settings empirically; (2) investigate the mechanisms that underlie the observed linguistic intergroup bias;

(3) define some of the boundary conditions; and (4) illustrate some of the consequences deriving from biased language use.

The Linguistic Category Model

Semin and Fiedler's (1988) linguistic category model, in its original formulation, distinguishes four levels of abstraction at which the same behavioral episode may be encoded. Descriptive action verbs (DAVs) such as *to call* or *to touch* represent the most concrete level and refer to single, observable episodes. At the second level of abstraction we find interpretive action verbs (IAVs) such as *to help* or *to cheat*, which describe a general class of behaviors (there are many ways to help) but that preserve the reference to a single behavioral episode. State verbs (SVs) describe a psychological state such as *hate* or *desire*; they have no direct reference to a specific behavioral episode or to a specific situation, but do refer to a specific object. At the highest level of abstraction are adjectives (ADJ), such as *aggressive* or *creative*, that describe highly abstract dispositions or characteristics of a person, thereby generalizing across specific behavioral events, across situations, and across objects. Thus, the same behavioral episode in which A hits B may be encoded as 'A hits B', as 'A hurts B', as 'A hates B' or as 'A is aggressive'. As becomes evident from this example, descriptions at different levels of abstraction carry different meanings. An abstract statement such as 'A is aggressive' implies great stability over time, suggesting that the person will behave similarly in the future, in different situations, and with other people. She or he would probably also be expected to show related aggressive behaviors such as kicking or pulling hair. Drawing such conclusions from a description at the concrete level would be much less likely.

Application to Intergroup Settings: The Linguistic Intergroup Bias (LIB)

We have recently suggested that this model may have a number of interesting implications for our understanding of intergroup biases in general and the transmisson and maintenance of stereotypic beliefs in particular (see Maass et al., 1989). It has long been known that people expect in-group members to display more desirable and fewer undesirable behaviors than out-group members (see, for example, Howard and Rothbart, 1980). They also are more likely to infer negative dispositions from undesirable out-group behaviors than from undesirable in-group behaviors (see, for example. Taylor and Jaggi, 1974; Pettigrew, 1979; Hewstone and Jaspars, 1984), suggesting that the evidence-to-inference link (Rothbart and Park, 1986) is considerably tighter when a behavior episode confirms preconceived ideas.

This is not as irrational as it may initially appear considering that stereotypes represent *probabilistic* expectancies. Thus, if we believe that Italians are lazy we obviously don't expect *all* Italians to *always* be either on strike or on vacation. Rather, we assume that Italians, compared to other nationalities, have a greater probability of engaging in lazy behaviors and a lower probability of engaging in industrious behaviors. Consequently, when we observe Italian citizens working hard and efficiently we do not need to revise our general concept of Italians because a probabilistic expectancy explicitly allows for a certain number of exceptions to occur.

There are at least two ways to reconcile unexpected behaviors with the general conception of the category: namely, the dissociation of the single, atypical member from the category as a whole; or the dissociation of the single act from the group member. It is this second mechanism where language comes into play. In fact, we suspect that stereotype-incongruent behaviors are interpreted as situationally and temporarily bound events that are largely unrelated to the actor's more enduring properties. As such, they are encoded in concrete terms without generalizing beyond the given information. In a sense, behavioral episodes that are incongruent with the general perception of social categories, and as such unexpected, are treated as local, transient events by simply shifting the level of analysis from the general to the specific. In contrast, stereotype-congruent behaviors will be described in abstract linguistic terms, thereby associating the single act with the actor's enduring properties or psychological state.

Experimental Demonstrations of the LIB

The first step in our research program was therefore to demonstrate the LIB in the most general case, in which people belong to mutually exclusive social groups and hold general negative expectations about out-group behaviors and positive expectations about in-group behaviors. The setting we selected for our first experiments (Maass et al., 1989: Experiments 1 and 2) was the so-called *palio*, an annual horse race competition in which members of different quarters of the city (in our case the city of Ferrara) compete against each other. The studies were run shortly before the *palio*, when in-group identification is particularly high and intergroup hostilities (such as reciprocal flag thefts or secret drugging of the other team's horses) are particularly frequent.

Members of the various *contrada* (teams) were presented with a series of cartoons in which either a member of their own *contrada* (in-group) or a competing *contrada* (out-group) performed a behavior. Half the cartoons portrayed socially desirable behaviors and half undesirable behaviors. In the first experiment, subjects were provided with four response alternatives for each episode, corresponding to the four levels of abstraction in the linguistic category model, and were asked to select the response alternative that, in their opinion, best described the scene. Obviously, we predicted that subjects would select abstract descriptions when in-group members performed desirable and when out-group members performed undesirable behaviors, while favoring concrete descriptions for desirable out-group and undesirable in-group behaviors. Our data (see Table 7.1) tend to confirm this prediction.

Table 7.1   *Mean level of abstraction as a function of group membership and social desirability*

	Desirability of behavior	
Membership of protagonist	desirable	undesirable
In-group	2.69	2.51
Out-group	2.47	2.82

Means are based on a 4-point scale with 1 indicating the lowest (DAV) and 4 indicating the highest level of abstraction (ADJ).

Source: Maass, A., Salvi, D., Arcuri, L. and Semin, G. (1989) Language use in intergroup contexts: The linguistic intergroup bias. *Journal of Personality and Social Psychology*, 57: 981–993; reproduced with permission from the American Psychological Association, 1990 (Experiment 1: multiple choice procedure).

In addition, we had asked our subjects to rate the positivity or negativity of each behavioral episode so that we were able to correlate abstraction with perceived positivity across episodes. These results provided further support for the LIB as they showed opposite correlations for in-group and out-group episodes: with increasing desirability of the episode, language became more abstract when referred to in-group protagonists ($r = 0.28$), but more concrete when referred to out-group protagonists ($r = -0.55$).

We then tested whether the results obtained with the multiple choice procedure would replicate using a more realistic free response format in which subjects were asked to briefly describe

Table 7.2   *Mean level of abstraction as a function of group membership and social desirability*

Membership of protagonist	Desirability of behavior	
	desirable	undesirable
In-group	2.63	2.75
Out-group	2.38	2.67

Means are based on a 4-point scale with 1 indicating the lowest (DAV) and 4 indicating the highest level of abstraction (ADJ).

Source: Maass, A., Salvi, D., Arcuri, L. and Semin, G. (1989) Language use in intergroup contexts: The linguistic intergroup bias. *Journal of Personality and Social Psychology,* 57: 981–993; reproduced with permission from the American Psychological Association, 1990 (Experiment 2: free response procedure)

each scene in their own words. As indicated in Table 7.2, the second experiment largely confirmed our previous findings. Again, subjects tended to encode the same desirable episodes at a higher level of abstraction when performed by an in-group member than when performed by an out-group member. However, contrary to our initial hypothesis and to the findings of the previous experiment, this tendency did not reverse for undesirable behaviors.

Meanwhile, the LIB has also partially been confirmed for a different social category, namely towns that have traditionally been in competition (see Lazzarato, 1989). Subjects in this study came from two small towns in the vicinity of Padua. Numerous historical documents indicate a pronounced rivalry between the two towns dating back to the early 1800s and culminating in the demand that the towns, formerly part of a common administration, be separated. Even in recent years, inhabitants of either town continue to strongly identify with their community, and inter-town hostility has not ceased entirely (as, for example, evidenced by the refusal of a post office employee to serve a client from the other town). Again, we used the cartoon paradigm in which inhabitants of either town were asked to briefly describe scenes depicting protagonists of either their own or the other town displaying either positive or negative behaviours. As can be seen in Table 7.3, the same undesirable behaviors were described in more abstract terms when displayed by an out-group than when displayed by an in-group member, whereas no differences emerged for desirable behaviors.

Taken together, the three experiment suggest that, in intergroup settings, language tends to be used in a biased fashion consistent

Table 7.3 *Mean level of abstraction as a function of group membership and social desirability*

	Desirability of behavior	
Membership of protagonist	desirable	undesirable
In-group	2.80	2.67
Out-group	2.82	3.01

Means are based on a 4-point scale with 1 indicating the lowest (DAV) and 4 indicating the highest level of abstraction (ADJ).

Source: Lazzarato, 1989: Experiment 4

with the LIB hypothesis. The three experiments reported here further suggest that this bias is more pronounced for episodes involving out-group than in-group members. People apparently process in-group episodes in an almost unbiased fashion, but they shift the level of analysis from the abstract to the concrete whenever they encounter unexpected out-group behaviors. Interestingly, this is quite in line with Wilder's (1986) contention that people hold an Aristotelian view of lawfulness for out-group members that allows for a great number of exceptions before the general rule has to be revised. Rather than revise the perception of the out-group in the face of disconfirming evidence, people are likely to regard such inconsistencies as single, exceptional instances largely unrelated to the general rule.

Taken together, the experiments reported so far illustrate the hypothesized language bias in intergroup settings, but they provide little information about the *mechanisms* that trigger the linguistic intergroup bias. The second step in our research program was therefore to identify the processes that are responsible for the observed phenomenon.

Mechanisms Underlying the Linguistic Intergroup Bias

We have initially proposed a model according to which people hold differential expectancies regarding in-group and out-group behaviors, which in turn determine the language representation of behavioral episodes. Expectancy-congruent observations are translated into abstract language that generalizes from the single act to more enduring properties of the actor. In contrast, expectancy-incongruent observations are described in concrete terms as single instances with clear situational and temporal constraints.

Besides our initial explanation, there are at least two alternative ways to account for the LIB, one derived from attribution theory, the other from social identity theory. From an *attributional perspective*, one may argue that our results simply reflect the linguistic expression of latent causal attributions. If concrete codings reflect implicit situational and abstract codings reflect implicit dispositional attributions, our findings could easily be interpreted as the linguistic manifestation of the well-known group-serving attributional bias (Hewstone and Jaspars, 1984).

Fortunately, the taxonomy proposed by the linguistic category model is not equivalent to the continuum of situational-to-personal causation, and the two models make, in part, different predictions that can be tested against each other. In fact, moving from DAVs to ADJs, there is no linear increase in implicit personal causation. neither do DAVs imply situational causation (the lack of interpretation is a defining feature of DAVs); nor do high levels of abstraction necessarily imply personal causation. This becomes particularly clear at the two intermediate levels of abstraction. Moving from IAVs to SVs, we observe an increase in abstraction but a decline in personal causation. Since Garvey and Caramazza's (1974) pioneering work on implicit causality, various studies on diverse languages and cultures have investigated the implicit causality of verbs embedded in subject–verb–object sentences and, with few exceptions, have found that the causality is regularly attributed to the subject when the verb is an IAV, but to the object when the verb is an SV (see, for example, Au, 1986; Brown, 1986; Brown and Fish, 1983; Franco et al., 1990; Voster, 1985).

For the two intermediate levels, then, the group-serving attributional bias (Hewstone and Jaspars, 1984) and the linguistic category model make exactly opposite predictions. The group-serving bias would predict that undesirable out-group and desirable in-group behaviors be attributed to the protagonist or logical subject of the sentence, thus favoring the use of IAVs (implying subject causation) over SVs (implying object causation). In contrast, the linguistic intergroup bias hypothesis predicts a higher level of abstraction for undesirable out-group and desirable in-group behaviors, suggesting a greater use of SVs than IAVs. These contradicting positions were tested in an experimental setting that explicitly encouraged causal thinking (Arcuri, Maass and Portelli, 1991).

Rather than simply to describe behavior episodes, subjects in this experiment were asked to provide explanations for a series of interpersonal episodes involving either in-group or out-group protagonists. The protagonist either resembled or differed from the subject on various social categories such as sex, town of residence,

Table 7.4 *Mean IAV to SV ratio as a function of group membership and social desirability*

	Desirability of behavior	
Membership of protagonist	desirable	undesirable
In-group	1.27	1.68
Out-group	2.39	0.99

Greater scores indicate that the ratio favors IAVs over SVs.

Source: from Arcuri et al., 1991

nationality, school affiliation, or preference for a certain sports team. Half of the episodes depicted successful interactions (for example, a basketball player encourages an injured player of the opposite team who subsequently continues playing), half-unsuccessful interactions (for example, two guys set up a tent together but, at some point, start arguing). Subjects were asked to indicated for each episode 'what the protagonist did to bring about this situation', either by selecting one of two response alternatives (one formulated as IAV, the other as SV), or by indicating that the two responses provided equally valid accounts.

From the attributional perspective, subjects should have favored IAVs for desirable in-group and undesirable out-group behaviors but SVs for the remaining combinations. Interestingly, they did not. Our findings (see Table 7.4) in fact show that people prefer IAVs when describing positive out-group and negative in-group behaviors *despite* the greater subject causation implicit in such statements. This suggests that attributional reasoning may sometimes be secondary to other concerns. Apparently, people choose abstract versus concrete language representations for reasons other than their attributional implications. Often, it may be more important to reveal whether or not a certain behavior reflects a stable characteristic or psychological state of the actor than to provide implicit information about its causation (see also Hamilton, 1988). More importantly, these results suggest that group-serving attributional biases provide an unlikely account of the linguistic intergroup bias observed in this and in our previous studies.

Besides the attributional and our own expectancy-based accounts there is yet another, primarily motivational explanation of the LIB which may be derived from *social identity theory* (Tajfel and Turner, 1979; Turner, 1987). From this perspective, the LIB may be interpreted as a subtle way of establishing an intergroup difference in favor of one's own group in an attempt to protect one's social identity. For example, when describing favorable out-group behaviors as single, isolated instances unrelated to the protagonist's enduring properties, people may engage in subtle out-group derogation consistent with a social identity perspective. Contrary to our own account, this explanation does not rely on the mediating role of differential expectancies.

The next step in our research program was therefore to test whether the LIB reflects an attempt to protect one's social identity, or whether it derives from differential expectations. Our interest in testing the two explanations against each other is not just motivated by academic curiosity, but also has important implications from an applied point of view. Although the two explanations often make converging predictions, they lead in some cases to exactly opposite predictions. If desire for a positive social identity . is at the basis of the linguistic intergroup bias, then such a bias should emerge whenever the individual's social identity is at stake (such as when groups are in direct competition, as in our experiments).

Yet if the LIB is mainly a function of differential expectancies, then predictions vary according to type and specificity of such expectancies. In certain intergroup settings, such as the ones reported so far, people have negative general views of the out-group without holding specific stereotypic expectancies about particular behavior patterns. Often, however, expectancies reflect well-defined stereotypes referring to very specific behavior patterns (for example, we expect Germans to be dogmatic, but not to be stupid). These are exactly the cases in which the two explanations make opposite predictions.

In fact, there are at least three situations in which predictions derived from the stereotypic expectancy perspective deviate from the more general intergroup bias perspective. First, since stereotypic expectancies are limited to specific behavior patterns, biases in language use should, according to the expectancy perspective, occur only for those behaviors that are directly relevant to the stereotype. Second, stereotypes may occasionally contain positive elements that are in contrast to the overall affective tone of the stereotype, as in the case of the intellectual achievements of Jews. Following a differential expectancy viewpoint, behaviors of Jews that are indicative of intelligence should be encoded at a high level of abstraction because they are expectancy-congruent. Yet non-Jews should prefer concrete language representations if they are mainly concerned with maintaining a positive social identity. Third, members of mutually exclusive social categories may occasionally hold converging stereotypic expectancies. A striking example are sex-stereotypes that are largely agreed on by male and female subjects (see, for example, Deaux, 1976). According to a differential expectancy perspective, both male and female subjects should encode sex-role incongruent behaviors ('feminine' behaviors of male protagonists or 'masculine' behaviors of female protagonists) in concrete terms independent of their valence.

We have recently made a first attempt to test the two approaches against each other (Maass et al., 1990). In this experiment, male and female subjects were presented with cartoons depicting male or female actors performing either desirable or undesirable behaviors. Half of these behaviors were typically masculine, half typically feminine (for example, *heavily insulting another driver* would constitute a negative, typically masculine behavior whereas *talking negatively about somebody behind his back* would constitute a negative, typically feminine behavior). Subjects described each episode, either by selecting one of four response alternatives corresponding to the four levels of the linguistic category model, or by describing the scene in their own words. Independent of the response mode, our results provide little support for the social identity perspective. According to this account, both males and females should have described positive behaviors of same-sex protagonists and negative behaviors of opposite-sex protagonists in abstract terms. This was not the case. Rather, subjects responded in a way that was largely consistent with the differential expectancy notion although effects were admittedly very small (see Table 7.5). Independent of the subject's own sex and the desirability of the action, subjects tended to encode sex-role congruent behaviors at a higher level of abstraction than sex-role incongruent behaviors.

Table 7.5 *Mean level of abstraction as a function of sex of protagonist and sex-typing of behavior*

| | Sex-typing of behavior | |
Sex of protagonist	masculine	feminine
Male	3.00	2.83
Female	2.85	2.88

Means are based on a 4-point scale with 1 indicating the lowest (DAV) and 4 indicating the highest level of abstraction (ADJ).

Source: Maass et al., 1990

This experiment provides first tentative evidence that the LIB is predominantly an expectancy-guided phenomenon. However, we do not exclude that self-protective motivations may prevail under different circumstances, such as when the subject's social identity is threatened or when groups are in direct competition. One of the next goals of our research program will therefore be to investigate whether different processes prevail in different situational contexts. It is conceivable that cognitive expectancy processes are at the basis of the LIB whenever people judge the behavior of in-group and out-group members from the perspective of an uninvolved observer, but that social identity protection becomes the driving force in competitive intergroup settings.

Boundary Conditions: Limitations of the LIB

We have now also begun to identify some of the limitations of the LIB. As noted earlier, we had already observed that the LIB is more pronounced for out-group than for in-group behaviors, a finding that is consistent with Wilder's (1986) notion that out-group expectations allow for more exceptions before a stereotype has to be revised.

In addition, we tested whether the LIB generalizes to situations in which people, rather than describe specific behavioral events, provide summary statements about in-group and out-group. Lazzarato (1989: Experiments 1 and 2) asked students with different majors (Law versus Political Science in Experiment 1, and Law versus Medical School in Experiment 2) to indicate one positive and one negative characteristic, action or behavior that they considered typical of Law (or Political Science) students. In line with our previous research, it was hypothesized that students would be willing to provide negative in-group and positive out-group descriptions, but that these would tend to be expressed at a lower level of abstraction than the remaining combinations. Contrary to our expectations, neither experiment confirmed this hypothesis. Since it was conceivable that our subjects did not hold sufficiently negative views of the out-group, the experiment was replicated using residents of two competing towns as subjects (Lazzarato, 1989: Experiment 3). Again, there was no evidence for biased language use when people were asked to simply describe positive and negative characteristics, actions or behaviors typical of the residents of either town. Interestingly, these same subjects *did* display the LIB when describing *concrete behavioral events* involving members of their own or the other town (Lazzarato, 1989: Experiment 4). Taken together, Lazzarato's studies suggest that the LIB is limited to situations in which people describe concrete behavioral episodes. When providing more general summary statements unrelated to specific events, people show little bias, probably due to the fact that they tend to shift their language overall toward the abstract pole of the continuum. Note that almost 60 per cent of the responses in Lazzarato's experiments (1989: Experiments 1, 2, 3) were expressed at the most abstract level, as adjectives. This is quite in line with the observation of other authors that there is a tendency toward abstraction in unrestricted, everyday communication (see also Fiedler et al., 1989; Grice, 1975). For our model, this suggests that the LIB is likely to be limited to settings in which *specific events* are communicated.

Implications of Abstract versus Concrete Language Use

The most interesting aspect of our model, we believe, are the consequences deriving from abstract versus concrete language use. We have argued earlier that biased language may contribute to the persistence of social stereotypes through a self-perpetuating cycle in which biased language use maintains or even aggravates initial intergroup biases.

Imagine the following example. A soccer fan is being observed as he leaves the soccer stadium after a match between Köln and Juventus; he gets into a fight with a spectator cheering for the opposite team and seriously injures his opponent. A news reporter may communicate this story at very different levels of abstraction. He may simply describe the behavior sequence, he may provide a interpretation, or he may ascribe abstract dispositions to the protagonist referring to him as an *aggressive* or *violent* person. Our own research suggests that an Italian sports reporter would more likely use more abstract terms if our juvenile delinquent was German than if he was Italian.

Since abstract language provides more information about the actor and implies greater temporal and cross-situational stability (see Semin and Fiedler, 1988), abstract language typically used for describing undesirable out-group and desirable in-group behaviors may bolster existing negative views of the out-group as well as positive views of the in-group. In particular, once a behavioral episode has been communicated in abstract terms it may induce the expectation that the same action be repeated in the future.

In order to test this hypothesis we presented subjects with statements formulated at different levels of abstraction that were taken from our *palio* studies reported earlier. Subjects were asked to rate how much information each sentence revealed about the protagonist and how likely it was that the protagonist would display the same behavior or trait in the future (Maass et al., 1989: Experiment 3). Our results demonstrate that with increasing level of abstraction the amount of information about the actor and the expectancy of repetition increase in a linear fashion.

This suggests that once a negative out-group or positive in-group behavior has been communicated in abstract linguistic terms, it influences information processing of both source and receiver of the communication. Thus, abstract information may serve as a schema that guides (and biases) subsequent information processing in ways that have still to be tested empirically.

Concluding Remarks

Although our research program is still at the beginning, we do have first evidence for biased language use in intergroup settings. Our research has repeatedly shown that people tend to describe expectancy-congruent episodes in abstract terms, but shift their analysis toward the concrete end of the continuum when they encounter expectancy-incongruent evidence. The fact that converging findings were obtained for different intergroup settings (*palio*, sex, nationality, town of residence, sport preference, school affiliation, and so on), for different response modes (multiple choice and free description) and for different tasks (simple descriptions as well as attributional accounts) further suggests that we are dealing with a pervasive phenomenon.

More importantly, we believe that our model may have a number of intriguing implications for the maintenance and interpersonal transmission of stereotypic beliefs in real life settings. For instance, one may envisage subtle language biases in the legal system, where witnesses may describe the observed event sequence in more or less abstract terms. Since the likelihood of repetition of a criminal act typically increases the severity of the sentence, abstract communications may contribute to more severe sentences. Along the same line, news reporters may inadvertently bias their news stories depending on whether or not the protagonist shares their own category membership. First indirect evidence for this idea comes from a recent international research program conducted by the Food and Agricultural Organization about the image of Africa in the mass media (see Pugliese, 1988). Besides the highly biased news story selection and the generally negative tone of the coverage, the report complained about a 'linguistic stereotype . . . in which phrases referring to Blacks are characterized by the predominance of nouns and the almost complete absence of verbs, at least in their active form, whereas the exact opposite occurs in reference to Westerners, denoted by action verbs' (Pugliese, 1988: 57). It remains to be seen whether more systematic analyses of mass media reports (for example, content analyses based on the linguistic category model) will confirm this observation.

Although many questions necessarily remain unanswered at such an early stage of inquiry, we hope that the present model will contribute to our understanding of the link between language and stereotyping and, in particular, that it will help to bridge the gap between intra-individual maintenance and inter-individual transmission of stereotypes.

Note

During the writing of this chapter, Anne Maass was visiting the University of Kiel, supported by an Alexander von Humboldt fellowship.

References

Arcuri, L., Maass, A. and Portelli, G. (1991) Linguistic intergroup bias and implicit attributions. Under review.

Au, T. (1986) A verb is worth a thousand words: The causes and consequences of interpersonal events implicit in language. *Journal of Memory and Language*, 25: 104–122.

Brown, R. (1986) Linguistic relativity. In S. H. Hulse and B. F. Green, Jr. (eds), *One Hundred Years of Psychological Research in America: G. Stanley Hall and the Johns Hopkins Tradition*, pp. 241–276. Baltimore: Johns Hopkins University Press.

Brown, R. and Fish, D. (1983) The psychological causality implicit in language. *Cognition*, 14: 237–273.

Deaux, K. (1976) *The Behavior of Women and Men*. Monterey, CA: Brooks/Cole.

Fiedler, K., Semin, G. R. and Bolten (1989) Language use and reification of social information: Top-down and bottom-up processing in person cognition. *European Journal of Social Psychology*, 19: 271–295.

Franco, F., Arcuri, L. and Cadinu, M. (1990) L'attribuzione di causalità nei verbi interpersonali: Una verifica sulla lingua italiana. [Causal attributions implicit in interpersonal verbs. A test in Italian language]. *Giornale Italiano di Psicologia*, 17: 159–174.

Garvey, C. and Caramazza, A. (1974) Implicit causality in verbs. *Linguistic Inquiry*, 5: 459–464.

Grice, H. P. (1975) Logic and conversation. In P. Cole and J. L. Morgan (eds), *Syntax and Semantics, vol. 3: Speech Acts*, pp. 365–372. New York: Seminar Press.

Hamilton, D. L. (1988) Causal attribution viewed from an information processing perspective. In P. Bar-Tal and A. W. Kruglanski (eds), *The Social Psychology of Knowledge*, Cambridge: Cambridge University Press.

Hewstone, M. and Jaspars, J. M. F. (1984) Social dimensions of attribution. In H. Tajfel (ed.), *The Social Dimension: European Developments in Social Psychology*, vol. II, pp. 379–404. Cambridge: Cambridge University Press.

Howard, J. and Rothbart, M. (1980) Social categorization and memory for ingroup and outgroup behavior. *Journal of Personality and Social Psychology*, 38: 301–310.

Lazzarato, G. (1989) L'uso del linguaggio nelle situazioni intergruppo: Applicazione del modello delle categorie linguistiche. Unpublished Master's Thesis.

Maass, A., Giordana, C. and Fontana, F. (1990) The linguistic intergroup bias: Is it a function of social identity protection or stereotypic expectations? Unpublished manuscript.

Maass, A., Salvi, D., Arcuri, L. and Semin, G. (1989) Language use in intergroup contexts: The linguistic intergroup bias. *Journal of Personality and Social Psychology*, 57: 981–993.

Pettigrew, T. F. (1979) The ultimate attribution error: Extending Allport's cognitive analysis of prejudice. *Personality and Social Psychology Bulletin*, 5: 461–476.

Pugliese, C. (1988) Quale imagine? *Nigrizia*, 106: 56–57.

Rothbart, M. and Park, B. (1986) On the confirmability and disconfirmability of trait concepts. *Journal of Personality and Social Psychology*, 50: 131–142.

Semin, G. R. and Fiedler, K. (1988) The cognitive functions of linguistic categories in describing persons: Social cognition and language. *Journal of Personality and Social Psychology*, 54: 558–568.

Tajfel, H. and Turner, J. C. (1979) An integrative theory of intergroup conflict. In W. S. Austin and S. Worchel (eds), *The Social Psychology of Intergroup Relations*, pp. 33–47. Monterey, CA: Brooks/Cole.

Taylor, D. M. and Jaggi, V. (1974) Ethnocentrism and causal attribution in a South Indian context. *Journal of Cross-cultural Psychology*, 5: 162–171.

Turner, J. C. (1987) *Rediscovering the Social Group: A Self-categorization Theory*. Oxford: Basil Blackwell.

Voster, J. (1985) Implicit causality in language: Evidence from Afrikaans. *South African Journal of Psychology*, 15: 62–67.

Wilder, D. A. (1986) Social categorization: Implications for creation and reduction of intergroup bias. In: L. Berkowitz (ed.) *Advances in Experimental Social Psychology*, vol. 19, pp. 291–355.

PART 4

COMMUNICATION AND SOCIAL COGNITION

8

Personal and Contextual Factors in Communication: A Review of the 'Communication Game'

C. Douglas McCann and E. Tory Higgins

Since its inception, social psychology has been concerned with examining the nature of interpersonal interaction and the types of social influence processes inherent in such contexts. This has led to a consideration of specific issues (such as impression formation, impression management, attitude formation and change) related to the acquisition and transmission of knowledge about self and others in interpersonal contexts. Given the central role played by interpersonal communication in such processes, it would seem evident that this type of focus would presuppose a concern with the nature of interpersonal communication itself.

Interestingly, up until the last few years, this has not been the case. Although some attention was directed toward understanding the nature of communication and its role in interpersonal inter-action (for example, Festinger, 1950; Krauss et al., 1968; Zajonc, 1960), most often communication was conceptualized simply as a vehicle for information transmission (for example, Hovland et al., 1953). This latter orientation resulted in little attempt to under-stand or examine its personal and interpersonal antecedents and consequences and has led to a restricted view of the role of communication in interpersonal interaction. Thus, little attention was devoted to developing a social psychology of communication and language use. More recently, however, social psychologists, along with scholars in sociology and communication studies, have increasingly turned their attention to a consideration of the inter-face between social psychology and communication (for example, Donohew et al., 1988; Giles and Robinson, 1990; Giles and

St Clair, 1985; Roloff and Berger, 1982). While there are many possible reasons for this resurgence of interest in social psychology and communication, one of the primary factors may be the ascendancy of the study of social information processing in social psychology. The *process* orientation adopted by those working in social cognition, along with the emphasis on the active nature of social participants and the focus on symbolic activity, has provided a framework that is compatible with the study of interpersonal communication (McCann and Higgins, 1990).

Our objective in this chapter is to review recent work conducted in the context of the 'Communication Game' model. This model was initially proposed by Higgins (1981), and was based in a social cognitive orientation toward interpersonal communication and its effects. Since that time, numerous investigations have addressed various aspects of the model and have served to clarify and extend its initial implications. We will review this work and will attempt to place it within the context of the developing interest in the study of social cognition and communication.

The 'Communication Game': A Social Cognitive View

The communication game model was developed in reaction to limitations evident in the 'information transmission' approach that had been particularly dominant in influencing research examining the social psychology of communication and language use (for reviews and critiques of this approach, see Higgins, 1981; and Krauss, 1987). This approach focused attention on issues related to communication accuracy and on communication as a vehicle for interpersonal persuasion (for example, Eagly and Himmelfarb, 1978; Hovland et al., 1953; McGuire, 1966, 1972; Mehrabian and Reed, 1968; Rosenberg and Cohen, 1966).

In this work, communication was conceptualized as a relatively linear (for example, Cherry, 1959; Devito, 1970; Shannon and Weaver, 1949) process focusing on source, message, and receiver characteristics as they impact on transmission/reception accuracy and/or persuasive impact. Communicative participants were presented as relatively passive participants in the process and as individuals who were motivated by concerns related simply to 'knowing the truth' or 'holding a correct position' on some specific issue (Higgins, Fondacaro and McCann, 1982). Early work in referential accuracy focused on examining general communication skills (for example, Flavell et al., 1968; Glucksberg et al., 1975; Rosenberg and Cohen, 1966), while work in persuasive communication focused on the effects of various source, message, and receiver characteristics on persuasion (for a review, see McGuire, 1972).

Although clearly important, it would appear that the overly static view, and the restricted role of communication conveyed by this work failed to promote significant further interest in the nature of communication itself, its personal and interpersonal antecedents and consequences, or in the active role played by participants in the process of interpersonal communication. The communication game model was developed in the context of this type of work and was designed initially as an attempt to underscore the important role played by a variety of personal and contextual (that is, interpersonal) factors in communication and the heuristic potential inherent in social cognitive approaches to communication and its effects.

The Communication Game

Although acknowledging the important contribution made by those working within the information transmission approach, the communication game model suggests that there are additional features of the communication process not highlighted by those models that are essential in a more comprehensive understanding of the nature of interpersonal communication.

This approach emphasizes the 'game-like' features of communication (for example, Burke, 1962; Garfinkel, 1967; Goffman, 1959; Wittgenstein, 1953) and the fact that communication is considered to be a form of purposeful social interaction that occurs within a socially defined context and that involves interdependent social roles. In addition, its 'game-like' features underscore the importance of considering the *rule-oriented* nature of interpersonal communication. This latter aspect necessitates consideration of the nature of the rules that are followed, and the tactics and strategies that are employed in attempts by individuals to obtain the goals they bring with them into their interpersonal interactions.

Our examinations of interpersonal communication in the context of the communication game model were guided by the implications of four general assumptions derived from the literature on the game-like features of language use in interpersonal contexts. First, rather than as serving only to transmit information, communication was seen as a multipurpose activity that functions, among other things, to develop, maintain, and strengthen interpersonal relationships (for example, Blumer, 1962; Garfinkel, 1967; Watzlawick et al., 1967). Second, communication was considered to be a process in which individuals collaboratively define the meaning or social reality of the interchange (for example,

Table 8.1   *Rules of the Communication Game*

Communicators should:	Recipients should:
1 take the audience's or recipient's characteristics into account 2 convey the truth as they see it 3 try to be understood (i.e., be coherent and comprehensible) 4 give neither too much nor too little information 5 be relevant 6 produce a message that is appropriate to the context and circumstances 7 produce a message that is appropriate to their communicative intent or purpose 8 assume that the message recipient is trying, as much as possible, to follow the rules of the communication game	1 take the communicator's characteristics into account 2 determine the communicator's communicative intent or purpose 3 take the context and circumstances into account 4 pay attention to the message and be prepared to receive it 5 try to understand the message 6 provide feedback (when possible) to the communicator concerning their interpretation or understanding of the message

Goffman, 1959; Rommetveit, 1974). Third, it was assumed that effective and efficient communication entails a continuous process of co-orientation and monitoring between participants along with accurate appraisal of each other's characteristics and intentions (for example, Cushman and Whiting, 1972; Mead, 1934; Piaget, 1926; Searle, 1970). Finally, communication was assumed to be a normatively based activity involving patterns of rules and conventions regarding appropriate language use and forms for distinct social roles and contexts (for example, Austin, 1962; Gumperz and Hymes, 1972; Peirce, 1940).

The notion that communicative interaction involves rule-following behavior is relatively common, and a review of the literature suggests several rules (see Table 8.1) of the communication game (for example, Austin, 1962; Cushman and Whiting, 1972; Grice, 1971; Gumperz and Hymes, 1972; Rommetveit, 1974; van Dijk, 1977; see Higgins, 1981, and Higgins, Fondacaro and McCann, 1982, for reviews).

The rules of the communication game presented in Table 8.1 are conceptualized as normative prescriptions for action in communicative interactions. Individuals socialized in similar cultural contexts are assumed to have available for use the same set of rules and, further, it is assumed that some of these rules will show variation across cultural and sub-cultural groups. In addition, it is assumed that the emphasis given to particular rules or sub-sets of rules will vary with features of the interpersonal context in which the communication takes place, the social roles the participants adopt, and as a result of both chronic and transitory differences in the personal goals individuals are attempting to achieve (for example, McCann and Higgins, 1984). Much of our own recent research has been directed at an attempt to examine the impact of these factors (for example, context and personal goals) on interpersonal communication and its social cognitive consequences.

This list of rules is not meant to imply that effective and efficient communication necessitates following all of these rules. In fact, in most communicative interactions it would be impossible to follow them all at the same time. In addition to the fact that some of the rules are mutually exclusive, it is also the case that different contexts, roles, relationships, and personal objectives lead to differential emphases on specific rules, to the exclusion of others. Rule-following behavior is clearly context dependent. It is also likely to be the case that the consequences of rule violation are also context dependent and may, in many cases, lead to a redefinition or termination of the interaction episode (for example, Davis, 1982). Thus, social cognitive processes related to decisions concerning which rules to follow are an important element of the communication game. In addition, it is expected that communication behavior will have important social cognitive consequences for the communicator him- or herself (for example, Higgins and Rholes, 1978). This issue is addressed more fully below.

In this review, we focus on the effects of communication role, interpersonal context, and personal goals as they impact on the nature of communicative behavior and its social cognitive consequences. Many of these issues have been considered by others working in this area, and we will review some of this work in the context of our discussion.

The Effects of Communication Roles

Any communicative interaction necessarily involves two interdependent social roles, that of communicator and recipient. According to the rules presented above, distinct sets of general normative prescriptions are associated with these two roles. Thus, for example, communicators are expected to be clear and concise (communicator rules 3 and 4), while message recipients are expected to be prepared for receiving the message (recipient rule 5). It is expected that in addition to affecting how individuals adopting these roles will approach any particular communicative interaction, it is also anticipated that following these rules will have implications for the participants' own memory and judgments of the stimulus information. One of our first studies (Higgins, McCann and Fondacaro, 1982) was designed, in part, to examine these issues. This research was based upon earlier work addressing the effects of 'cognitive tuning' (for example, Brock and Fromkin, 1968; Cohen, 1961; Harkins et al., 1977; Harvey et al., 1976; Leventhal, 1962; Zajonc, 1960).

This early work was designed to examine the implications of adopting either a speaker (that is, transmitter) or listener (that is, receiver) role on the way in which individuals represented the social information they were communicating about. In his innovative work, Zajonc (1960) suggested that communicators, in order to fulfill their communication task, required relatively differentiated, unified and organized cognitive representations of the stimulus information in order to produce an effective (that is, clear, coherent, and comprehensible) message for their listeners. Recipients or listeners, on the other hand, because of their particular role requirements, were obligated to represent the information they already had about the issue or communication topic in a relatively unorganized, non-unified, and undifferentiated manner. Thus, the communicator and recipient roles were assumed to influence the type of cognitive representation that the role players formed of the information they had about the topic.

All subjects in Zajonc's study received the same information about the topic and were then assigned the roles of speaker or listener. Before actually communicating, subjects in both roles were asked to complete several measures assessing their cognitive representation of the information they had been given earlier. The results of this study supported Zajonc's hypotheses about the types · of distinct representations held by speakers and listeners in anticipation of communication. Speakers were found to represent the information in a highly organized and differentiated manner. Listeners, on the other hand, tended to maintain a representation of the information that was more flexible and undifferentiated. Subsequent research has replicated and extended these results (for example, Brock and Fromkin 1968).

Our own view of this work, however, suggested that the cognitive tuning studies involved more than just differences in normatively based prescriptions for individuals adopting communicator or recipient roles. More specifically, it was clear that communicator and recipient roles, as operationalized in this research, also differed in the extent to which they anticipated receiving additional information regarding the topic. Both speakers and listeners are exposed to the same set of stimulus information with listeners, *but not speakers*, expecting to receive additional information about the topic from their communication partner (that is, the communicator). It is reasonable to assume that individuals expecting to receive additional information (that is, the listeners) will resist forming unified and organized representations of the information until they believe that they possess all the relevant information at their disposal. Thus, it is possible that the confounding of communication role with expectation of additional information in the traditional cognitive tuning research may have obscured the nature of the underlying causes for at least some of the effects typically observed in that work.

We examined this issue (Higgins, McCann and Fondacaro, 1982) by orthogonally manipulating both communication role and anticipation of additional information. Speakers and listeners were exposed to the same stimulus information that was to serve as the basis of their communication activity, with half of each group expecting to receive additional information about the topic from the experimenter. All subjects were then asked to write out their impressions of the person described in the stimulus information. These impressions were scored in terms of the number of positive and negative labels that were included in the impressions. The information subjects had been exposed to initially was evaluatively ambiguous. We assumed that unified, organized and coherent impressions would be indexed by the tendency to use more of one type of evaluative label (that is, positive or negative) than the other. Relatively non-unified and undifferentiated impressions would be reflected in more of a tendency to use relatively equal numbers of positive and negative labels in participants' impressions. The results of our analysis of labels indicated a positivity bias in general, with all subjects tending to employ more positive than negative labels. Further analysis, however, indicated that this positivity bias was not evident in all four conditions (that is, all combinations of Speaker–Listener × Expectation–No Expectation of additional information). In both speaker conditions, a more unified and coherent impression was observed. This pattern of results is entirely consistent with the implications of past work on cognitive tuning. Also consistent with this work, a less unified and more undifferentiated representation was evident for listeners who expected *additional* information. Finally, in contrast to the implications of traditional work in cognitive tuning, the impressions of listeners who did not expect additional information were similar to both groups of speakers, in that they manifested a more differentiated and unified representation of the original stimulus information.

The results of this study indicated that the representations formed by speakers were primarily influenced by the communication role they adopted. In general, therefore, it would appear that the rules and roles associated with interpersonal communication can have an important impact on the social cognitive processes of participants. In addition, it is also necessary to consider the implications of additional features of the communication context – in this case, the status of participants in terms of their expectations for receiving additional information about the topic. Interesting here is the fact that the expectation of additional information had little effect on the cognitive representations formed by speakers. This can be taken to reflect the powerful nature of this more *active* social role in that it appears to have overwhelmed the potential effects of this contextual variation. Speakers, above all else, must be cognitively prepared to deliver a message to their listener. The listener role, on the other hand, accords more flexibility in terms of its immediate role requirements in these types of situations.

Contextually Adapted Encoding and Social Cognitive Effects

The notion that effective communication necessitates consideration of the characteristics of one's communicative partner or message recipient has been well recognized and extensively researched (Brown, 1986; Brown and Fraser, 1979; Danziger, 1976; Flavell et al., 1968; Giles and Hewstone, 1982; Krauss, 1987; Kraut and Higgins, 1984; McCann and Higgins, 1990).

Traditional work in this area has addressed a number of specific concerns. One central line of research in developmental psychology has been concerned with the developmental antecedents of perspective-taking as a necessary communication skill (for example, Delia and O'Keefe, 1979; Flavell et al., 1968; Higgins, 1977; Higgins, Fondacaro and McCann, 1982; Piaget, 1926). In this line of investigation, it is assumed that development of the ability to take the role and perspective of others is a prerequisite skill for effective interpersonal communication. Interest here has focused specifically on development of the cognitive structures and processes that are assumed to underlie this skill.

Another large body of research has focused on register variation, 'in which language structure varies in accordance with the occurrence of its use' (Ferguson, 1983: 154). While some of this work has examined the use of highly specialized types of language forms, for example the innovative work by Ferguson on sports announcer talk, other work has examined language use as a function of audience attributes. A prototypic example of this is the research on the nature and use of 'baby talk', 'foreigner talk', and related language forms (for example, Bell, 1982; Caporael et al., 1983; DePaulo and Bonvillian, 1978; Ferguson, 1975, 1977; Freed, 1981; Gelman and Shatz, 1977; Gleason and Weintraub, 1978; Snow, 1977; Snow and Ferguson, 1977). This work, in general, has tended to focus on the effects of highly salient and easily categorizable audience characteristics (McCann and Higgins, 1990) on language use.

Some more recent – and unique – work in social psychology has begun to examine, from a slightly different perspective, some of the parameters of context-biased adaptation in language use. For example, Tetlock (1985) has proposed a social contingency model of social judgment and choice that has been recently extended to examine the effects of 'accountability' on knowledge representation in anticipation of communicative activity (for example, Tetlock et al., 1989). In this line of research, Tetlock and his colleagues suggest that variation in the extent to which the communicator is committed to a specific viewpoint and knowledge of the specific views held by the audience can serve to influence the extent to which communicators adopt a variety of information processing approaches which, in turn, have been found to influence the nature of the stored representation formed by communicators.

In another intriguing line of research, Vallacher et al. (1989) have extended their early work on action-identity theory (for example, Vallacher and Wegner, 1985; Wegner and Vallacher, 1987) to consider the effects of the variation in the difficulty of the persuasive task facing communicators, due to the similarity or differences between their views and that held by the audience, on communication effectiveness. The application of their model to such situations has led to support for the non-obvious prediction that communicators may function more effectively in difficult communication situations if their communication is subjected to some type of contextual disruption. They suggest that social actions such as communicating can be cognitively represented by the actor in many different ways, ranging from those that are relatively abstract (such as influencing someone, personal evaluation) to those that are more concrete (such as choosing the right words). In some situations, the identifications adopted by a speaker may actually be non-optimal from a performance standpoint. In difficult situations (for example, communicating to a skeptical audience) we often represent the situation in terms of 'personal evaluation' where a more concrete focus on choosing the right words might be more functional. Additionally, they suggest that contextual disruptions tend to make salient lower level action identifications (such as choosing the right words) which, in the end, may result in more effective performance. Their recent research has provided support for these formulations (Vallacher et al., 1989). The full implications of their model have yet to be examined across a range of communication situations.

In our own work on the issue of contextually adapted communication and language use, we have adopted a different orientation toward the issues raised by a consideration of this topic. As with the work just described, however, our orientation stresses the potential social cognitive effects of modifying one's message production for the context in which it occurs.

Message Modification in the Communication Game

As discussed above, previous research conducted in a variety of areas has served to illustrate the fact that communicators tend to adapt their verbal encoding of information to suit their communication context. One focus in this research has been an examination of the tendency of communicators to modify their messages to suit the attitudinal characteristics of their audience (for example, Manis et al., 1974; Newtson and Czerlinsky, 1974; Zimmerman and Bauer, 1956). Of particular concern to us in our own initial research, however, was a consideration of the social cognitive effects of such message modification. This issue had not been systematically addressed by previous work.

It is assumed that individuals attempt to tune or modify their messages in order to promote effective communication and to avoid social conflict or embarrassment. In addition to these *intended* effects, we assumed that the communicators' messages would tend to influence their own reconstructive memory for the stimulus information that served as the basis of the message, as well as influencing any subsequent social judgments they made based upon their representation.

Higgins and Rholes (1978) first examined these issues. Subjects communicated a description of a target person they had read about to a listener who they were told either liked or disliked the target person. The subjects' role in this task was to summarize the information they had read about the target for the listener. All subjects had initially been exposed to the same set of evaluatively ambiguous stimulus information about the target. Higgins and Rholes hypothesized that subjects would modify their messages to suit the characteristics of their audience by, for example, using more negative than positive trait labels in their descriptions for a listener who supposedly disliked the target and more positive than negative labels in their descriptions for a listener who supposedly liked the stimulus person. Analysis of the messages provided strong support for these expectations.

All subjects were later asked to reproduce the original stimulus information 'word for word' and to indicate their own personal attitude toward the target person. Higgins and Rholes reasoned that because of the effects of categorization on memory (for example, Bartlett, 1932; Higgins et al., 1977; Neisser, 1967), subjects' own memory and attitudes would tend to become (over time) evaluatively consistent with the attitudes of their listeners, and that this evaluative consistency would be a function of the biased nature of the messages they had produced for their listeners. The results of their analyses confirmed these expectations. Thus, for example, subjects communicating to a listener who supposedly liked the target person included more positive than negative distortions of the original information in their reproductions of it, while the reverse pattern was revealed for subjects who had communicated to a listener who disliked the target person. A subsequent study extended this work by showing a conceptually similar pattern of message modification and social cognitive effects when audience variation was based upon *informational* (that is, listeners possessed either the same or different information from the speaker) rather than *attitudinal* (that is, listeners either liked or disliked the target person) attributes (Higgins, McCann and Fondacaro, 1982).

These initial studies (Higgins and Rholes, 1978; Higgins, McCann and Fondacaro, 1982) were taken as strong support for the assumptions underlying the Communication Game model. Subsequently, this work has been extended in several directions. For example, in a recent set of studies, Sedikides (1990) examined the relative influence of the social cognitive effects of message modification as outlined above, and the effects of temporary activation of cognitive constructs (see Higgins and King, 1981, and McCann and Higgins, 1984, for reviews) on the impressions we form of others. Recent models of social information processing (for example, Srull and Wyer, 1989; Wyer and Srull, 1986) have emphasized the role played by accessible constructs in the encoding and retrieval of social information.

Sedikides presented his subjects with a communication task similar to those described above (for example, by Higgins and Rholes, 1978) in which they were required to communicate their descriptions of a target person to a listener who either liked or disliked or held a neutral attitude toward the target person. Subjects had previously been exposed to a priming manipulation (see Higgins et al., 1977) designed to make accessible either positive or negative, applicable and inapplicable (to the target information they had received) cognitive constructs. For subjects in the neutral audience condition, primed applicable cognitive constructs were found to influence subjects' subsequent impressions of the target person in ways that were consistent with the results of past research on construct accessibility (for example, Higgins et al., 1977). In the other two audience conditions, however, the effects of temporary construct activation as a result of the priming manipulation were found to be overridden by the social cognitive effects of message modification. Thus, regardless of priming condition (that is, positive or negative), subjects' final impressions were found to be evaluatively consistent with the messages they had tailored to suit the attitudinal characteristics of their audience. This study, therefore, serves to underscore the importance of the factors highlighted by our own previous work on the Communication Game model.

In our own extensions of the work described above, we have examined the implications of the communicator's personal goals, the nature of the relationship between the communicator and recipient, and the effects of multiple contexts, on rule-following behavior and its social cognitive consequences. We briefly review each of these research directions below.

The Role of Personal Goals and the Nature of the Relationship in the Communication Game

One of the issues highlighted in the communication game is the notion that in any particular communicative interaction, individuals are usually unable to follow all of the general rules of communication. As discussed above, the emphasis given to any specific communication rule is a function of several factors including the nature of the communication context (that is, audience attitude). Another factor that is expected to influence rule choice are the goals adopted by communicative participants. It is assumed that the goals emphasized by individuals in any particular communicative interaction are a function both of relatively transitory concerns and of chronic characteristics of the individuals involved (for example, McCann and Higgins, 1984).

This type of goal-oriented perspective on communication is consistent with a great deal of previous research emphasizing the strategic nature of interpersonal interaction (for example, Argyle and Kendon, 1967; Athay and Darley, 1981; Goffman, 1959; Higgins, 1981; Miller et al., 1960; Srull and Wyer, 1989).

Past work has suggested that social interaction is initiated in pursuit of a variety of personal and interpersonal goals, including such things as determining the accuracy of one's definition of social reality (for example, Festinger, 1954; Schachter, 1959); initiating, defining and maintaining social relationships (for example, Devine et al., 1989; Ruesch and Bateson, 1968; Watzlawick et al., 1967); face work (for example, Goffman, 1959); personal identity concerns (for example, Eastman, 1985; Street and Giles, 1982); persuasion (for example, Schank and Abelson, 1977); and entertainment (for example, Tubbs and Moss, 1977). More recent work in this area has turned to a consideration of the interrelationships of such goals, attempting, for example, to uncover the general categories or dimensions underlying prototypic personal goals (for example, Clark and Delia, 1979; Danziger, 1976; Dillard, 1989; Dillard et al., 1989; Giles and Hewstone, 1982; McCann and Higgins, 1988; Seibold et al., 1985). The results of much of this work are consistent with Clark and Delia's (1979) suggestion that the goals adopted by communicative interactants generally are related to identity, instrumental and interpersonal objectives, broadly defined.

In addition to this work examining the general goals adopted by individuals in their interactions with others, other recent work has begun to examine the types of strategies followed when particular goals are made salient (for example, Cody and McLaughlin, 1985). An excellent example of this work is the research conducted on social influence goals (for example, Dillard, 1989; Rule et al., 1985). Our own work on the issue of personal goals in communication has considered their relation to rule-following behavior and its social cognitive consequences.

McCann and Hancock (1983), for example, were interested in examining the effects of individual differences in self-monitoring and communication. In that study, they had high and low self-monitoring individuals (Snyder, 1979) communicate about a target person to a listener who supposedly either liked or disliked the target. Self-monitoring is an individual difference construct that is related to a concern with face goals, emphasizing a concern with creating a desired opinion of oneself in the eyes of another (Snyder, 1974, 1979).

High self-monitors tend to adopt a very 'pragmatic' approach to social interaction and are, therefore, particularly concerned with the social appropriateness of their behavior in specific social settings. Thus, they tend to be very attentive to the cues available in social situations, including the characteristics of their partners, and have exhibited a tendency to use these cues to shape and guide their own behavior (for example, Snyder and Monson, 1975). Low self-monitors, on the other hand, are particularly concerned with maintaining and expressing their own personal identity, beliefs and attitudes (for example, Zanna et al., 1980). They tend to pay little attention to social comparison information or other contextual cues and, overall, tend to act in what is referred to as a more 'principled' manner (Snyder, 1979). That is, they tend to act in ways that are consistent with their own attitudes and beliefs.

The relevance of this construct to the types of contextual cues discussed above is clear. One of the more salient aspects of the communication context is the listener and his or her characteristics. McCann and Hancock reasoned that, because of their greater sensitivity to and use of contextual cues, it would be the high self-monitoring individuals who would tend to manifest more message modification in such settings and thus be subject to its social cognitive effects. The results of the study provided support for this reasoning. Analysis of the messages produced by subjects for their listeners revealed, as expected, that it was only the high self-monitors who engaged in significant message modification in the direction of their listener's attitudes toward the target person. In addition, and again as expected, it was only the impressions of the high self-monitors that tended to be evaluatively consistent with the attitudes of their listeners.

The results of this study indicate the importance of considering the role of personal goal orientation in studying the nature of interpersonal communication and its effects. High self-monitors, because of their concern with the social appropriateness of their behavior, apparently placed more emphasis on communication rules taking into consideration attributes associated with their partner (that is, communicator rule 1 in Table 8.1). Low self-monitors, on the other hand, apparently tended to place more emphasis on rules underscoring the importance of message accuracy and telling the truth as they saw it (that is, communicator rule 2). These patterns of behavior were also found to have unintended effects on subjects' own personal evaluations of the information they were communicating about. The importance of considering the nature of *communicator characteristics* and their relevance to the communication context is also highlighted by the results of another of our recent studies (Higgins and McCann, 1984).

Thus far, our consideration of the effects of context has focused primarily on the effects of listener or audience characteristics. Another relevant contextual feature relates to the nature of the relationship between the communicator and message recipients. One important dimension characterizing interpersonal relationships has to do with the relative status or social power of the partners. Previous formulations have suggested that equal versus unequal status is an important consideration when attempting to understand the dynamics of interpersonal relationships.

The issue of relative status also has implications for our understanding of rule-following behavior in the context of the Communication Game. We might expect, for example, that if individuals do exhibit a tendency to engage in message modification in response to the characteristics of their audience, that this tendency would be heightened in communications directed toward high-status others as compared to messages for equal-status others. Recent research in communication and social cognition has served to indicate the importance of status in communicative interactions (for example, Cansler and Stiles, 1981; Holtgraves et al., 1989).

Sensitivity to the implications of relative status, however, is also likely to be a function of the communicator's own personal orientation. More specifically, there is a substantial literature indicating that high authoritarians are much more responsive to high-status others than are low authoritarians (for example, Adorno et al., 1950; Berg and Vidmar, 1975). The implications of individual differences in authoritarianism for the effects of status on message modification are clear; high authoritarians should be more likely to evidence message modification for high-status others compared to equal-status others, while low authoritarians should be much less likely to show this pattern of differential message modification.

These issues were addressed in a study by Higgins and McCann (1984) in which high and low authoritarians were required to communicate a message about a target person they had read about to a listener who supposedly either liked or disliked the target person. In addition, their listener was described as being either a high-status other (that is, a senior Ph.D. student) or someone of equal status (that is, another freshman student). Subjects' written messages were scored for the number of positive and negative distortions of the original stimulus information that were included in them. The amount and nature of message distortion was used as an index of message modification in response to audience characteristics (that is, positive or negative attitude toward the target person discussed in the message).

In addition, we also asked subjects after either a brief (20 minute) or long (2 week) delay to reproduce the original stimulus information they had read about the target person, to give their own impressions of the target, and to indicate their own attitudes toward the target. We varied the delay between message production and dependent measure collection in order to evaluate more systematically the prediction, derived from previous work on categorization effects, that individuals will exhibit an increasing tendency *over time* to use their prior judgments and encoding as a basis for reconstructing and evaluating the original stimulus input to which they were exposed (for example, Bartlett, 1932; Higgins and Rholes, 1978). Subjects' reproductions and impressions were scored by assessing the number of positive and negative distortions of the original stimulus information that were included in them, and their own attitudes toward the target person were assessed by means of their responses to an 11-point Likert-type scale ranging from +5 (Extremely Desirable) to −5 (Extremely Undesirable).

An analysis of subjects' messages revealed strong support for our expectations. Under conditions of equal status, both high and low authoritarian subjects modified their messages to suit the attitudinal characteristics of their audience by using more positive than negative distortions when communicating to a listener who liked the target person and more negative than positive distortions when communicating to someone who supposedly disliked him. This serves to replicate the results of the study conducted by Higgins and Rholes (1978). In the high-status condition, however, it was only the high authoritarians who tended to engage in significant message modification. This effect is consistent with past formulations suggesting the heightened sensitivity of high authoritarians to high-status others. In addition, analyses of variance conducted on the number of positive and negative distortions included in subjects' impressions and reproductions, as well as analyses of their attitudes, indicated that the previously documented social cognitive effects of message modification were increasingly manifested as a function of temporal delay.

In addition to these analyses, we also conducted another set of analyses in order to systematically evaluate our assumptions regarding the *mediating* role accorded to messages in this formulation. The model makes the assumption that subjects' impressions, reproductions and attitudes are influenced primarily by their prior verbal encoding of the information for their message recipient and not by the attitude of their message recipient *per se*. In order to evaluate this, we conducted a path analysis (Pedhauzur, 1982), the results of which are displayed in Figure 8.1. Here we present the standardized partial regression coefficients for the paths between audience attitude, subjects' messages, reproductions, impressions, and the subjects' own attitudes. The analyses for all subjects (Panel A) and for high authoritarians alone, who were more influenced by audience attributes (Panel B), support our assumptions concerning the important mediating role accorded to messages. The analyses reveal few significant direct paths from audience attitude to measures of subjects' representation and evaluation of the original

A. All Subjects

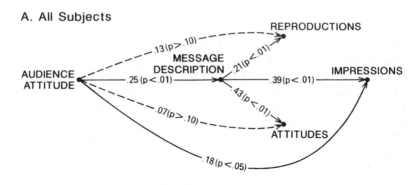

B. High Authoritarian Subjects

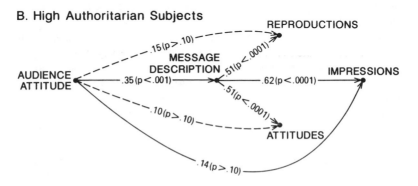

Figure 8.1 *Path analysis (with standardized partial regression coefficients) of relations among audience attitude, message description, reproductions, impressions, and attitudes (from Higgins and McCann, 1984).* © Douglas McCann.

stimulus information. Rather, the effects of audience attitudes appear to be mediated by message production itself.

In addition to indicating the importance of considering the effects of personal orientation and features of the relationship in the communication game, the studies reviewed above serve to provide more direct evidence for the social cognitive processes that are assumed to underlie the effects of rule-following behavior on memory and judgment. The implications of this work served as the basis for our most recent study (McCann et al., 1991) in this area, which focused on the effects of successive audiences on the processes discussed above.

The Effects of Successive Audiences on Encoding and Judgment

As is clear from the discussion presented above, a great deal of attention has been directed at examining the effects of context on interpersonal communication. Particularly relevant here is the work examining the effects of audience characteristics. In our own work, as well as that of others, only the effects of an initial audience are considered. An important issue that has yet to be addressed concerns the effects on individuals communicating to successive audiences. Two interrelated issues are raised in this context. First, given that individuals have been found to modify their messages for an initial audience, what would be the effect of having to produce a message for a second audience? Would individuals also evidence message modification for a second audience, whose attitudinal characteristics might or might not be similar to those of the initial audience? Second, given the demonstrated social cognitive effects of message modification, what are the implications of communicating to successive audiences on communicators' own memory and evaluation?

We examined these issues in a recent study (McCann et al., 1991) in which subjects who had been exposed to the same set of information about a target person were required to deliver messages to each of two successive audiences. As was the case with our previous research, our subjects were led to believe that each of these message recipients either liked or disliked the target person subjects were to describe. As an additional factor in this experiment, we included a variable *inter-message delay* between subjects' production of the two messages. One half of the subjects (Brief Inter-message Delay) experienced a short delay (10 minutes) between delivering their two messages, while the other half of the subjects delivered their second message (Long Inter-message Delay) one week after their first message. In this study, speakers engaged in face-to-face communication with the listeners. The listeners were experimental confederates whose behavior in the interaction was carefully scripted and monitored. Subjects' verbal messages were tape recorded and transcribed for the analyses presented below.

In addition to our interest in the effects of these factors on the nature of subjects' messages, we were also interested in examining the social cognitive effects of subjects' message productions. Accordingly, one week after the second message, all subjects were required to give us their own personal impressions of the target person and to indicate their attitude toward him on a seven-point Likert-type scale (that is, from 1 = Dislike to 7 = Like).

Previous research on audience effects had suggested several

possible sets of predictions. Some of the past work in this area seemed to suggest that the characteristics of the first audience would be most important in shaping subjects' messages (for example, Zimmerman and Bauer, 1956). This expectation concerning the emphasis given to first audience characteristics in message production is also consistent with a large body of research emphasizing the fact that individuals are motivated to maintain personal consistency in such situations (for example, Festinger, 1957; Hovland et al., 1957). Thus, there was some evidence to suggest that all our subjects would modify their messages for their first audiences, and that this message bias would then be evident in their second messages regardless of the attitudinal characteristics of their second message recipient. On this basis, we would also expect that subjects' cognitive representations and evaluations of the original stimulus information would tend to be evaluatively consistent with the attitudes of their first (not second) audience.

The communication game, however, would generally predict rule-based message modification to suit the characteristics of both audiences with subjects' evaluations of the original information tending to be evaluatively consistent with the attitudes of their most recent audience. A different set of predictions, however, are derived from a consideration of the implications of the variable time delay between messages for the types of social cognitive processes that are assumed by the communication game to underlie message effects and their social cognitive consequences (for example, Higgins and McCann, 1984).

As discussed above, our previous research has indicated that message modification has been found to influence subjects' cognitive representations and evaluations of the original stimulus information that their messages are based upon. This research also indicates, however, that the tendency of subjects to base their reconstruction of the original stimulus information partially on their messages increases with increasing temporal delay, as their memory for the original details decays or becomes less accessible (Higgins and McCann 1984; Higgins and Rholes, 1978) and as the (message) modified representation becomes increasingly consolidated (for example, Crowder, 1976). This consideration leads to two distinct sets of predictions for subjects in the Brief and Long Inter-message Delay conditions.

We assumed that subjects in the Brief Inter-message Delay condition, because of the short time interval between message productions, would have accessible for use in their second messages a relatively accurate representation of the original stimulus information they had read. These subjects were expected to display substantial message modification for their second audience. Thus, Brief Inter-message Delay subjects were expected to show message modification in the context of both recipients. In addition, it was expected that their own subsequent impressions and attitudes measured one week after the second messages would evidence evaluative consistency with the attitudes of their *second (and most recent) message recipient*.

Our expectations for subjects in the Long Inter-message Delay condition, however, were quite different. Given the increased delay between message productions and the increased social cognitive effects of such message modification that is assumed to occur during the delay, we expected that these subjects would have accessible a more biased representation of the original stimulus information and would, therefore, be less likely (and able) to engage in substantial message modification to suit the attitudinal characteristics of their second message recipient. In fact, we anticipated that their second messages would continue to be evaluatively consistent with the attitudinal characteristics of their *first* message recipients. In addition, we expected that their own personal impressions and attitudes would tend to evidence evaluative consistency with their first, rather than their second, message recipient. Thus, in summary, we expected to observe a message-based *primacy* effect for subjects in the Long Inter-message Delay condition, and a message-based *recency* effect for subjects in the Brief Inter-message Delay condition.

Subjects' messages were transcribed and subsequently analyzed for the number of positive and negative trait labels that were included in them. In addition, subjects' written impressions of the target person were analyzed for the number of positive and negative distortions of the original target person information that were included in them. Each of these measures, along with subjects' attitudes toward the target person, were initially analyzed by means of a First Audience Attitude (Like or Dislike) × Second Audience Attitude (Like or Dislike) × Inter-message Delay (Brief or Long) analysis of variance.

Analysis of subjects' messages revealed strong support for our assumptions. Whereas all subjects evidenced significant message modification in the context of the attitudinal characteristics of their *first* message recipient, it was only the subjects in the Brief Inter-message Delay condition who modified their messages to suit the attitudes of their *second* audience. Thus, the pattern of message modification exhibited by our communicators depended critically on the length of the delay between their message productions for the successive audiences. This pattern of results is consistent with the assumptions of the communication game with regard to the types of social cognitive processes that are implicated in such contexts.

In addition, our analyses of subjects' impressions and attitudes provided further support for the assumptions of the communication game. Analysis of impression distortions indicated no significant effects for subjects in the Brief Inter-message Delay condition, but did reveal, as expected, a significant effect of First Audience Attitude for the impressions held by subjects in the Long Inter-message Delay condition. Thus, the impressions of subjects in this condition were found to be evaluatively consistent with the attitudes of their first audience, even though a second message had been delivered about the same topic subsequent to that initial message. Finally, an analysis of subjects' attitudes indicated, as expected, a significant effect of Second Audience Attitude on the attitudes held by subjects in the Brief Inter-message Delay condition, and a marginally significant ($p<0.10$) effect of First Audience Attitude on the attitudes expressed by subjects in the Long Inter-message Delay condition. Thus, depending upon whether subjects had experienced a long or short delay between message productions, their own personal attitudes tended to be evaluatively consistent with the attitudes of either their first or second audience, respectively. The results of the impression and attitude measures, taken together, provide strong support for the assumptions of the communication game with regard to the types of social cognitive processes that are assumed to underlie the effects of verbal encoding on representation and evaluation.

In addition to the analyses just described, we conducted another set of analyses in order to clarify the nature of the processes that are assumed to underlie these effects. While the interpretations of the effects for Brief Inter-message Delay subjects is relatively straightforward, the interpretation for Long Inter-message Delay subjects is more complicated. Again, we assumed that the messages produced for their first audiences would mediate subsequent messages, impressions and attitudes. In order to evaluate these assumptions, we conducted a path analysis examining the partial regression coefficients for the paths linking successive context attributes (that is, audience attitudes), messages, attitudes and impressions (see Figure 8.2). The results of this analysis provide clear support for our assumptions regarding the critical *mediating* role assigned to *first messages* for subjects in this condition. Few direct effects of first message audience are revealed. Rather, it would appear that first audience attributes influence second messages, impressions and attitudes, primarily through their

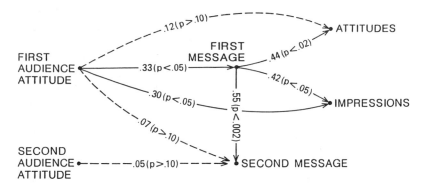

Figure 8.2 *Path analysis (with standardized partial regression coefficients) of relations among successive audience attitudes, messages, impressions, and attitudes for Long Inter-message Delay subjects (from McCann et al., 1991).* © Copyright Douglas McCann.

influence on the nature of the first messages produced by subjects for that initial audience. It is also clear from this analysis that second audience attitudes had little effect on subjects' impressions and personal attitudes. This work serves to extend past work on audience effects both by considering and examining the effects of successive audiences on message production, and in terms of its consideration of the social cognitive consequences of message modification produced in such contexts.

Summary and Conclusions

Although the central importance of language and communication to issues of concern to social psychologists has long been recognized, little attempt has been made until recently to systematically consider the nature of social communication and its effects. In large measure, the current interest in communication on the part of social psychologists can be traced to the recent emphasis on social information processing (McCann and Higgins, 1990). Social cognitive models, with their emphasis on process, symbolic activity, and the active nature of social participants, have provided a framework and context that is compatible with a systematic consideration of the nature and effects of interpersonal communication.

The communication game model of interpersonal communication was developed in this context and has proven to be a heuristic framework from which to approach various aspects of social communication. It emphasizes the rule-oriented nature of interpersonal communication and focuses attention on the factors that affect the behavior of communicative participants in any particular situation. More specifically, it focuses attention on the influence of features of the interpersonal context and participant attributes on communication and its effects.

In addition to this focus, however, the communication game emphasizes the importance of considering the cognitive processes underlying message production, and the types of social cognitive effects that message production can have on communicators and message recipients. More than anything, it is this latter aspect of the communication game model, as well as of other current social cognitive models of communication, that has served to renew interest in communication on the part of scholars working in social psychology. It would appear that the general ascendancy of social cognitive models in social psychology has provided an arena in which it is possible to explore the relevance of interpersonal communication to issues of traditional interest to social psychology.

Note

Preparation of this paper was facilitated by a grant awarded to the first author by the Social Sciences and Humanities Research Council of Canada (#410-87-0099), and by a National Institute of Mental Health Grant (MH39429) awarded to the second author. We would like to acknowledge the helpful comments of Alexander MacKenzie and Klaus Fiedler on an earlier draft.

References

Adorno, T. W., Frenkel-Brunswick, E., Levinson, D. J. and Sanford, R. N. (1950) *The Authoritarian Personality*. New York: Harper.

Argyle, M. and Kendon, A. (1967) The experimental analysis of social performance. In L. Berkowitz (ed.), *Advances in Experimental Social Psychology*, vol. 3, pp. 55–99. New York: Academic Press.

Athay, M. and Darley, J. M. (1981) Toward an interaction-centered theory of personality. In N. Cantor and J. F. Kihlstrom (eds), *Personality, Cognition, and Social Behavior*, pp. 281–308. Hillsdale, NJ: Erlbaum.

Austin, J. L. (1962) *How to Do Things with Words*. Oxford: Oxford University Press.

Bartlett, F. C. (1932) *Remembering*. Cambridge: Cambridge University Press.

Bell, A. (1982) Radio: The style of news language. *Journal of Communication*, 32: 150–164.

Berg, K. S. and Vidmar, N. J. (1975) Authoritarianism and recall of evidence about criminal behavior. *Journal of Research in Personality*, 9: 147–154.

Blumer, H. (1962) Society as symbolic interaction. In A. M. Rose (ed.), *Human Behavior and Social Processes*, pp. 58–72. London: Routledge & Kegan Paul.

Brock, T. C. and Fromkin, H. L. (1968) Cognitive tuning set and behavioral receptivity to discrepant information. *Journal of Personality*, 36: 108–125.

Brown, R. (1986) *Social Psychology* (2nd edition). New York: Free Press.

Brown, P. and Fraser, C. (1979) Speech as markers of situation. In K. R. Scherer and H. Giles (eds), *Social Markers in Speech*. Cambridge: Cambridge University Press.

Burke, K. (1962) *A Grammar of Motives and a Rhetoric of Motives*. Cleveland: World.

Cansler, D. C., and Stiles, W. B. (1981) Relative status and interpersonal presumptuousness. *Journal of Experimental Social Psychology*, 17: 459–476.

Caporael, L. R., Lukaszewski, M. P. and Culbertson, G. H. (1983) Secondary baby talk: Judgments by institutionalized elderly and their caregivers. *Journal of Personality and Social Psychology*, 44: 746–754.

Cherry, C. (1977) *On Human Communication*. Cambridge, MA: MIT Press.

Clark, R. A. and Delia, J. C. (1979) Topoi and rhetorical competence. *Quarterly Journal of Speech*, 65: 187–206.

Cody, M. J. and McLaughlin, M. L. (1985) The situation as a construct in interpersonal communication research. In M. L. Knapper and G. R. Miller (eds), *Handbook of Interpersonal Communication*, pp. 263–312. Beverly Hills: Sage.

Cohen, A. R. (1961) Cognitive tuning as a factor affecting impression formation. *Journal of Personality*, 29: 235–245.

Crowder, R. G. (1976) *Principles of Learning and Memory*. Hillsdale, NJ: Erlbaum.

Cushman, D. and Whiting, G. C. (1972) An approach to communication theory: Toward consensus on rules. *Journal of Communication*, 22: 217–238.

Danziger, K. (1976) *Interpersonal Communication*. New York: Pergamon Press.

Davis, D. (1982) Determinants of responsiveness in dyadic interaction. In W. Ickes and E. Knowles (eds), *Personality, Roles and Social Behavior*, pp. 85–140. New York: Springer-Verlag.

Delia, J. G. and O'Keefe, B. J. (1979) Constructivism: The development of communication in children. In E. Wartella (ed.), *Children Communicating*, pp. 157–185. Beverly Hills: Sage.

DePaulo, B. M. and Bonvillian, J. D. (1978) The effects on language development of the special characteristics of speech addressed to children. *Journal of Psycholinguistic Research*, 7: 189–211.

Devine, P. G., Sedikides, C. and Furhman, R. W. (1989) Goals in social information processing: The case of anticipated interaction. *Journal of Personality and Social Psychology*, 56: 680–690.

Devito, J. A. (1970) *The Psychology of Speech and Language*. New York: Random House.

Dillard, J. P. (1989) Types of influence goals in personal relationships. *Journal of Personal Relationships*, 6: 293–308.

Dillard, J. P., Segrin, C. and Harden, J. M. (1989) Primary and secondary goals in the production of interpersonal influence messages. *Communication Monographs*, 56: 19–38.

Donohew, L., Sypher, H. E. and Higgins, E. T. (eds). (1988) *Communication, Social Cognition, and Affect*. Hillsdale, NJ: Erlbaum.

Eagly, A. H. and Himmelfarb, S. (1974) Current trends in attitude theory and research. In S. Himmelfarb and A. Eagly (eds), *Readings in Attitude Change*. New York: Wiley.

Eastman, C. (1985) Establishing social identity through language use. *Journal of Language and Social Psychology*, 4: 1–20.

Ervin-Tripp, S. M. (1969) Sociolinguistics. In L. Berkowitz (ed.), *Advances in Experimental Social Psychology*. New York: Academic Press.

Ferguson, C. A. (1975) Toward a characterization of English foreigner talk. *Anthropological Linguistics*, 17: 1–14.

Ferguson, C. A. (1977) Baby talk as a simplified register. In C. A. Ferguson and C. Snow (eds), *Talking to Children: Language Input and Acquisition*, pp. 209–235. Cambridge: Cambridge University Press.

Ferguson, C. A. (1983) Sports announcer talk: Syntactic aspects of register variation. *Language in Society*, 12: 153–172.

Festinger, L. (1950) Informal social communication. *Psychological Review*, 57: 271–282.

Festinger, L. (1954) A theory of social comparison processes. *Human Relations*, 7: 117–140.

Festinger, L. (1957) *A Theory of Cognitive Dissonance*. Stanford, CA: Stanford University Press.

Flavell, J. H., Botkin, P. T., Fry, C. L., Wright, J. W. and Jarvis, P. E. (1968) *The Development of Role-taking and Communication Skills in Children*. New York: Wiley.

Freed, B. (1981) Foreigner talk, baby talk, native talk. *International Journal of the Sociology of Language*, 28: 19–40.

Garfinkel, H. (1967) *Studies in ethnomethodology*. Englewood Cliffs, NJ: Prentice-Hall.

Gelman, R. and Shatz, M. (1977) Appropriate speech adjustment: The operation of conversational constraints on talk to two year olds. In M. Lewis and L. Rosenblum (eds), *Interaction, Conversation, and the Development of Language*, pp. 116–145. New York: Wiley.

Giles, H. and Hewstone, M. (1982) Cognitive structures, speech and social situations: Two integrative models. *Language Sciences*, 4: 187–219.

Giles, H. and Robinson, W. P. (eds) (1990) *The Handbook of Language and Social Psychology*. Chichester: Wiley.

Giles, H. and St Clair, R. N. (1985) *Recent Advances in Language, Communication, and Social Psychology*. Hillsdale, NJ: Erlbaum.

Gleason, J. B. and Weintraub, S. (1978) Input language and the acquisition of communication competence. In K. E. Nelson (eds), *Children's Language*, pp. 171–222. New York: Garden Press.

Glucksberg, S., Krauss, R. M. and Higgins, E. T. (1975) The development of referential communication skills. In F. Horowitz, E. Hetherington, S. Scarr-Salapatek and G. Siegel (eds), *Review of Child Development Research*, vol. 4. Chicago: University of Chicago Press.

Goffman, E. (1959) *The Presentation of Self in Everyday Life*. Garden City, NY: Doubleday & Co.

Grice, H. P. (1971) Meaning. In D. D. Steinberg and L. A. Jakobovits (eds), *Semantics: An Interdisciplinary Reader in Philosophy, Linguistics, and Psychology*. London: Cambridge University Press.

Gumperz, J. J. and Hymes, D. (eds) (1972) *Directions in Sociolinguistics: The Ethnography of Communication*. New York: Holt, Rinehart & Winston.

Harkins, S. G., Harvey, J. H., Keithly L. and Rich, M. (1977) Cognitive tuning, encoding, and the attribution of causality. *Memory and Cognition*, 5: 561–565.

Harvey, J. H., Harkins, S. G., and Kagehiro, D. K. (1976) Cognitive tuning and the attribution of causality. *Journal of Personality and Social Psychology*, 34: 708–715.

Higgins, E. T. (1977) Communication development as related to channel, incentive, and social class. *Genetic Psychology Monographs*, 96: 75–141.

Higgins, E. T. (1981) The 'communication game': Implications for social cognition and persuasion. In E. T. Higgins, M. P. Zanna and C. P. Herman (eds), *Social Cognition: The Ontario Symposium*, vol. 1, pp. 343–392. Hillsdale, NJ: Erblaum.

Higgins, E. T., Fondacaro, R. A. and McCann, C. D. (1982) Rules and roles: the 'communication game' and speaker–listener processes. In W. P. Dickson (ed.), *Children's Oral Communication Skills*, pp. 289–312. New York: Academic Press.

Higgins, E. T. and King, G. A. (1981) Accessibility of social constructs: Information processing consequences of individual and contextual variability. In N. Cantor and J. F. Kihlstrom (eds), *Personality, Cognition, and Social Interaction*, pp. 69–121. Hillsdale, NJ: Erlbaum.

Higgins, E. T. and McCann, C. D. (1984) Social encoding and subsequent attitudes, impressions, and memory: 'Context-driven' and motivational aspects of processing. *Journal of Personality and Social Psychology*, 47: 26–39.

Higgins, E. T., McCann, C. D. and Fondacaro, R. A. (1982) The 'communication game': Goal-directed encoding and cognitive consequences. *Social Cognition*, 1: 21–37.

Higgins, E. T. and Rholes, W. S. (1978) 'Saying is believing': Effects of message modification on memory and liking for the person described. *Journal of Experimental Social Psychology*, 14: 363–378.

Higgins, E. T., Rholes, W. S. and Jones, C. R. (1977) Category accessibility and impression formation. *Journal of Experimental Social Psychology*, 13: 141–154.

Holtgraves, T., Srull, T. K. and Socall, D. (1989) Conversational memory: The effects of speaker status on memory for the assertiveness of conversational remarks. *Journal of Personality and Social Psychology*, 56: 149–160.

Hovland, C. I., Campbell, E. H. and Brock, T. C. (1957) Primacy and recency in impressions. In C. I. Hovland, W. Mandell, E. H. Campbell, T. C. Brock, A. S. Luchins, A. R. Cohen, W. J. McGuire, I. L. Janis, R. Feieraben and N. H. Anderson (eds), *The Order of Presentation in Persuasion*, pp. 33–54. New Haven, CT: Yale University Press.

Hovland, C. I., Janis I. L. and Kelley, H. H. (1953) *Communication and Persuasion: Psychological Studies of Opinion Change*. New Haven, CT: Yale University Press.

Krauss, R. M. (1987) The role of the listener: Addressee influences in message formulations. *Journal of Language and Social Psychology*, 6: 81–89.

Krauss, R. M., Vivekananathan, P. S. and Weinheimer, S. (1968) Inner speech and external speech: Characteristics of communication effectiveness of socially and nonsocially encoded messages. *Journal of Personality and Social Psychology*, 9: 292–300.

Kraut, R. E. and Higgins, E. T. (1984) Communication and social cognition, In R. S. Wyer and T. K. Srull (eds), *Handbook of Social Cognition*, vol. 3, pp. 67–128. Hillsdale, NJ; Erlbaum.

Leventhal, H. (1962) The effects of set and discrepancy on impression change. *Journal of Personality*, 30: 1–15.

McCann, C. D. and Hancock, R. D. (1983) Self-monitoring in communicative interactions: Social-cognitive consequences of goal-directed message modification.

Journal of Experimental Social Psychology, 19: 109–121.

McCann, C. D. and Higgins, E. T. (1984) Individual differences in communication: Social cognitive determinants and consequences. In H. E. Sypher and J. L. Applegate (eds), *Understanding Interpersonal Communication: Social Cognitive and Strategic Processes in Children and Adults*, pp. 53–79. Beverly Hills: Sage.

McCann, C. D. and Higgins, E. T. (1988) Motivation and affect in interpersonal relations: The role of personal orientations and discrepancies. In L. Donohew, H. E. Sypher and E. T. Higgins (eds), *Communication, Social Cognition, and Affect*, pp. 53–79. Hillsdale, NJ: Erlbaum.

McCann, C. D. and Higgins, E. T. (1990) Social cognition and communication. In H. Giles and P. Robinson (eds), *Handbook of Language and Social Psychology*, pp. 13–32. Chichester: Wiley.

McCann, C. D., Higgins, E. T. and Fondacaro, R. A. (1991) Primacy and recency in communication and self-persuasion: How successive audiences and multiple encodings influence subsequent judgments. *Social Cognition* 9: 47–66.

McGuire, W. J (1966) Attitudes and opinions. *Annual Review of Psychology*, 17: 475–514.

McGuire, W. J. (1972) Attitude change: The information processing paradigm. In C. G. McClintock (ed.), *Experimental Social Psychology*. New York: Holt, Rinehart & Winston.

Manis, M., Cornell, S. D. and Moore, J. C. (1974) Transmission of attitude-relevant information through a communication chain. *Journal of Personality and Social Psychology*, 30: 81–94.

Mead, G. H. (1934) *Mind, Self, and Society*. Chicago: University of Chicago Press.

Mehrabian, A. and Reed, H. (1968) Some determinants of communication accuracy. *Psychological Bulletin*, 70: 356–381.

Miller, G. A., Gallanter, E. and Pribram, K. H. (1960) *Plans and the Structure of Behavior*. New York: Holt.

Neisser, U. (1967) *Cognitive Psychology*. New York: Appleton-Century-Crofts.

Newtson, D., and Czerlinsky, T. (1974) Adjustment of attitude communications for contrasts by extreme audiences. *Journal of Personality and Social Psychology*, 30: 829–837.

O'Keefe, B. J. and Delia, J. G. (1985) Psychological and interactional dimensions of communicative development. In H. Giles and R. N. St Clair (eds), *Recent Advances in Language, Communication, and Social Psychology*, pp. 41–85. Hillsdale, NJ: Erlbaum.

Pedhauzur, E. J. (1982) *Multiple Regression in Behavior Research: Explanation and Prediction* (2nd edition). New York: Holt, Rinehart & Winston.

Peirce, C. S. (1940) Logic as semiotic: The theory of signs. In J. Buchler (ed.), *The Philosophy of Peirce: Selected Writings*. London: Routledge & Kegan Paul.

Piaget, J. (1926) *The Language and Thought of the Child*. New York: Harcourt Brace.

Roloff, M. E. and Berger, C. R. (1982) *Social Cognition and Communication*. Beverly Hills: Sage.

Rommetveit, R. (1974) *On Message Structure: A Framework for the Study of Language and Communication*. New York: Wiley.

Rosenberg, S. and Cohen, B. D. (1966) Referential processes of speakers and listeners. *Psychological Review*, 73: 208–231.

Ruesch, J. and Bateson, G. (1968) *Communication: The Social Matrix of Psychiatry*. New York: W. W. Norton.

Rule, B. G., Bisanz, G. L. and Kohn, M. (1985) Anatomy of a persuasion schema: Target, goals and strategies. *Journal of Personality and Social Psychology*, 48: 1123–1140.

Schachter, S. (1959) *The Psychology of Affiliation*. Stanford: Stanford University Press.

Schank, R. and Abelson, R. (1977) *Scripts, Plans, Goals, and Understanding*. Hillsdale, NJ: Erlbaum.

Searle, J. R. (1970) *Speech Acts: An Essay in the Philosophy of Language*. Cambridge: Cambridge University Press.

Sedikides, C. (1990) Effects of fortuitously activated constructs versus activated communication goals on person impressions. *Journal of Personality and Social Psychology*, 58: 397–408.

Seibold, D. R., Cantril, J. G., and Meyers, R. A. (1985) Communication and interpersonal influence. In M. L. Knapper and G. R. Miller (eds), *Handbook of Interpersonal Communication*, pp. 551–611. Beverly Hills: Sage.

Shannon, C. E. and Weaver, W. (1949) *The Mathematical Theory of Communication*. Urbana, IL: University of Illinois Press.

Snow, C. E. (1977) Mother's speech research: From input to interaction. In C. E. Snow and C. A. Ferguson (eds), *Talking to Children*, pp. 31–49. Cambridge: Cambridge University Press.

Snow, C. E. and Ferguson, C. A. (eds) (1977) *Talking to Children*. Cambridge: Cambridge University Press.

Snyder, M. (1974) The self-monitoring of expressive behavior. *Journal of Personality and Social Psychology*, 30: 526–537.

Snyder, M. (1979) Self-monitoring processes. In L. Berkowitz (ed.), *Advances in Experimental Social Psychology*, vol. 12, pp. 86–128. New York: Academic Press.

Snyder, M. and Monson, T. C. (1975) Persons, situations, and the control of social behavior. *Journal of Personality and Social Psychology*, 32: 637–644.

Srull, T. K. and Wyer, R. S. (1989) Person memory and judgment. *Psychological Review*, 96: 58–83.

Street, R. L. and Giles, H. (1982) Speech accommodation theory: A social cognitive approach to language and social behavior. In M. E. Roloff and C. R. Berger (eds), *Social Cognition and Communication*, pp. 193–226. Beverly Hills: Sage.

Tetlock, P. E. (1985) Accountability: The neglected social context of judgment and choice. In B. Stau and L. Cummings (eds), *Research in Organizational Behavior*, vol. 1, pp. 297–332. Greenwood, CT: JAI Press.

Tetlock, P. E., Skitka, L. and Boettiger, R. (1989) Social and cognitive strategies for coping with accountability: Conformity, complexity and bolstering. *Journal of Personality and Social Psychology*, 58: 397–408.

Tubbs, S. L. and Moss, S. (1977) *Human Communication* (2nd edition). New York: Random House.

Vallacher, R. R. and Wegner, D. M. (1985) *A Theory of Action Identification*. Hillsdale, NJ: Erlbaum.

Vallacher, R. R., Wegner, D. M. and Somoza, M. P. (1989) That's easy for you to say: Action identification and speech fluency. *Journal of Personality and Social Psychology*, 56: 199–208.

van Dijk, T. A. (1977) Context and cognition: Knowledge frames and speech act comprehension. *Journal of Pragmatics*, 1: 211–232.

Watzlawick, P., Beavin, J. H. and Jackson, D. D. (1967) *Pragmatics of Human Communication*. New York: W. W. Norton.

Wegner, D. M. and Vallacher, R. R. (1987) The trouble with action. *Social Cognition*, 5: 179–190.

Wittgenstein, L. (1953) *Philosophical Investigations*. New York: Macmillan.

Wyer, R. S. and Srull, T. K. (1986) Human cognition in its social context. *Psychological Review*, 93: 322–359.

Zajonc, R. B. (1960) The process of cognitive tuning and communication. *Journal of Abnormal and Social Psychology*, 61: 159–167.

Zanna, M. P., Olson, J. M. and Fazio, R. H. (1980) Attitude–behavior consistency: An individual difference perspective. *Journal of Personality and Social Psychology*, 38: 432–440.

Zimmerman, C. and Bauer, R. A. (1956) The effect of an audience on what is remembered. *Public Opinion Quarterly*, 20: 238–248.

9

Communicative Influences in Standardized Question Situations: The Case of Implicit Collaboration

Fritz Strack and Norbert Schwarz

A communication that is structured by questions and answers is probably the most important form of human interaction. Typically, such communications occur in social settings that give participants a large degree of freedom to provide their contributions in a format they find appropriate. As an example, questioners and respondents in most situations may choose to be more or less specific, to be elliptical or redundant, to ask for feedback about an earlier contribution. This freedom has been found to play an important role in the process of understanding what is meant.

However, there exist situations in which questioners and respondents are not free but severely restricted in their contributions. Such 'standardized question situations' are the focus of the present chapter. We shall discuss them as a special case of natural conversations and present findings suggesting that such a perspective may be fruitful to help us better understand a great number of influences that have been labelled 'response effects'.

Collaboration and Understanding: Natural Conversations and Standardized Questioning

Natural Conversations

Some 25 years ago, Robert Krauss and his colleagues (for example, Krauss and Weinheimer, 1964, 1966) developed an experimental paradigm to study how people understand each other in a social setting. In their experimental task, two subjects were provided with a set of 'nonsense figures' that had to be named or described by one subject and identified on the basis of this description by the other. Using this paradigm, the authors were able to show that in the course of the communicative interaction, the participants became both more accurate and more efficient in the identification task. The efficiency increased (that is, fewer words were needed to describe the figure) if the speaker received explicit or implicit feed-back from the listener.

More recently, a variant of this procedure was employed by Herbert Clark and his collaborators (for example, Schober and Clark, 1989; Clark and Wilkes-Gibbs, 1986) as a prototype for the process of understanding in natural conversations. On the basis of this identification task, these authors developed a 'collaborative theory of reference' (Schober and Clark, 1989). This collaborative perspective implies that speakers and listeners actively interact and give each other feedback to ensure that what is meant is also understood. It allows active participants to understand more accurately and faster than a third person who is not participating but only overhearing a conversation (see, Schober and Clark, 1989). Moreover, this view emphasizes that understanding is very functional with respect to a certain interactional goal, namely to identify a particular referent. This perspective suggests that the required 'depth' of interpretation is determined by the hearer's confirmed success in finding out what the speaker means (Clark and Wilkes-Gibbs, 1986). If the identification is unsuccessful, the speaker may vary her description based on the agreement that has so far been reached. This way, each conversational interaction generates its own idiosyncratic language that is 'grounded' (Schober and Clark, 1989) in the history of the collaboration and may therefore be difficult to comprehend by an overhearer.

A similar perspective is proposed by Garrod and Anderson (1987) who criticize that in both psychology and linguistics speakers and listeners are treated as 'isolated individuals' despite the fact that speaking and listening occurs in a 'broader inter-actional framework of dialogue'.

These approaches demonstrate very convincingly that to understand what is meant, it is not sufficient to decipher what a particular word or a sentence 'means', much rather, it is necessary to go beyond the linguistic units to find out what the *speaker* means; that is, the intended meaning of an utterance. Thus, it is not sufficient that listeners match concepts to words. Rather, it is necessary that they correctly infer the 'communicative intention' of the speaker. Meanwhile, this 'pragmatic' analysis is undisputed for natural conversations (for example, Levinson, 1983), and the studies by Krauss, Clark and their colleagues suggest that collaborative interaction that consists of feedback and tuning of one's contributions to the particular needs of the recipient is an effective vehicle to identify the communicator's intention.

Such collaboration, however, seems to require a social situation that is largely unconstrained. Most importantly, the situation must provide the possibility that recipients of a communication express their level of understanding either directly or indirectly in such a way that the speaker may infer it. This can be accomplished by comparing the recipient's interpretation with one's intention, remedying specific deficits, and tuning subsequent messages to the particular interpretive needs of the listener. These behavioral options, however, require a relatively unstructured situation that does not prescribe a certain format in which participants have to provide their contributions. This requirement is largely fulfilled in natural situations where participants in a conversation have a maximum amount of freedom in how they conduct their verbal interaction. Other forms of conversation, however, do not share these features.

Standardized Questioning

Specifically, there are situations in which communication occurs in a largely constrained fashion. That is, questioners have to present their contributions in a format that cannot be modified according to the interpretive needs of recipients. Moreover, such needs cannot even be recognized because responses have to be provided in a predetermined format. In some cases, such as in survey interviews, this format may provide the option to give a 'don't know' answer, but it usually does not provide the possibility to check 'don't understand'. Communicative interactions that do have constraints of this sort can be described as 'standardized question situations' (see Strack, in press).

Such standardized questioning plays an important role in modern society because it has certain advantages. Primarily, it facilitates answers that are given in a certain format to be aggregated and compared. This, of course, is an essential ingredient of social and psychological measurement of all kinds, which includes social surveys and psychological testing in the form of structured interviews, self-administered questionnaires, or experiments (see Brown, 1983).

The present reasoning suggests, however, that such standardization is an impediment to effective understanding. If the degrees of behavioral freedom are restricted by the requirements of standardization, then the respondent cannot provide the questioner with feedback about her understanding of the intended meaning of a contribution (here: the intended content of a question), and the questioner cannot tune his contributions to the interpretational needs of the respondent.

But does standardization preclude collaboration? If it is true that the collaboration between questioner and respondent is a necessary ingredient in the process of understanding, one may wonder if it is entirely precluded in standardized situations.

Collaboration and the Metatheories of Standardized Questioning

To understand whether and how collaboration may be effective under standardized conditions, we shall examine the two most important metatheories that underlie measurement through standardized questioning, namely psychometric test theory and the not so explicitly articulated theory of survey measurement. To find out how understanding in such situations is theoretically conceived, it is interesting to compare the two theoretical rationales and their psychological underpinnings. For this purpose, the two positions will be presented in a somewhat simplified form.

Psychometric Testing

Psychometric testing is based on the behavioristic assumption that the answer to a question is simply a response elicited by a stimulus; that is, the question (for a more complete account of psychometric test theory, see Lord and Novick, 1974). The response consists of two components: a 'true-value' component and an 'error' component. Psychometric test theory further assumes that the error is randomly determined and its dispersion around the 'true value' will approximate a normal distribution with increasing number of questions. Because the 'error' (that is, the deviation from the 'true value' that is associated with one particular question) is considered to be 'random', psychometricians do not focus on the content or the wording of a particular question. Multiple measurement, many questions tapping the same phenomenon, is the route by which the psychometrician approaches the true value. The validity does not hinge on one single question but solely on the covariations of the response with other behaviors; that is, response behaviors under standardized conditions (for a related discussion, see Abelson, 1984).

Moreover, the respondents do not even have to know their 'true value'. For example, if a psychometrician wants to find out if the respondent is extraverted or a type-A person, it is not necessary that the respondent has an idea what this concept refers to or where he or she would be allocated on that dimension. Thus, the psychometrician is not primarily interested in how a question is understood and how an answer is generated. As a consequence, the issue of collaboration does not arise.

Survey Research
A rather different metatheory underlies standardized questioning in survey situations. Although survey researchers use a similar terminology (for example, the terms 'true value' and 'error'; see Lessler, 1984), their approach to measurement is quite different. On the surface, this is reflected in the fact that, unlike psychometricians, survey researchers often use one single question to address a particular phenomenon and that they do care extensively about the content of a question and about how it is worded (for example, Belson, 1981; Payne, 1951; Schuman and Presser, 1981; Sudman and Bradburn, 1982). Still, as for psychometricians, it is their goal to capture respondents' 'true values'. How is that possible without multiple measurements? What is the rationale behind this logic?

Table 9.1   *The 'Introspection theory' of standardized question situations*

Assumption
Features of respondent
    (a) 'objective' (age, gender, income . . .) – objective criterion
    (b) 'subjective' (beliefs, attitudes, evaluations . . .) – *no* objective criterion

Claim
Immediate access to 'true value' of features

Method of access
Introspection

Source of error
Respondents lie if goal of reporting 'true value' is less desirable than other goals (e.g., make a good impression)

As summarized in Table 9.1, the metatheory of survey responding[1] has four components that refer to features of the respondent, to a psychological process that guarantees validity, and to a possible source of error. We shall discuss each of them in turn.

The starting point is the assumption that respondents possess certain features. These features are either 'objective', like a specific age and gender, or 'subjective', like a certain attitude and belief. The only difference between the two classes is the existence of external criteria for the 'objective' features, and the absence of external criteria for the 'subjective' ones. Thus, the 'true value' of respondents' age can be checked by inspecting their birth certificates while the 'true value' of a specific attitude cannot be examined by such means.

Such objective validation, however, is not a necessary criterion for survey measurement because its internal validity is guaranteed by the method of accessing the 'true value'. It is assumed that independent of whether external criteria exist or not (that is, whether the features are 'objective' or 'subjective'), respondents have immediate access to their 'true value'. Quite succinctly, Martin (1984: 298) summarized this position as follows: 'There is a fundamental assumption in survey research that respondents can give valid reports of their own subjective states'. Just as respondents can report their 'true' age, they can describe their 'true' attitude 'with candor and accuracy' (Campbell, 1981: 23).

What is the psychological mechanism that guarantees such a privileged, immediate and unbiased access to one's own subjective features? It is the method of introspection.[2] As Martin (1984: 298) put it: 'It might be assumed . . . that respondents base their reports on introspective self-examination'. If it is true that respondents *can* access the 'true values' of their subjective features, 'errors' are only possible in this conceptualization if respondents do not *want* to communicate their 'true values', if they do not tell the truth (although they know it); that is, if they lie. Thus, if the respondents' *competence* is ruled out as a determinant of error it is their *motivation* that must be held responsible for deviations from the truth. Almost exclusively, the influence that affects respondents' motivation not to communicate their 'true values' is assumed to be 'social desirability'; that is, the desire to make a positive impression, or at least to avoid a negative one (see DeMaio, 1984).

In this metatheory, collaboration occurs primarily at a motivational level, in that the respondent complies with what the questioner wants her to do, and that is to tell the truth. While this is an important insight, this introspective theory limits theorizing in the survey methodology domain to addressing only one aspect of collaboration. This shortcoming makes it difficult for the metatheory of survey research to explain a substantial body of findings bearing on the impact of question wording and question context (for example, Schuman and Presser, 1981). Specifically, survey researchers found that rather innocuous variations like changes in the order in which questions are asked may have enormous effects on respondents' answers (for research examples, see Belson, 1981; Payne, 1951; Schuman and Presser, 1981; Schwarz and Sudman, 1992). In explaining these so-called 'response effects', survey methodologists realized the limits of their metatheory: it proved rather implausible to invoke changes in respondents' motivation to collaborate and tell the truth as the major variable underlying the impact of question wording and question context (see Hippler and Schwarz, 1987; Strack and Martin, 1987).

An Alternative Metatheory

In the face of these shortcomings, we would like to suggest an alternative conceptualization of standardized question situations that is based on a joint consideration of cognitive and communicative processes (see Schwarz and Strack, 1991a,b; Strack, 1992; Strack and Martin, 1987; Tourangeau, 1984). This metatheory readily acknowledges motivational variations of collaboration that concern the respondents' self-presentation. In the suggested conceptualization, however, it is recognized that collaboration is not only relevant for the act of communication. More importantly, collaboration is regarded to be essential in the act of question understanding. In our conceptualization, we assume that standardized question situations constitute a particular type of communication in which the participants – that is, the questioner and the respondent – pursue certain goals and that this pursuit is guided by certain rules.

Several authors have identified such goals and studied their pursuit and its psychological consequences. In the characterization of what he called the 'communication game', Higgins (1981; see also McCann and Higgins, this volume) made a distinction between goals that are determined by the requirements of the task in which the participants find themselves (typically, the transmission of information), and goals that are extraneous to the particular task, like the goal to entertain, to maintain a social relationship, to save one's face, or to make a good impression.

Table 9.2 *The 'Communication theory' of standardized question situations (SQS)*

Assumption
SQS is particular goal-directed interaction. Interaction is cooperative if questioner and respondent:
   (a)   pursue matching *goals*
   (b)   follow the same *rules*

Possible goals

Questioner	Respondent
obtain information	provide requested information
	make a good impression
	confirm the presumed hypothesis
fix a date	fix a date

Thesis
Participants are typically *motivated* to cooperate

As depicted in Table 9.2, this 'implicit collaboration' in standardized situations is successful if two requirements are fulfilled:

Questioners and respondents must pursue matching goals, and they must follow the same rules. The first requirement is similar to motivational collaboration as it is implied in the introspection theory. However, we claim that matching the goals of questioners and respondents is more difficult in natural than in standardized question situations. In natural situations, more complex inferences are often required to identify the immediate and the more remote goals of the questioner (see Jones, 1964). Fortunately, in standardized question situations, things are somewhat less difficult. While standardized situations have the disadvantage of imposing constraints on the participants, they have the advantage of being more explicit about the goal of the questioner. In standardized situations, it is the questioner's goal to obtain information. The respondent can either collaborate by matching this goal and trying to provide the requested information, or not collaborate by pursuing alternative goals, like making a positive impression. This mismatch of goals is exactly the type of error that is held to be central in the 'introspection theory'.

In our communication approach, however, we assume that respondents are generally motivated to collaborate; that is, that they try to pursue the matching goal of providing the questioner with the desired information. The problem lies more in the fulfillment of this goal. And that is where the constraints of the situation enter into the picture.

To address these constraints, let us first return to a natural, unconstrained communication in which participants try to identify the meaning of an utterance. In this situation, they have to observe certain shared rules in generating their contributions. These rules may be syntactic, semantic and pragmatic in character. In our discussion, we are focusing on the last type of rules and shall discuss them in more detail in the next section. These pragmatic rules are important because they allow the respondent to go beyond the linguistic information given and infer the communicative intention of the questioner.

Obeying such rules seems to be particularly important if constraints in the communication situation prevent the contributors from providing feedback about the reached level of understanding and preclude the questioner helping the respondent either directly or indirectly by tuning subsequent messages to the particular needs of the respondent.

If one applies this reasoning to standardized situations, it seems that because explicit help and feedback is less available, respondents depend more on cues that allow pragmatic inferences (about the intended meaning) on the basis of the rules of communication.

Table 9.3 *The Gricean 'Cooperative Principle'*

Maxim of Quantity
Make your contribution as informative as is required, but not more informative
than is required.

Maxim of Quality
Try to make your contribution one that is true.

Maxim of Relation/Relevance
Make your contribution relevant to the aims of the ongoing conversation.

Maxim of Manner
Be clear.

Source: adapted from Clark and Clark, 1977

Interestingly, this has rarely been recognized by theorists of psychological measurement.

The Gricean Rules of Conversation   What exactly are the rules of communication? Most important are the postulates that are subsumed under the 'cooperative principle' of the linguist Paul Grice (1975). Table 9.3 gives a synopsis of this principle as it was summarized by Clark and Clark (1977: 122). The Maxim of Quantity requires participants in a conversation to select their contributions such that they contain neither too much nor too little information. The Maxim of Quality requires them to tell the truth. The Maxim of Relation/Relevance requires participants to relate their contributions to each other. And the Maxim of Manner requires them to be clear and to avoid obscurity (for an in-depth discussion of the Gricean maxims, see Levinson, 1983).

What does it mean to observe the maxims of communication in a standardized question situation? How can these rules for natural, unrestricted conversations be translated into standardized situations? To illustrate this, let us use the Gricean Maxim of Relevance (or Relation) and the postulate of Quantity and describe a series of studies we have conducted on the issue.

Empirical Evidence: Conversational Maxims and Question Answering in Standardized Situations

The Maxim of Relation

The Maxim of Relation asks participants in a conversation to make their contribution relevant to what has been contributed before. The following example comes from Levinson (1983: 97). If the question 'Can you tell me the time?' is followed by 'Well, the milkman has come', then the communicative intention of the second utterance can only be understood if the listener can safely assume that it really refers to what has been said before; that is, the inquiry about the correct time.

In a much less dramatic sense, the respondent in a standardized situation must be able to assume that the response categories or the response scale refers to the preceding question. If this rule is being obeyed, the respondent may use the response categories as a cue to infer the intended meaning of a question (see, Schwarz, 1990; Schwarz and Hippler, in press). Suppose, for example, that respondents are asked to indicate how frequently they were 'really irritated' recently. Before the respondent can give an answer, he or she must decide what the researcher means by 'really irritated'. Does this refer to major irritations such as fights with one's spouse, or does it refer to minor irritations such as having to wait for service in a restaurant? If the respondent has no opportunity to ask the interviewer for clarification, or if a well-trained interviewer responds, 'Whatever you feel is really irritating', he or she might pick up some pertinent information from the questionnaire. One such piece of information may be the frequency range provided by the scale.

For example, respondents who are asked to report how often they are irritated on a scale ranging from 'several times daily' to 'less than once a week' may relate the frequency range of the response alternatives to their general knowledge about the frequency of minor and major annoyances. Assuming that major annoyances are unlikely to occur 'several times a day', they may consider instances of less severe irritation to be the target of the question, in contrast to respondents who are presented a scale ranging from 'several times a year' to 'less than once every three months'. Experimental data support this assumption (Schwarz et al., 1988). Respondents who reported their experiences on the former scale subsequently reported less extreme examples of annoying experiences than respondents who were given the latter scale. Thus, the type of annoying experiences that respondents reported was determined by the frequency range of the response alternatives in combination with respondents' general knowledge, rather than by the wording of the question *per se*, reflecting that respondents used an apparently formal feature of the question to interpret its meaning, much as the Maxim of Relation would entitle them to do. From an applied point of view, this finding indicates that the same question combined with different frequency scales is likely to assess different experiences.

In a related vein, Schwarz, Knäuper, Clark, Hippler and Noelle-Neumann (1991) observed that respondents may use the numeric values of a rating scale to interpret the meaning of the scale's labels. Specifically, a representative sample of German adults was asked, 'How successful would you say you have been in life?', accompanied by an 11-point rating scale ranging from 'unsuccessful' to 'very successful'. However, in one condition the numeric values of the rating scale ranged from 0 (unsuccessful) to 10 (very successful), whereas in the other condition they ranged from −5 (unsuccessful) to +5 (successful). The results showed a dramatic impact of the numeric labels. Whereas 34 per cent of the respondents endorsed a value between 0 and 5 on the 0 to 10 scale, only 13 per cent endorsed one of the formally equivalent values between −5 and 0 on the −5 to +5 scale. Subsequent experiments indicated that this difference reflects differential interpretations of the term 'unsuccessful'. When 'unsuccessful' is combined with the numeric value '0' respondents interpret it to reflect the absence of success. However, when the same term is combined with the numeric value '−5', they interpret it to reflect the presence of failure.

This different interpretation of the same term as a function of its accompanying numeric is also reflected in inferences that judges draw on the basis of a report given along a rating scale. For example, in one of our experiments a fictitious student reported his academic success along one of the above scales, checking either a '−4' or a '2'. As expected, judges who were asked to estimate how often this student had failed an exam assumed that he failed twice as often when he checked a '−4' than when he checked a '2', although both values are formally equivalent along 11-point rating scales of the type described above.

In combination, these findings indicate that respondents use the related format in which their responses have to be provided to draw inferences about the intended meaning of the question as well as the meaning of answers given in response to it. However, the operation of the Maxim of Relation is not limited to the use of response formats in question interpretation. Rather, the same maxim does also allow respondents to use the content of apparently related questions to disambiguate the meaning of subsequent ones.

A study by Strack et al. (1991: Experiment 1) illustrates this phenomenon. Suppose a respondent is asked whether she is in favor of or in opposition to an 'educational contribution'. The respondent may want to find out what exactly the questioner has in mind. An inference about the intended meaning may be based on the content of the preceding question, provided the questioner observes the Maxim of Relevance and asks such questions in temporal proximity that are related in their content. Thus, if the ambiguous attitude question is preceded by an unambiguous knowledge question, the content of this preceding item may provide the basis for a pragmatic inference.

In this study, we asked respondents in a preceding question to estimate either the average allowance Swedish students obtain from their government or, alternatively, the average tuition fee an American student has to pay. The results were as predicted. German student respondents expressed more favorable attitudes toward the ambiguous 'educational' contribution' when the preceding question was about receiving money than when it was about having to pay money. This difference was particularly pronounced if the interpretation was consistent with the content of the preceding question.

Of course, this finding could have also been caused by a simple priming effect that occurred not even on a conscious level (cf. Bargh and Pietromonaco, 1982). However, the fact that there was an assimilation effect despite respondents being aware of the 'priming episode' suggests that the influence was more likely to have occurred on an inferential basis (see Strack et al., 1990).

These experimental examples indicate that the Gricean Maxim of Relevance can be applied to standardized question situations and its assumed obedience can be the basis for pragmatic inferences.

The Maxim of Quantity

Another aspect of collaboration in a standardized situation is the Maxim of Quantity. In natural conversations, this rule requires participants to tune their contributions to the particular informational needs of their partners. That is, a contribution should add new information to what is already known, but it should not be redundant. In other words, it should build on the 'common ground' (Clark, 1985) that has been established between speaker and hearer. This is often reflected by the use of the definite versus the indefinite article. The definite article should be used if the target of the description can be assumed to be known to the recipient. For example, if a particular waiter had been previously mentioned in a story, the speaker may (and should) subsequently refer to 'the' waiter. This is also true if the speaker can assume some knowledge about the situation in which the target plays a role. Thus, even before a waiter is mentioned, the speaker should use the definite article if the listener can be assumed to know that waiters play a role in a particular setting. Thus, if it is clear that the described event occurs in a restaurant, the definite article should be used for aspects that are genuine component parts of the restaurant setting (like waiters, menus, bills) even without explicit previous reference (see Schank and Abelson, 1977).

Of course, the specific realization of the cooperative principle depends on the dynamics of the particular interaction. The 'common ground' is partly a function of the information conveyed so far, and to determine the appropriate 'quantity' of information requires one to take one's previous contributions into account. Clark and Haviland (1977) have termed this the 'given–new contract', which is described (Clark, 1985: 197) as follows:

> In using given and new information the speaker has good reason to believe that the given information designates a referent that the addressees can identify uniquely on the basis of their common ground and that the new information designates information, to be attached to that referent, that is not already part of their common ground.

How can this Maxim of Quantity operate in a standardized question situation and guide pragmatic inferences? Let us return to a natural conversation in which you are first asked 'How is your wife?' followed by the second question 'And how is your family?' What exactly is the questioner referring to? More precisely, is 'family' meant to include the respondent's wife or not? In this case, the obedience of Grice's Maxim of Quantity would allow the respondent to infer that 'family' does *not* refer to his wife because otherwise the answer would be redundant. Note that this is not the case if the two questions were asked in the reverse order.

Applied to a standardized question situation, the Maxim of Quantity should be relevant if two questions overlap in their content and the interpretation of a subsequent question may be based on the content of the preceding question. This is the case if a specific question precedes a more general one and their contents are in a subset–superset relationship. This rule should also apply if the contents are very similar and there is an intersection between the two. Note, however, that the Maxim of Quantity in its form of the given–new contract presupposes that the Maxim of Relation is being followed. In other words, only if a subsequent question is seen as related to a previous one does it make sense to obey the given–new contract.

In our example of a question and its response categories, it is obvious that they are related. However, in standardized situations, it is not guaranteed that two succeeding questions are related. Frequently, such a perception is even actively avoided by placing items at different positions in the questionnaire or by interspersing filler items. Thus, it seems that the perception of relatedness can be manipulated and used for experimental purposes. That is, an experimental induction of the perception of relatedness should determine the operation of the Gricean Maxim of Quantity. This was attempted in a series of studies.

We would like to begin with the case of a specific and a general question that stand in a part–whole relationship. In one of our experiments (Strack et al., 1988: Experiment 2), the specific question was subjects' happiness with their dating, and the general question their happiness with life in general. What are the predictions about mutual influence that can be generated? From a merely cognitive priming perspective (see Higgins et al., 1977; Srull and Wyer, 1979, 1980), we would predict that the specific question activates certain contents that are subsequently more accessible. More specifically, if respondents think about the quality of their dating, this information should subsequently be salient when the question about happiness in general is to be answered. As a result, the answers should be highly correlated. Such an assimilation effect, however, should only be observed if the Maxim of Quantity is not applied. If it is, then the respondents should try to be informative and should not provide the same information that they have previously given. This rule, however, should only be applied if the two questions are perceived as related to each other; that is, if they are placed in the same conversational context.

To test these predictions, we asked undergraduate students to participate in a short survey on 'student issues'. Among a set of university-related questions, respondents were asked how happy they were with life in general and how happy they were with their dating. In a control condition, the two questions were asked in the general–specific order, whereas in a priming condition, the specific question was asked before the general one. To reduce the visual relatedness of both questions, the question about happiness with dating was asked at the end of the first page of the questionnaire and the general one about happiness with life in general at the beginning of the next page.

In a third condition, the 'communication' condition, the specific–general order was maintained but in addition it was made clear that the two questions were related to each other. We did this by using the following lead-in: 'We are now asking two questions about your life, (a) happiness with dating, (b) happiness with life in general.'

As shown in Table 9.4, the correlation of the dating and the life-satisfaction questions was lowest ($r = 0.16$) in the general–specific control condition where neither a priming nor a communication effect is expected. The correlation was dramatically increased ($r = 0.55$) in the specific–general priming condition, reflecting the

Table 9.4 *Happiness with dating, and happiness with life in general*

Control	Priming	Conversation
general–dating	dating–general	dating–general + context
$r = 0.16$	$r = 0.55$	$r = 0.26$

Source: Strack et al., 1988

increased cognitive accessibility of information bearing on respondents' dating. However, the correlation dropped again to $r = 0.26$ when the two questions were asked in the same order but were placed in a joint conversational context. Our communication analysis suggests that the Maxim of Quantity in the form of the given–new contract caused subjects in the latter condition not to include the content of the specific question in the answer to the general one.

The evidence, of course, is indirect and therefore, we conducted a conceptual replication (Schwarz, Strack and Mai, 1991). Specifically, German adults who had either a spouse or a partner were asked how satisfied they were with their current relationship and how satisfied they were with their life as a whole. Three conditions of the previous experiment were replicated. In these conditions, the order and the conversational context were varied. In addition, there were two new conditions in which the respondents were explicitly instructed to do what we assumed they did spontaneously as a function of the Maxim of Quantity, namely to include or exclude the redundant information. Thus, we explicitly requested them to either *exclude* or *include* the content of the specific question when they rated their satisfaction with life in general.

In this follow-up study, the previous pattern of correlation coefficients was clearly replicated. The correlation was significantly higher ($r = 0.67$) under the 'priming' condition than under either the 'conversation' ($r = 0.18$) or the 'control' ($r = 0.32$) condition. More importantly, the correlation coefficients under the conditions where respondents were explicitly instructed to include ($r = 0.61$) or exclude ($r = 0.20$) the specific content matched exactly the conditions under which we assumed that the Maxim of Quantity induced them to do the same. In combination, this set of findings suggests that respondents in standardized situations observe the Maxim of Quantity when they answer specific and general questions whose content is related in a part–whole manner. However, the impact of the given–new contract is not limited to this type of question sequence.

Extending the above line of research, we (Strack, Schwarz and Wänke, 1991: Experiment 2) applied the same logic to contents that are semantically similar. The prediction is that respondents who follow the Maxim of Quantity and apply the given–new contract should differentiate between two semantically similar concepts more than respondents who do not apply this conversational rule. This should again be a function of the conversational context in which the two questions are placed. The (perhaps somewhat counterintuitive) empirical consequence is that answers to questions about happiness and satisfaction should be more similar if the two questions stand in no contextual relationship. And this should be particularly the case if they are part of two different questionnaires. On the other hand, their answers should be more different if the Maxim of Relation applies and the two questions are perceived as belonging to the same conversational context.

To test this prediction, we asked respondents to indicate on a response scale how happy they were with their own life as a whole and how satisfied they were with it. Under one condition, the two questions were part of different questionnaires. The happiness question was asked as the last item of a questionnaire that was part of an experiment in which subjects had to ascribe different emotions to a target person. Then, a second questionnaire followed that had to do with characteristics of people who participate in experiments. The two assessments were even made more distinct by different color of the paper, different typeface, and so on. As intended, subjects did not perceive the two questionnaires to be related in any manner. In the context conditions, we simply drew a box around the two questions on which we wrote: 'Here are two questions about your life'.

We predicted that the answers should be more similar if the two questions are perceived to be unrelated and part of different questionnaires, and that they should be more different if they are perceived to be related and the Maxim of Quantity is invoked.

The correlation between the two questions was almost perfect ($r = 0.96$) when respondents reported their happiness and their satisfaction in two different questionnaires. However, it dropped significantly ($r = 0.65$) if the two questions were seen as related. Inspection of the mean ratings revealed that there was almost no difference between 'happiness' and 'satisfaction' in the 'two questionnaires' condition, and a relatively large difference under the 'communication context' condition. This suggests that respondents are more likely to base their answers on the distinct aspects of two content domains if they follow a rule that requires them to be informative.

Conclusions

We began this chapter by referring to some classic work on the dynamics of understanding by Krauss and his colleagues (for example, Krauss and Weinheimer, 1966) and to the more recent rediscovery of the Kraussian perspective by psychologists of language like Herbert Clark and collaborators (for example, Clark and Wilkes-Gibbs, 1986). In this perspective, human understanding was portrayed as a genuinely social and truly interactive endeavor that is based on the collaboration of the participants. We have noted that in this type of collaboration, it was essential that communicators were not restricted in their interactions because the speakers would utilize feedback from the respondent to tune subsequent contributions to the understanding that has been reached so far. We pointed out that this type of collaboration is precluded if questions and answers have to be given in a pre-determined format; and the question arises whether a collaboration occurs in such 'standardized question situations' and, if so, how a collaboration under constrained conditions can be conceptualized. We consulted meta-theories of standardized questioning and noted that they had little to say or were incomplete with respect to collaboration or understanding in general. At the same time, these theories are not capable of dealing with certain 'response effects' that have been frequently reported by survey researchers. Therefore, we reconceptualized standardized question situations as a special type of communication in which collaboration between participants occurs implicitly by (a) matching the goals, and (b) following the same rules. We have argued that – unlike in natural communications – the first requirement (that is, matching the goals) is somewhat less problematic in standardized question situations; though for the introspection theory, non-matching goals are the central source of error. It is the application of the conversational rules that needs to be understood. Under the assumption that both respondents and questioners in a survey situation do cooperate and pursue the goal of seeking versus providing information, we applied some of the conversational rules that have been formulated by Paul Grice (1975) and found that they can account for response effects that are, on the surface, the result of contextual variations. Both the Maxim of Relevance and the Maxim of Quantity seem to be operating in such situations and help us explain effects that have previously only been described.

At the same time, as a psychologist, one notes that communicative influences have also been largely ignored in standardized experimental situations (for an exception, see Hilton and Slugoski, 1986; and the contributions in Schwarz and Strack, 1991b). It seems that future studies that focus on the communicational rules *experimental* subjects apply to infer what they are meant to do might be helpful both to test the determinants of social interactions and to provide more parsimonious explanations for implicit demands of the experimental situation (see Orne, 1962).

Notes

The research reported in the present chapter was supported by grants from the Deutsche Forschungsgemeinschaft to the authors (Str 264/2 and Schw 278/2).
1. The characterization of the metatheory of survey responding is based on various parts of the handbook edited by Turner and Martin (1984).

2. In this chapter, we cannot review the extensive literature on introspection. For a more recent general discussion of the issue, see Lyons, 1986. For a more empirically oriented treatment of the topic, see Nisbett and Wilson, 1977; Ericsson and Simon, 1980.

References

Abelson, R. P. (1984) Psychological measurement: An introduction to the subjective domain. In C. F. Turner and E. M. Martin (eds), *Surveying Subjective Phenomena*, vol. 1, pp. 117–125. New York: Russell Sage Foundation.

Bargh, J. A. and Pietromonaco, P. (1982) Automatic information processing and social perception: The influence of trait information presented outside of conscious awareness on impression formation. *Journal of Personality and Social Psychology*, 43: 437–449.

Belson, W. A. (1981) *The Design and Understanding of Survey Questions*. Aldershot: Gower.

Brown, F. (1983) *Principles of Educational and Psychological Testing*. New York: Rinehart & Winston.

Campbell, A. (1981) *The Sense of Well-being in America*. New York: Russell Sage.

Clark, H. H. (1985) Language use and language users. In G. Lindzey and E. Aronson (eds), *Handbook of Social Psychology*, vol. 2, pp. 179–232. New York: Random House.

Clark, H. H. and Clark, E. V. (1977) *Psychology and Language. An Introduction to Psycholinguistics*. New York: Harcourt Brace Jovanovich.

Clark, H. H. and Haviland, S. E. (1977) Comprehension and the given–new contract. In R. O. Freedle (ed.), *Discourse Production and Comprehension*. Norwood, NJ: Ablex.

Clark, H. H. and Wilkes-Gibbs, D. (1986) Referring as a collaborative process. *Cognition*. 22: 1–39.

DeMaio, T. J. (1984) Social desirability and survey measurement: A review. In C. F. Turner and E. Martin (eds), *Surveying Subjective Phenomena*, vol. 2, pp. 257–282. New York: Russell Sage Foundation.

Ericsson, K. A. and Simon, H. A. (1980) Verbal reports as data. *Psychological Review*, 87: 215–225.

Garrod, S. and Anderson, A. (1987) Saying what you mean in a dialogue: A study in conceptual and semantic co-ordination. *Cognition* 27: 181–218.

Grice, H. P. (1975) Logic and conservation. In P. Cole and J. L. Morgan (eds), *Syntax and Semantics 3: Speech Acts*, pp. 41–58. New York: Academic Press.

Higgins, E. T. (1981) The 'communication game': Implications for social cognition and persuasion. In E. T. Higgins, C. P. Herman and M. P. Zanna (eds), *Social Cognition: The Ontario Symposium*, vol. 1, pp. 343–392. Hillsdale, NJ: Erlbaum.

Higgins, E. T., Rholes, W. S. and Jones, C. R. (1977) Category accessibility and impression formation. *Journal of Personality and Social Psychology*, 13: 141–154.

Hilton, D. J. and Slugoski, B. R. (1986) Knowledge-based causal attribution: The abnormal conditions focus model. *Psychological Review*, 93: 75–88.

Hippler, H. H. and Schwarz, N. (1987) Response effects in surveys. In Hippler, H. J., Schwarz, N. and Sudman, S. (eds), *Social Information Processing and Survey Methodology*, pp. 102–122. New York: Springer.

Jones, E. E. (1964) *Ingratiation*. New York: Appleton-Century-Crofts.

Krauss, R. M. and Weinheimer, S. (1964) Changes in reference phrases as a function of frequency of usage in social interaction: a preliminary study. *Psychonomic Science*, 1: 113–114.

Krauss, R. M. and Weinheimer, S. (1966) Concurrent feedback, confirmation, and the encoding of referents in verbal communication: *Journal of Personality and Social Psychology*, 4: 343–346.

Lessler, J. T. (1984) Measurement error in surveys. In C. F. Turner and E. M. Martin (eds), *Surveying Subjective Phenomena*, vol. 2, pp. 405–440. New York: Russell Sage Foundation.

Levinson, S. (1983) *Pragmatics*. Cambridge: Cambridge University Press.

Lord, F. M. and Novick, M. R. (1974) *Statistical Theories of Mental Test Scores*. Reading, MA: Addison-Wesley.

Lyons, W. (1986) *The Disappearance of Introspection*. Cambridge, Massachusetts: MIT Press.

Martin, E. (1984) The tasks posed by survey questions. In C. F. Turner and E. Martin (eds), *Surveying Subjective Phenomena*, vol. 1, pp. 295–300. New York: Russell Sage Foundation.

Nisbett, R. E. and Wilson, T. D. (1977) Telling more than we can know: Verbal reports on mental processes. *Psychological Review*, 84: 231–259.

Orne, M. (1962) On the psychology of the psychological experiment: With particular reference to demand characteristics and their implications. *American Psychologist*, 17: 776–783.

Payne, S. L. (1951) *The Art of Asking Questions*. Princeton: Princeton University Press.

Schank, R. C. and Abelson, R. P. (1977) *Scripts, Plans, Goals, and Understanding*. Hillsdale, NJ: Erlbaum.

Schober, M. F. and Clark, H. H. (1989) Understanding by addressees and overhearers. *Cognitive Psychology*, 21: 211–232.

Schuman, H. and Kalton, G. (1985) Survey methods. In G. Lindzey and E. Aronson (eds), *Handbook of Social Psychology*, vol. I. New York: Random House.

Schuman, H. and Presser, S. (1981) *Questions and Answers in Attitude Surveys.* Orlando, FL: Academic Press.

Schwarz, N. (1990) Assessing frequency reports of mundane behaviors: Contributions of cognitive psychology to questionnaire construction. In C. Hendrick and M. S. Clark (eds), *Research Methods in Personality and Social Psychology* (*Review of Personality and Social Psychology*, vol. 11), pp. 98–119. Beverly Hills, CA: Sage.

Schwarz, N. and Hippler, H. J. (in press) Response alternatives: The impact of their choice and ordering. In P. Biemer et al. (eds), *Measurement Error in Surveys.* Chichester: Wiley.

Schwarz, N., Knäuper, B., Clark, L., Hippler, H. J. and Noelle-Neumann, E. (1991) The impact of rating scale values on question interpretation. *Public Opinion Quarterly*, 30: 618–630.

Schwarz, N. and Strack, F. (1991a) Context effects in attitude surveys: Applying cognitive theory to social research. In W. Stroebe and M. Hewstone (eds), *European Review of Social Psychology*, vol. 2. Chichester: Wiley.

Schwarz, N. and Strack, F. (eds) (1991b) Social cognition and communication: Human judgment in its social context. Special issue of *Social Cognition*, 9.

Schwarz, N., Strack, F. and Mai, H. P. (1991) Assimilation and contrast effects in part–whole question sequences: A conversational logic analysis. *Public Opinion Quarterly* 55: 3–23.

Schwarz, N., Strack, F., Müller, G. and Chassein, B. (1988) The range of response alternatives may determine the meaning of the question: Further evidence on informative functions of response alternatives. *Social Cognition*, 6: 107–117.

Schwarz, N. and Sudman, S. (eds) (1992) *Context Effects in Social and Psychological Research.* New York: Springer-Verlag.

Srull, T. K. and Wyer, R. S. (1979) The role of category accessibility in the interpretation of information about persons: Some determinants and implications. *Journal of Personality and Social Psychology*, 37: 1660–1672.

Srull, T. K. and Wyer, R. S. (1980) Category accessibility and social perception: Some implications for the study of person memory and interpersonal judgments. *Journal of Personality and Social Psychology*, 38: 841–856.

Strack, F. (1992) Order effects in survey research: Activative and informative functions of preceding questions. In N. Schwarz and S. Sudman (eds), *Context Effects in Social and Psychological Research.* New York: Springer-Verlag.

Strack, F. (in press) *Urteilsprozesse in standardisierten Befragungen: kognitive und kommunikative Einflüsse.* Heidelberg: Springer-Verlag.

Strack, F. and Martin, L. L. (1987) Thinking, judging, and communicating: A process account of context effects in attitude surveys. In H. J. Hippler, N. Schwarz and S. Sudman (eds), *Social Information Processing and Survey Methodology*, pp. 123–148. New York: Springer.

Strack, F., Martin, L. L. and Schwarz, N. (1988) Priming and communication: Social determinants of information use in judgments of life satisfaction. *European Journal of Social Psychology*, 18: 429–442.

Strack, F., Schwarz, N., Bless, H., Kübler, A. and Wänke, M. (1990) Remember the priming events! Episodic cues may determine assimilation vs. contrast effects. Manuscript submitted for publication.

Strack, F., Schwarz, N. and Wänke, M. (1991) Semantic and pragmatic aspects of context effects in social and psychological research. *Social Cognition*.

Sudman, S. and Bradburn, N. M. (1982) *Asking Questions. A Practical Guide to Questionnaire Design*. San Francisco: Jossey-Bass.

Tourangeau, R. (1984) Cognitive sciences and survey methods. In T. B. Jabine et al. (ed.), *Cognitive Aspects of Survey Methodology: Building a Bridge between Disciplines*, pp. 73–100. Washington, DC: National Academy Press.

Turner, C. F. and Martin, E. (eds) (1984) *Surveying Subjective Phenomena*, vols. 1 and 2. New York: Russell Sage Foundation.

PART 5

WORDS, REASONING AND PRESUPPOSITIONS IN SOCIAL COGNITION

10

Counterfactual Reasoning

Terry Kit-fong Au

Edward Sapir (1949: 162) argued, 'Language is a guide to "social reality," ' . . . No two languages are ever sufficiently similar to be considered as representing the same social reality.' His student Benjamin Lee Whorf (1956: 213) further asserted, 'The world is presented in a kaleidoscopic flux of impressions which has to be organized . . . largely by the linguistic systems in our minds.' Together, Sapir and Whorf formulated one of the best-known hypotheses about the relation between language and cognition. The Sapir–Whorf hypothesis appears to have two tenets: (1) *Linguistic Relativity*: Structural differences between two languages will generally be paralleled by non-linguistic cognitive differences in the native speakers of the two languages. (2) *Linguistic Determinism*: The structure of a language strongly influences or fully determines the way its speakers perceive and reason about the world.

Empirical tests of the Sapir–Whorf hypothesis, thus far, have focused exclusively on Linguistic Relativity. The reason is clear. It is extremely difficult to establish a causal relation between language and thought, but it may be easier to show a parallel between them. Some of the early findings at first seemed to support a weak form of Linguistic Relativity. That is, they seemed to suggest that it was easier to express and think about certain concepts in one language than in another (for example, Brown and Lenneberg, 1954; Carroll and Casagrande, 1958; Lenneberg and Roberts, 1956). But such findings turned out to be quite problematic (see, for example, Au, 1988; Brown, 1976, 1986; Rosch, 1977).

Yet, as Bloom (1981) pointed out, previous studies of Linguistic

Relativity focused almost entirely on color terms and shape classifiers. Since it is possible to code color and shape with both linguistic and non-linguistic schemas, it is no wonder that the research findings with color terms and shape classifiers have given little compelling support for the Sapir–Whorf hypothesis. As cognition moves to more abstract domains, language may exert its most dramatic effects on cognition. In this new research direction, Bloom examined counterfactual reasoning in speakers of two unrelated languages, namely, English and Chinese. Bloom's findings at first seemed quite impressive.

English, like other Indo-European languages, has a distinct counterfactual construction, the subjunctive, whereas other languages like Chinese do not. When commenting on the present in English, one may say, 'If I were you, I would go home and read Jane Austen right now.' When talking about the past, one may say, 'If I had been there, this would not have happened.' That is, when entertaining a counterfactual, the verb tense is pushed further into the past. So, the past tense is used for counterfactuals about the present; the past perfect tense is used for counterfactuals about the past. These linguistic constructions might put some psychological distance between the reality and the counterfactual world.

There are no tense markers for verbs in Chinese. In order to say something like 'If I had been there yesterday, this would not have happened,' one can say, for instance, 'Yesterday, I not being there. If I being there, this will not happen.' In order to interpret a counterfactual statement, Bloom (1981) argued, Chinese speakers have to remember that the premise is not true, but if it were true, then the implication(s) would be true. If a counterfactual has many implications and a lot of distracting details, by the time Chinese speakers get to the end of such a long and complex counterfactual statement, they may have forgotten that the premise is false in the first place, and as a result, they may not realize that the implications are also counterfactual. In English, by contrast, every counterfactual implication is marked as counterfactual with, for example, a *would* (for the present) or *would have* (for the past). Bloom, then, hypothesized that it should be easier to deal with long and complex counterfactual statements in English, and that English speakers should be more inclined to think counterfactually than Chinese speakers. This hypothesis is in essence a special case of linguistic relativity. It states that the lack of a distinct counterfactual marker in the Chinese language should be associated with Chinese speakers' difficulty and reluctance to think counterfactually.

Bloom's Test of Linguistic Relativity

Bloom set out to test his hypothesis by asking some Chinese and English speakers in Hong Kong, Taiwan, and the United States to read a counterfactual story. The subjects were then asked whether the implications discussed were true. He conducted a number of studies (Bloom, 1981, 1984), and I will summarize only his most dramatic findings here.

In one study, English speakers in the US read a counterfactual story about an eighteenth-century European philosopher, Bier. The story went like this: Bier could not read Chinese, but if he had been able to do so, he would have been influenced by certain Chinese philosophical works, and he would thus have been able to synthesize Western and Chinese views and make several important contributions to Western philosophy (for the actual text, see Version Two of the Bier story in Bloom, 1981: 27). When asked whether Bier actually made the contributions discussed in the story, 98 per cent of the native English speakers responded that Bier did not do so. In other words, virtually all of these English speakers appreciated that the implications of the story were contrary to fact. When Bloom gave a Chinese version of this story to native Chinese speakers in Hong Kong and Taiwan, only 6 per cent of the Chinese speakers gave a counterfactual interpretation to the story (Bloom, 1981).

If Bloom's findings turned out to be valid, they would be very compelling support for the Sapir–Whorf hypothesis. Sapir and Whorf were interested in how the structure of language might shape fundamental and pervasive aspects of thinking such as perception of social reality, concept of time, causality, the ontological distinction between object and event, and so forth. And counterfactual reasoning seems fundamental and pervasive indeed in human thinking. Consider regret, for instance. If regret is a universal emotion, then counterfactual reasoning must also be universal. Imagine that a mother sent her child to run an errand, and the child was seriously hurt in an accident. The mother would no doubt wish she had not asked her child to run that errand. More generally, when one regrets some past action and wishes things have turned out otherwise, one has to engage in counterfactual reasoning. If Bloom is correct, then Chinese speakers should be less likely to feel regret than English speakers.

On the other hand, I am skeptical about Bloom's findings precisely because counterfactual reasoning seems so important and fundamental in human thinking. How could such a fundamental aspect of thinking be at the mercy of the presence or absence of a distinct linguistic marker such as the subjunctive? Would a Chinese mother really feel less regret than an English-speaking mother in the situation just described, because of the syntactic differences in their languages? It seems very unlikely that counterfactual reasoning would be difficult in any culture. One way or the other, speakers of any language should have ways to think and talk about the counterfactual world readily.

Empirical Evidence against Bloom's Claims

Recall that when Bloom gave Version Two of his Bier story to Chinese and English speakers, he found a marked difference in the rate of counterfactual responses in these two groups (6 per cent versus 98 per cent, respectively). He considered this version of the story to be the most complex and to contain the most distracting details among his stimulus materials, and indeed this version also elicited the most dramatic support for his hypothesis. Bloom (1984) took these findings as evidence for language having the greatest effect on thinking when the materials are complex and demanding.

The problem with these findings is that the counterfactual in the Chinese version of this story was not expressed properly. Some of the hypothetical markers were missing. Recall that one way to express counterfactuality in Chinese is to use the construction *A not being the case, If A being the case, then B will/may/can be the case.* *Then* can be rendered in Chinese as *jiu*; however, *jiu* has two different senses. When *jiu* is followed by a hypothetical marker such as *will, may* or *can*, it means 'then', as in 'If A, then B'. However, when *jiu* is followed by *is* or *are* (*shi* in Chinese in both cases), it means 'precisely'. In Bloom's Version Two of the Bier story, *what would have most influenced him would have been . . .* was rendered in Chinese as something that means 'what influenced him most was precisely . . .' Another example of a mistake in expressing the if–then conditional in the Chinese version was that *once influenced by that Chinese perspective, Bier would then have synthesized . . .* was rendered in Chinese as 'Therefore, it was not until after Bier had been influenced by the Chinese perspective that he synthesized . . .' The problem in this case is that Bloom used the Chinese word *cai*, which also has two senses. When followed by a hypothetical marker such as *will, may* or *can, cai* is an adverb of contingency as in 'Only if A, then B.' Without a hypothetical marker, it is an adverb of time as in 'not until then' or 'just then' (see Chao, 1968, for further analysis of the if–then conditional in Chinese). Hypothetical markers are also missing in several other places in the Chinese Version Two of the Bier story. The overall

result is that the Bier story was told in the factual mode rather than
the counterfactual mode in Chinese.

In a series of studies (Au, 1983, 1984), I tried to evaluate several
alternative explanation of Bloom's findings. Let me summarize here
what I consider to be the most telling study. That study examined
the effects of language (English versus Chinese) and hypothetical
markers (present versus absent) on the tendency to give a counterfactual interpretation to the Bier story (Experiment 1 in Au, 1984).
I used Bloom's Chinese and English Version Two of the Bier Story.
In addition, a revised Chinese version was created by adding
appropriate hypothetical markers to Bloom's Chinese version; a
revised English version was created by rewriting a few phrases and
clauses of Bloom's English version so that it read like Bloom's
Chinese version (that is, with hypothetical markers missing). The
two Chinese versions were randomly assigned to 86 Chinese speakers
in Hong Kong, and the two English versions to 51 English speakers
in the United States. The results are summarized in Table 10.1.

Table 10.1   *The effects of language and hypothetical markers
on the counterfactual response rate*

	Hypothetical markers	
	Present	Absent
Chinese	81%	23%
	(N = 42)	(N = 44)
English	88%	16%
	(N = 26)	(N = 25)

When the hypothetical markers were present in the story, over 80
per cent of the subjects gave a counterfactual interpretation to the
story, regardless of whether it was written in Chinese or English.
And when the hypothetical markers were absent, less than a
quarter of the subjects responded counterfactually in either
language. These results suggest that the low counterfactual
response rate for Bloom's Chinese Version Two clearly cannot be
taken as evidence for language having profound effects on thought
in challenging situations. In other words, thus far there is still no
compelling support for the Sapir–Whorf hypothesis. Several other
studies have likewise revealed that when the counterfactuals are
expressed correctly in Chinese, native Chinese speakers seem to
have little difficulty in thinking counterfactually (Au, 1983, 1984;
Liu, 1985; see also Cheng, 1985; Takano, 1989; Vorster and Schuring, 1989, for critiques of Bloom's methodology).

Counterfactual Reasoning in Everyday life

Consider again the view that counterfactual reasoning is so fundamental and pervasive in human thinking that it is unlikely to be
difficult to do, regardless of what language one speaks. One way
or the other, speakers of every language should be able to think
and talk readily about possible worlds that are contrary to fact.
But how fundamental and pervasive is counterfactual reasoning in
everyday life?

According to Bloom, counterfactual reasoning is very alien to
the Chinese culture. Bloom reported that his

> informal content analysis of a leading Chinese newspaper in Taiwan
> conducted over a three week period uncovered only one example of the
> use of what one might call counterfactual argument, expressed by the
> circumlocution: 'X is not the case; but if X then Y,' and that turned
> out to be in a translation of a speech by Henry Kissinger. (1981: 18)

However, at least two factors may have conspired to lead Bloom
to this conclusion. First, counterfactual speculations found in
American newspapers, for instance, are often criticisms of or
satirical remarks on public policies, such as what the US or some
other government should have done or could have done. Because
of the different standards for media censorship in Taiwan and the
US, journalists and columnists in Taiwan may be less willing to
discuss counterfactual scenarios of what their government should
or could have done. Second, there are a number of ways to mark
counterfactuality in Chinese. The one Bloom focused on (not X, if
X then Y) is but one of them. Some examples in Classical Chinese
are *wei, shi,* and *jie* (for example, Eifring, 1988; Garrett, 1983–85;
Wu, 1987; Yen, 1977). Some examples in Modern Chinese are *bu
shi, hai yiwei, yaobushi,* and *yaoshi . . . zao jiu/zenme hui . . . le*
(Eifring, 1988; Ramsey, 1987; Wu, 1987). Since Bloom focused on
only the 'not X, if X then Y' construction, he may have missed
many counterfactual remarks and hence seriously underestimated
the prevalence of counterfactual remarks in the everyday life of
Chinese speakers.

An important question remains: how prevalent is counterfactual
reasoning in everyday life in various cultures? What I would like
to do next is to consider some mental activities that seem to require
counterfactual thinking and to be human universals. If there are
many exemplars of such mental activities, one can argue that
speakers of all languages ought to be able to think and talk about
counterfactual possibilities readily.

Consider frustration. When we are frustrated or upset about
something that has happened, we often cannot help but consider

how things could have turned out all right (but did not!). Not only do people seem to conjure up such counterfactual scenarios after some misfortune, but they also seem to rely on how readily such scenarios come to mind when they judge how upsetting the misfortune is. Kahneman and Tversky (1982) examined whether undesirable outcomes that can be easily undone by constructing a counterfactual scenario would tend to elicit stronger affective reactions. For instance, they asked English-speaking adults, 'Mr C and Mr D were scheduled to leave the airport on different flights, at the same time. They traveled from town in the same limousine, were caught in a traffic jam, and arrived at the airport 30 minutes after the scheduled departure time of their flights. Mr D is told that his flight left on time. Mr C is told that his flight was delayed, and only left 5 minutes ago. Who is more upset?', 96 per cent of the subjects said that Mr C should be more upset than Mr D, although their objective situations (that is, both have missed their flights) and their expectations (that is, both had expected to miss their planes) were identical. According to Kahneman and Tversky, subjects agree that Mr C will be more upset because it is easier to imagine a counterfactual scenario in which Mr C managed to make up 5 minutes and hence could catch the flight than to construct a counterfactual scenario in which Mr D managed to make up 30 minutes to catch his flight.

Kahneman and Tversky (1982) have also examined the role of counterfactual reasoning in regret. They asked English-speakers, 'Mr Jones almost never takes hitch-hikers in his car. Yesterday he gave a man a ride and was robbed. Mr Smith frequently takes hitch-hikers in his car. Yesterday he gave a man a ride and was robbed. Who do you expect to experience greater regret over the episode?'; 88 per cent said that Mr Jones would experience greater regret than Mr Smith. In other words, people are most apt to regret actions that are out of character. This is perhaps because it is easier to imagine – contrary to fact – that someone did not do something that he or she would not normally do anyway. In these and other demonstrations, Kahneman and Tversky have shown that English-speakers not only tend to construct counterfactual scenarios when they encounter their or other people's misfortunes, but they also rely on the availability of such counterfactual scenarios to judge how much regret or frustration might be experienced in those unfortunate situations (see also Kahneman and Miller, 1986).

The role of counterfactuals in everyday reasoning has been further explored in other studies. For instance, Miller and McFarland (1986) found people would recommend more compensation for victims of fates for which a positive counterfactual alternative was highly available. Several studies also examined the role of counterfactuals in causal attribution (for example, Dunning and Parpal, 1989; Hilton and Slugoski, 1986; Trabasso and Sperry, 1985; Trabasso et al., 1989; Wells and Gavanski, 1989). For instance, Wells and Gavanski (1989) found that people seem to use the availability of a counterfactual alternative to a prior event to determine its causal role in a subsequent event. In one study, for instance, a woman was described as having died from an allergic reaction to a meal ordered by her boss. When the boss was described as having considered another meal without the allergic ingredient, people tended to judge his action played a larger causal role in the death than if the alternative meal that he had considered was also said to have the allergic ingredient. In another study, a paraplegic couple was described as having died in an auto accident after having been denied a taxi ride. People tended to see the taxi-driver as a stronger cause of the deaths when his taking the couple would have undone the accident than when it would not have. So, counterfactual alternatives are actively used by people in evaluating events.

In addition to sympathy and causal attribution, other kinds of emotions and everyday reasoning such as resentment and predicting personal events also seem to be affected by the availability of relevant counterfactual alternatives (for example, Folger, 1984; Hoch, 1985). Even in the absence of experimental data, it should not be difficult to see that when we feel lucky, grateful, or vindictive, we are likely to have engaged in counterfactual reasoning too (see also Lewis, 1973; Hofstadter, 1979, 1985). In order to feel lucky that things have turned out well, one must be able to appreciate that things could have turned out badly. Otherwise, one will be just blessed but will not necessarily feel lucky. Likewise, when one is grateful to someone, one is likely to think, 'If it weren't for her help, I wouldn't have accomplished this.' Or, when we feel vindictive, we may think, 'If only he had listened to me, he wouldn't be in this mess now.'

Moreover, counterfactual reasoning is central to historical analyses, regardless of whether the history was political or personal. Indeed, most of Chinese historical writing describes how some strategists' brilliant manoeuvres (verbal or military) in ancient and modern China got various small states, warlords, or political parties out of many disastrous dilemmas. Those strategists often tried to convince their clients by discussing mistakes of past rulers and various might-have-beens and should-have-beens (Wu, 1987). It seems, then, whenever we try to persuade someone to learn from past mistakes – be those mistakes his or her own or someone else's – we are likely to go over various might-have-beens and should-have-beens.

No doubt, one can argue that the experiments on everyday reasoning discussed here were all done with English-speaking adults, and so it remains to be seen whether speakers of Chinese or other languages that lack a distinct counterfactual marker would behave like the English-speakers in these experiments. Nonetheless, if regret, frustration, sympathy, causal attribution, gratitude, and feeling vindictive permeate the everyday life of people from all cultures, counterfactual reasoning has to be fundamental and pervasive in human thinking as well.

Counterfactual Thoughts in Children

When we read a story, or see a movie or a drama, we usually cannot help but immerse ourselves in some counterfactual world. When we daydream and engage in wishful thinking, we will also be thinking counterfactually. Young children also have their share of fantasy, often manifested in pretend play. Such play emerges around one year of age and becomes more complex during the next several years. Moreover, children also become more explicit in separating the pretend world from the real one (for example, Bretherton, 1984; Fein, 1981; Piaget, 1962; Rubin et al., 1983). By age three, children are quite good at making an explicit distinction between pretense and reality. In one study, for instance, 3-year-olds were asked:

> What is this [curved straw] really and truly? Let's pretend this is a telephone, I'll take a turn; then you can take a turn. Ring. Ring. Hello. I'm fine. Goodbye . . . Now I'll ask you two different questions. I'll ask you about what I'm pretending this is right now and about what it really and truly is. Here's the first question. What is this really and truly? Is it really and truly a telephone or really and truly a straw? What am I pretending this is right now? Am I pretending this is a straw or pretending this is a telephone?

About two-thirds of the 3-year-olds consistently succeeded in keeping track of the pretend and real identities of various objects (Flavell et al., 1987).

Not only can young children distinguish the identity of an entity in the real world and that in a pretend – or counterfactual – world, but they also seem able to reason within both the real and counterfactual worlds. Reilly (1983) read stories such as *The Three Little Pigs* to children. After each story, she showed a child a picture depicting a scene in the story. For instance, the child might see the straw house which had been blow down by the wolf. The child was then asked, 'What if the straw house had been made of bricks?' If a child could reason counterfactually *and* use the subjunctive correctly, the child should give a response such as 'It would have stayed okay.' In this study, 92 per cent of the 4-year-olds were able to think about the counterfactual alternatives offered by the experimenter and gave reasonable responses (for example, saying that the house would be okay). Interestingly, while these children could reason counterfactually, they had not yet acquired the subjunctive construction in English. Instead of using *would have* + *verb* to talk about a counterfactual alternative to a past event, the 4-year-olds generally simply used *would* + *verb*. In fact, in Reilly's study, only children who were six or older used expressions such as *woulda* and *would've* when they talked about counterfactual alternatives of past events. It seems, then, that young children can think and talk about counterfactual possibilities before they can use the English subjunctive. But it remains unclear whether the 4-year-olds in Reilly's study could comprehend the subjunctive even though they could not produce it themselves. To address this issue, I examined to what extent young children's ability to reason counterfactually depends on the use of the subjunctive by other people. In addition, I tried to extend Flavell et al.'s (1987) findings. Their work has shown that young children can keep track of the real and pretend identities of an object. My study examined whether children can use the real and pretend identities to reason factually and counterfactually.

Ten English-speaking 4-year-olds participated in this experiment. They were randomly assigned to one of two conditions, with 2 boys and 3 girls (mean age = 4;6, ranging from 4;0 to 4;10) in each condition. In one condition, the experimenter used the subjunctive construction to invite children to reason about some pretend situations. In the other condition, she used the simple if–then conditional.

In the Subjunctive Condition, each child was asked, for instance, 'Is this [a straw] a pencil? Let's pretend that it's a pencil. If this were a pencil, what could you do with it? Now let's stop pretending. Is this really and truly a pencil? Can you really [whatever the child had said earlier one could do with a pencil] with it?' In the Simple Conditional Condition, the analogous test item was identical except that the subjunctive was replaced by a simple if-then conditional. So, a child would be asked instead, 'If this is a crayon, what can you do with it? . . .' If the subjunctive is more effective in signaling counterfactuality to children than the simple if–then conditional, children in the Subjunctive Condition should do better. Each child was given four test items, and the other three items had to do with pretending that a strip of cardboard was a toothbrush, pretending that the child had wings, and pretending that a wooden block was a train. The four test items were randomized and counterbalanced across children.

The results were very straightforward. All ten children responded appropriately on all test items. That is, the 4-year-olds could keep the real and pretend worlds separate and reason counterfactually as well as factually. This was the case regardless of whether the experimenter used the English subjunctive or the simple if–then conditional when she questioned children about the pretense. Here is a sample protocol. The child was 4 years and 9 months old, and she was in the Simple Conditional Condition.

Is this [a straw] a pencil? *No.*
Let's pretend that it is a pencil. If this is a pencil, what can you do with it? *Write with it.*
Is this really and truly a pencil? *No.*

Is this [a wooden block] a big choo choo train? *No.*
. . . If this is a big choo choo train, what can it carry? *Give rides.*
Is this really and truly a big choo choo train? *No.*
Can it really give rides? *No.*

Is this [a strip of cardboard] a toothbrush? *No.*
. . . If this is a toothbrush, what can you do with it? *Brush your teeth.*
Is this really and truly a toothbrush? *No.*
Can you really brush your teeth with it? *No. It has germs. They can make you sick.*

Do you have wings? *No.*
. . . If you have wings, what can you do? *Fly.*
Do you really and truly have wings? *No.*
Can you really fly? *No. Just birds* [can fly].

Together, these experimental findings, along with Flavell et al.'s (1987) and Reilly's (1983), suggest that English-speaking children can distinguish between reality and pretense well before they can produce the subjunctive. While 3- and 4-year-olds can make the real–pretend distinction quite well, children do not use the subjunctive reliably till age 6 or so. They can reason about the reality and some contrary-to-reality situations appropriately when requested to do so, regardless of whether their conversation partners used the subjunctive in requesting them to think about a counterfactual situation.

When left to their own devices, young children also seem remarkably adept at keeping pretense and reality separate in their pretend play. Giffin (1984) identified several features of pretend play that show such early competence. For one thing, children often define their actions verbally while enacting them nonverbally. Such underscoring is similar to the convention of the soliloquy in traditional theater. It is usually unnecessary in real life actions but is often useful in pretense play. It helps playmates to figure out what everybody is supposedly doing in the play. Giffin (1984) noticed that some types of underscoring remarks were rhythmically chanted (for example, 'Wash–wash–wash' accompanied by rubbing clothes or 'Cooky–cooky–cooky' accompanied by stirring motions above a pot). Here are two more examples of underscoring observed by other researchers.

(1) 2;0 (The child pretended that he was driving a tractor into a tunnel.) *Rrrrrrrrrrrrr. Dege degedegedege . . . Broom broom. Engine broke down.* (Later on, the child pretended to put petrol in his tractor.) *Ssssssssssssss.* (Dunn & Dale, 1984: 141)

(2) 2;0 (The child pretended to read a book to a baby, who was actually her older sister.) *I read. I read.* (Dunn and Dale, 1984: 142)

Giffin (1984) also observed young children prompting each other in their pretense play. In general, the prompts are very brief. When children prompt their playmates, they momentarily abandon their character voice and posture. Instead, they assume their own voice, often at lowered volume. According to Giffin, a lowered but normal voice indicates that the children are no longer speaking within the play frame, but rather speaking about the play. By changing their voice and posture, then, children can keep the reality and pretense separate in their communication.

(3) Three-and-a-half years (The child told her older sister, who was pretending to be the child's daughter, how to talk in the pretense play.) *You didn't talk like that. You say* [sweetly] *What's the matter, Mother?* (The older sister imitated in a honeyed voice, 'What's the matter, Mother?' and the pretend play continued. Giffin, 1984: 97)

Garvey and Berndt (1977) also reported that a 39-month-old girl played the role of mother to her baby doll and the role of wife to her 33-month-old husband. To cap it all, she prompted the 'husband' on how to enact the father role. (For more examples of prompting, see Garvey and Berndt, 1977; Giffin, 1984).

Other evidence for children's distinguishing between reality and pretense comes from their formal pretend proposals and exits from the make-believe world. For instance, young children often begin their pretend play by saying 'Let's pretend (or say, or play) we are

. . .' (Giffin, 1984: Matthews, 1977). Children also mark their exits from the pretend world explicitly. For instance, they may say, 'I'm not the dad,' 'I'm not dead,' 'That's not a car,' 'It's not cake any more,' and 'Please don't push me 'cause I'm not the dragon any more.' (Matthews, 1978).

In short, children from quite early on can distinguish the reality from some counterfactual world such as a make-believe world created in their play. Moreover, they can go back and forth between the two worlds and reason quite consistently within each world. They can coordinate their factual and counterfactual thoughts with their playmates without relying on the English subjunctive. Instead, they use a variety of devices such as underscoring, prompting, proposing to pretend, and declaring their exits of the make-believe world. (For further discussion of how children manage the boundary between reality and make-believe, see for example Bateson, 1956; Bretherton, 1984, 1989; Garvey and Kramer, 1989; Wolf and Pusch, 1982.)

Diary records of young children also reveal that children begin to talk about counterfactual possibilities from very early on. Wellman (1985) reported spontaneous verbal expressions of the real–pretend distinction in a boy's speech from age two on. Importantly, young children's counterfactual thoughts are not limited to make-believe. Bates (1976) noted that children in their second year of life sometimes mark the nontruth of their behavior with a remark such as 'No no.' Bowerman (1986) pointed out that when children use *about to* or *almost* to comment on a situation that came close to occurring but has not actually occurred, the children are entertaining some counterfactual alternatives to the reality. Some examples are:

(4) 1;10 (The mother had just caught a pitcher that the child had set down on the edge of a sandbox.) *Almost fall!* (Bowerman, 1986: 290)

(5) 2;9 (The child was looking for her slippers.) *I was about ready to say I can't find my other one, but I found it.* (Markman, n.d.)

(6) 4;0 (The child frequently asked her mother to teach her to read, and often played word games. One day the child proposed to switch roles with the mother.) *You be me and I'll be you, and I'll teach you to read.* (The child then gave the mother some letters and the mother read them.) *That's almost right sweetheart! Very good, you almost got it.* (Markman, n.d.)

Example (6) is especially interesting because the four-year-old implicitly entertained a counterfactual alternative (that is, the mother actually 'got it right') within a more global counterfactual context (that is, the pretense that the child was the mother and vice versa).

Bowerman (1986) also noted that young children sometimes use *thought* and *wish* as counterfactual markers.

(7) 2;0 (The child was upset when she found that the mother had screwed the nipple on her bottle; she liked to do this herself.) *I thought me do that!* (Bowerman, 1986: 290)

(8) 1;11 (The child ate a brown bread crumb and commented on her misperception.) *I thought I ate an ant.* (Mother: 'What was it?' *Bread!* (Markman, n.d.)

(9) 2;1 (The mother drew a face on a napkin in the child's lunchbox to surprise her. Later in the evening, the mother told the child that it was her, not the father, who had done that. The mother asked, 'Who did you think put the face on the napkin?') *Daddy.* (Mother asked, 'Who really put the face on the napkin?') *Mommy* (Markman, n.d.)

(10) Three-and-a-half years (The child prompted another child what to do in their pretend play.) *Pretend you thought I was alive but I was dead.* (Giffin, 1984: 99).

These examples suggest that by age two, children can comment on their wrong ideas, which are thoughts about some counterfactual alternatives to the reality. Example (10) illustrates that young children can even instruct others to entertain a counterfactual alternative within a more global counterfactual context, namely, their pretend play. Together, Examples (6) and (10) suggest that young children can embed different kinds of counterfactual thoughts (for example, an almost occurred event, misperception) in a more global counterfactual context.

Young children sometimes also talk about their wishes for some desirable but contrary-to-fact situations.

(11) 2;1 (The child and the mother were chatting.) *I wish Christy* [the child's name] *have a car. I wish me have a airplane.* (Bowerman, 1986: 290).

Like adults, even young children sometimes feel lucky that things have turned out well. Note that in order to feel lucky, one has to realize that some misfortunes – be they major or minor – could have occurred but did not occur. Here is an example of a 3-year-old congratulating herself for her good luck.

(12) 3;9 (The mother explained to the child that lox [smoked salmon] was a treat because it was very expensive.) *How much?* (Mother: 'About $15 a pound.') *I'm glad I'm not with you when you buy that.* (Mother: 'Why?') *Because it takes too long.* (Mother: 'Why does it take longer to buy something expensive?') *Because you spend that much time giving that much money. But two pieces of money wouldn't spend that much time.* (Markman, n.d.)

Together, data from experiments and diary records converged to suggest that from very early on, young children are capable of entertaining counterfactual alternatives. From around age two years on, they talk about events that could have and almost occurred but did not actually occur. They talk about their wishes for some desirable but contrary-to-fact situations. They also talk about their misperceptions, namely, their false beliefs that some counterfactual events actually took place. By age three or so, they can reliably distinguish pretense from reality. Experimental and observational studies of pretense play have demonstrated that by age four, children not only can readily shift back and forth between the real and the pretend world, but they also can reason quite consistently within each of these two worlds. Importantly, children's early competence in counterfactual reasoning is not limited to the domain of pretense play. As just noted, they comment on their wishes and misperceptions and on events that nearly occurred. Moreover, they sometimes also congratulate themselves for their good luck. Along with others (for example, Bowerman, 1986; Lyons, 1977), I would argue that to think and talk about such matters requires the ability to entertain counterfactual alternatives to reality. Well before they have acquired the subjunctive, then, children seem to engage in counterfactual reasoning in their everyday life.

Implications for the Relation between Language and Social Cognition

One reason why Sapir and Whorf's view on language and thought is so fascinating has to do with the kind of thought Sapir Whorf were interested in. To them, language is a guide to social reality (Sapir, 1949), and our world views depend on how our languages happen to dissect the kaleidoscopic flux of impressions presented to us (Whorf, 1956). Conducted in this spirit, Bloom's (1981) work on counterfactual reasoning was likewise fascinating. Because counterfactual thinking seems to be both fundamental and pervasive in human thinking, if Bloom's claim about the importance of having a distinct linguistic marker for counterfactual turned out to be valid, his work would be extremely compelling support for the Sapir–Whorf hypothesis.

Close scrutiny of Bloom's work, however, has revealed many methodological problems. Indeed, when the counterfactual is expressed correctly in Chinese, Chinese speakers seem to have little difficulty in counterfactual reasoning (Au, 1983, 1984; Liu, 1985). What is the moral of this research story about counterfactual reasoning? One may read this story as yet another variation of the theme 'Support for the Sapir–Whorf hypothesis: Found and lost (again)' (see, for example, Au, 1988; Brown, 1976, 1986; Rosch, 1977). As a result, one may conclude that this hypothesis is unlikely to receive support in future tests. On the other hand, it is possible that researchers simply have not yet found an appropriate domain to test this hypothesis. Thus far, linguistic relativity has been tested in domains such as color terms, shape classifiers, and counterfactuals. Since there are numerous other logical possibilities, support for the Sapir–Whorf hypothesis may turn up in some other domains.

What I tried to do in this chapter, in some sense, is to turn Bloom's hypothesis on its head. Bloom was interested in whether the absence of a distinct counterfactual marker in a language would make speakers of that language less inclined to reason counterfactually. In other words, he was interested in whether and how the structure of a language can shape its speakers' thinking. What I aimed to do, instead, is to explore to what extent the nature of our thinking can shape our language. Note that evidence for cognitive constraints on language is not directly against the Sapir–Whorf hypothesis (Au, 1988). Cognition shaping language does not pre-empt language shaping cognition.

To explore the cognitive basis of linguistic markers for counterfactuals, I have argued that counterfactual reasoning is an integral part of everyday life for children as well as adults. In order to experience emotions such as regret, frustration, gratitude, sympathy, feeling lucky or unlucky, we need to entertain some counterfactual alternatives to the reality. In order to fantasize, to enjoy pretense play, fictions, and dramas, we need to enter some counterfactual worlds. In order to learn from past mistakes, we need to consider what might have been and should have been. These many and varied aspects of social cognition all seem to require counterfactual reasoning, and importantly, seem to be universal across cultures. How can something so fundamental and pervasive in human thinking be at the mercy of the presence or absence of a distinct counterfactual marker in our languages? One way or the other, each language must have some way or ways to mark counterfactuality and to allow its speakers to think and talk counterfactually. In other words, where there is a will (or necessity) to communicate, there is a way.

Note

I am grateful to Ellen Markman for sharing her diary data with me. Gregory Murphy offered helpful comments on an earlier version of this essay; Jennifer DeWitt offered valuable assistance in data collection. I thank Eve Clark and John Flavell for alerting me to several important papers on counterfactual thoughts in children.

References

Au, T. K. (1983) Chinese and English counterfactuals: The Sapir–Whorf hypothesis revisited. *Cognition*, 15: 155–187.

Au, T. K. (1984) Counterfactuals: In reply to Alfred Bloom. *Cognition*, 17: 289–302.

Au, T. K. (1988) Language and cognition. In R. L. Schiefelbusch and L. L. Lloyd (eds), *Language Perspectives: Acquisition, Retardation, and Intervention*, second edition, pp. 125–146, Austin, TX: Pro-ed.

Bates, E. (1976) *Language and Context: The Acquisition of Pragmatics*. New York: Academic Press.

Bateson, G. (1956) The message 'This is play.' In B. Schaffner (ed.), *Group Processes: Transactions of the Second Conference*, pp. 145–241. New York: Josiah Macy Jr. Foundation. (Reprinted in R. E. Herron and B. Sutton-Smith (eds), *Child's Play*. New York: Wiley, 1971).

Bloom, A. H. (1981) *The Linguistic Shaping of Thought: A Study in the Impact of Language on Thinking in China and the West*. Hillsdale, NJ: Lawrence Erlbaum.

Bloom, A. H. (1984) Caution – the words you use may affect what you say: a response to Au. *Cognition*, 17: 275–287.

Bowerman, M. (1986) First steps in acquiring conditionals. In E. C. Traugott, A. ter Muelen, J. S. Reilly and C. A. Ferguson (eds), *On Conditionals*, pp. 285–307. Cambridge: Cambridge University Press.

Bretherton, I. (1984) Representing the social world in symbolic play: Reality and fantasy. In I. Bretherton (ed.), *Symbolic Play: The Development of Social Understanding*, pp. 3–41. New York: Academic Press.

Bretherton, I. (1989) Pretense: The form and function of make-believe play. *Developmental Review*, 9: 383–401.

Brown, R. (1976) Reference: In memorial tribute to Eric Lenneberg. *Cognition*, 5: 125–153.

Brown, R. (1986) Linguistic relativity. In S. H. Hulse and B. F. Green, Jr. (eds), *One Hundred Years of Psychological Research in America: G. Stanley Hall and the Johns Hopkins Tradition*, pp. 241–276. Baltimore, MD: Johns Hopkins University Press.

Brown, R. W. and Lenneberg, E. H. (1954) A study in language and cognition. *Journal of Abnormal and Social Psychology*, 49: 454–462.

Carroll, J. B. and Casagrande, J. B. (1958) The function of language classifications in behavior. In E. E. Maccoby, T. M. Newcomb and E. L. Hartley (eds), *Readings in Social Psychiatry*, pp. 18–31. New York: Holt, Rinehart and Winston.

Chao, Y. R. (1968) *A Grammar of Spoken Chinese*. Berkeley: University of California Press.

Cheng, P. W. (1985) Pictures of ghosts: A critique of Alfred Bloom's *The Linguistic Shaping of Thought*. *American Anthropologist*, 87: 917–922.

Dunn, J. and Dale, N. (1984) I a daddy: 2-year-olds' collaboration in joint pretend with sibling and with mother. In I. Bretherton (ed.) *Symbolic Play: The Development of Social Understanding*, pp. 131–158. New York: Academic Press.

Dunning, D. and Parpal, M. (1989) Mental addition versus subtraction in counterfactual reasoning: On assessing the impact of personal actions and life events. *Journal of Personality and Social Psychology*, 57: 5–15.

Eifring, H. (1988) The Chinese counterfactual. *Journal of Chinese Linguistics*, 16: 193–217.

Fein, G. G. (1981) Pretend play in childhood: An integrative review. *Child Development*, 52: 1005–1118.

Flavell, J. H., Flavell, E. R. and Green F. L. (1987) Young children's knowledge about the apparent–real and pretend–real distinctions. *Developmental Psychology*, 23: 816–822.

Folger, R. (1984) Perceived injustice, referent cognitions, and the concept of comparison level. *Representative Research in Social Psychology*, 14: 88–108.

Garrett, M. (1983–85) Theoretical buffalo, conceptual kangaroos, and counterfactual fish: A review of Alfred Bloom's *The Linguistic Shaping of Thought*. *Early China*. 9–10: 220–236.

Garvey, C. and Berndt, R. (1977). Organization of pretend play. *JSAS Catalogue of Selected Documents in Psychology*, 7: Manuscript 1589.

Garvey, C. and Kramer, T. (1989) The language of social pretend play. *Developmental Review*, 9: 364–382.

Giffin, H. (1984) The coordination of meaning in the creation of a shared make-believe reality. In I. Bretherton (ed.), *Symbolic Play: The Development of Social Understanding*, pp. 73–100. New York: Academic Press.

Hilton, D. J. and Slugoski, B. R. (1986) Knowledge-based causal attribution: The abnormal conditions focus model. *Psychological Review*, 93: 75–88.

Hoch, S. J. (1985) Counterfactual reasoning and accuracy in predicting personal events. *Journal of Experimental Psychology: Learning, Memory, and Cognition*, 11: 719–731.

Hofstädter, D. R. (1979) *Gödel, Escher, Bach: An Eternal Golden Braid*. New York: Basic Books.

Hofstädter, D. R. (1985) *Metamagical Themas: Questing for the Essence of Mind and Pattern*. New York: Basic Books.

Kahneman, D. and Miller, D. T. (1986) Norm theory: Comparing reality to its alternatives. *Psychological Review*, 93: 136–153.

Kahneman, D. and Tversky, A. (1982) The simulation heuristic. In D. Kahneman, P. Slovic and A. Tversky (eds), *Judgment under Uncertainty: Heuristics and Biases*, pp. 201–208. New York: Cambridge University Press.

Lenneberg, E. H. and Roberts, J. M. (1956) The language of experience: A study in methodology. *International Journal of Linguistics*, memoir 13, supplement 22: 1–33.

Lewis, D. (1973) *Counterfactuals*. Cambridge, MA: Harvard University Press.

Liu, L. G. (1985) Reasoning counterfactually in Chinese: Are there any obstacles? *Cognition*, 21: 239–270.

Lyons, J. (1977) *Semantics*, vol. 2, Cambridge: Cambridge University Press.

Markman, E. M. (n.d.) Diary records of an English-speaking child.

Matthews, W. S. (1977) Modes of transformation in the initiation of fantasy play. *Developmental Psychology*, 13: 211–216.

Matthews, W. S. (1978) Breaking the fantasy frame: An analysis of the interruptions and terminations of young children's fantasy play episodes. Paper presented at the meeting of the Eastern Psychological Association, March, 1978. Washington, DC.

Miller, D. T. and McFarland, C. (1986) Counterfactual thinking and victim compensation: A test of norm theory. *Personality and Social Psychology Bulletin*, 12: 513–519.

Piaget, J. (1962) *Play, Dreams and Imitation in Childhood*. New York: Norton.

Ramsey, S. R. (1987) *The Languages of China*. Princeton: Princeton University Press.

Reilly, J. S. (1983) What are conditionals for? *Papers and Reports in Child Language Development*, 22: 1–8.

Rosch, E. (1977) Linguistic Relativity. In P. N. Johnson-Laird and P. C. Wason (eds), *Thinking: Readings in Cognitive Science*, pp. 501–519. Cambridge: Cambridge University Press.

Rubin, K. H., Fein, G. G. and Vandenberg, B. (1983) Play. In E. M. Hetherington (ed.), P. H. Mussen (series ed.), *Handbook of Child Psychology: Vol. 4. Socialization, Personality, and Social Development*, pp. 693–774. New York: Wiley.

Sapir, E. (1949) In D. G. Mandelbaum (ed.), *Selected Writings of Edward Sapir in Language, Culture and Personality*. Berkeley and Los Angeles: University of California Press.

Takano, Y. (1989) Methodological problems in cross-cultural studies of linguistic relativity. *Cognition*, 31: 141–162.

Trabasso, T. and Sperry, L. L. (1985) Causal relatedness and importance of story events. *Journal of Memory and Language*, 24: 595–611.

Trabasso, T., Van den Broek, P. and Suh, S. Y. (1989) Logical necessity and transitivity of causal relations in stories. *Discourse Processes*, 12: 1–25.

Vorster, J. and Schuring, G. (1989) Language and thought: Developmental perspectives on counterfactual conditionals. *South African Journal of Psychology*, 19: 34–38.

Wellman, H. M. (1985) The origins of metacognition. In D. L. Forrest-Pressley, G. E. MacKinnon and T. G. Waller (eds), *Metacognition, Cognition and Human Performance*, pp. 1–31. New York: Academic Press.

Wells, G. and Gavanski, I. (1989). Mental simulation of causality. *Journal of Personality and Social Psychology*, 56: 161–169.

Whorf, B. L. (1956). In J. B. Carroll (ed.), *Language, Thought and Reality: Selected Writings of Benjamin Lee Whorf*. Cambridge, MA: MIT Press.

Wolf, D. and Pusch, J. (1982). The origins of autonomous texts in play boundaries. In L. Galda and A. Pellegrini (eds), *Play Language and Stories*, pp. 63–77. Norwood, NJ: Ablex.

Wu, K. M. (1987). Counterfactuals, universals, and Chinese thinking – A review of the linguistic shaping of thought: A study in the impact of language on thinking in China and the West. *Philosophy East and West*, 37: 84–94.

Yen, S. L. (1977). On the negative *wei* in Classical Chinese. *Journal of the American Oriental Society*, 97: 469–481.

11

Psychological Significance of Seemingly Arbitrary Word-Order Regularities: The Case of Kin Pairs

William J. McGuire and Claire V. McGuire

The research program described here investigates thought processes, particularly thought accessibility, by using an overlooked tool, the ubiquitous but puzzling word-order regularities shared by most native speakers of a language where no explicit rule or recognized function is served by using one ordering over another. Examples are numerous in all parts of speech although our studies focus mainly on noun and adjective instances. Most commonly paired noun expressions (two nouns joined by 'and' or 'or') show asymmetrical ordering preferences, often quite extreme. In the familiar domain of kin pairs, when several hundred English speakers were given five minutes to write down 'kin x and kin y' expressions where the two kin would often be mentioned together, 75 per cent of the sibling pair mentions were in the 'brother and sister' order, and 82 per cent of the parent pairings were in the 'mother and father' order. In the food-pair domain, 91 per cent of joint occurrences are ordered 'apples and oranges' and 95 per cent 'cream and sugar.' In the domain of familiar objects, 100 per cent of their co-occurrences are ordered 'knife and fork' and 96 per cent 'hat and coat.' Adjective series (two or more adjectives modifying a noun) exhibit similarly ubiquitous and asymmetrical ordering preferences. When several hundred English speakers were given five minutes to write down familiar-sounding 'adjective x, adjective y, noun' expressions, they almost invariably listed size adjectives before color adjectives ('long white dress' rather than 'white long dress') and listed color adjectives before materials adjectives ('white silk dress' rather than 'silk white dress'). Our research program uses these seemingly arbitrary ordering regularities to provide insight into the accessibility and processing of thoughts.

Three aspects of these word-order regularities make them an attractive research tool. First, they are very common, manifested in diverse speech instances and showing high across-speaker uniformity, suggesting that they reflect deep and shared psychological processes. Secondly, these regularities are mysterious, serving no obvious function nor even conforming to any arbitrary rule. *Ad hoc* principles can be suggested to account for them, but counterinstances abound and their adaptive purpose is unclear. Such mysteriousness promises that uncovering their underlying psychological processes will provide novel insights. A third feature that makes these ordering asymmetries an attractive research tool is that they fluctuate reliably with numerous situational and dispositional variables. For example, when the formal parental terms are paired in natural speech the ordering 'mother and father' is used in 79 per cent of the utterances, and when the fond terms are used they are ordered 'mom and dad' in 91 per cent of the pairings. In formal English literature of the twentieth century, on the other hand, there is a reverse male primacy in naming parents, with the 'father and mother' ordering being used in 82 per cent of the pairings. Such responsiveness to formality and other context variables makes these word-order regularities a sensitive tool for detecting effects of independent-variable manipulations.

Two restrictions in our research program deserve mention at the outset. First, at this stage we have studied formally only English-language data. Secondly, we are using an eclectic, inclusive strategy, not seeking to explain all word-order regularities by one or two broad principles, but hypothesizing a wide range of independent-variable determinants, both semantic and phonological, that account for these regularities.

Types of Word-Order Regularities

We shall distinguish the arbitrary type of word-order regularities that we are studying here by first mentioning four other types of more purposeful word-order regularities that do not concern us in this program. A type that may reflect the structure of the human thinking apparatus includes those that show up as cross-language universals or as uniform ontogenetic maturational trends. Greenberg (1966) and Jakobson (1971) include among across-language universals the rule that the subject precedes the object. The Braine (1965) and Bever et al. (1965a,b) conjecture, that what the child learns is primarily the proper locations of words in sentences, has evoked speech research on the acquisition of word order (Brown and Bellugi, 1964; Buium, 1974; Moeser, 1975). A standardized word ordering, even if only arbitrary, is needed for efficient language acquisition if it is the case that children first learn the meaning of whole sentences and only later discriminate the component words as having separate atomistic meanings (Donaldson, 1987; Quine, 1987), rather than first learning the meanings of atomistic words as theorized by behaviorists.

A second set of ordering regularities are those prescribed in low-inflected languages that permit alternative word orderings to convey different meanings, as when 'John loves Mary' and 'Mary loves John' have different meanings. The confusions or deliberate misleadings that can arise are legendary in oracular prophecies, such as the witch's amphibolous forecast in Shakespeare's *Henry IV*, 'The duke yet lives that Henry shall depose.'

Word-order regularities of a third type are those imposed by grammatical rules which may be precise even when their purpose is unclear. For example, French grammar meticulously prescribes which adjectives precede versus follow the nouns they modify. One might expect that a few simple rules with adaptive function should suffice to partition adjectives into the two classes but the rationale has so far eluded a century of research (Waugh, 1977), resembling the futile search for a few meaningful rules that will account for the gender of nouns in French or in German. Even if one cannot formulate a few elegant principles that account for such grammatical prescriptions, the ordering rules are at least explicit.

Aesthetic considerations give rise to a fourth type of word-order regularities, most obviously in metrical poetry whose rhythm is based on accentuation or vowel length. Poetic license allows conserving meter even at the cost of using word orderings that violate grammatical and semantic conventions. The use of atypical word orders for psychological effect or to communicate subtle meanings deserves more study.

A fifth case, the only one studied in the research program reported here, involves word-order regularities that most people observe spontaneously and effortlessly, but seem to serve no function nor conform to any prescription. Almost everyone says 'knife and fork' rather than 'fork and knife,' and 'flimsy wooden fence' instead of 'wooden flimsy fence.' When asked why, people typically give a near-tautological explanation such as 'Everybody says it that way,' or 'It sounds better that way.' If pushed, people often offer generalizations to account for a narrow set of cases – 'One always says the male before the female,' or 'You always name the more expensive item first,' or 'People always say first the one they like better,' but counterexamples can readily be found for most of these *ad hoc* descriptive generalizations. Such ubiquitous word-order regularities deserve study because their pervasiveness, mysteriousness, and sensitivity promise to clarify thought processes. Some research has been done on the topic (Cooper and

Ross, 1975; Enkvist and Kohonen, 1976; Pinker and Birdsong, 1979) but surprisingly little relative to the pervasiveness and mysterious nature of these seemingly arbitrary orderings.

The Strategic Planning of Programmatic Word-Order Research

We have been arguing in recent years (McGuire, 1983, 1986, 1989) that teaching of research methodology currently ignores whole domains of issues; for example, it focuses on research tactics (methodological details that arise in individual experiments) to the exclusion of research strategy (issues that arise in planning a whole program of research which give meaning to the individual experiments). As a corrective, we have in this work on arbitrary word-order regularities engaged explicitly in strategic planning of an overall program of research. We began by blocking out the total research space by defining the three orthogonal 'edges' that can define any domain to be investigated. These three defining edges, shown in Figure 11.1, are multiple domains in which word-order regularities occur × multiple classes of hypothesized determinants of the orderings × multiple methods of investigation; that is, the dependent variables × the independent variables × the methods.

Multiple Domains of Word-Order Regularities: The Dependent Variables
These arbitrary word-order regularities show up in all parts of speech, as sketched in the vertical axis of the Figure 11.1 block. Primacy regularities in noun-pairs are prevalent across meaning domains, for example, in pairs of kin ('wife and mother,' 'husband and wife'), individual celebrities ('Antony and Cleopatra,' 'Victoria and Albert'), foods ('lettuce and tomatoes,' 'gin and tonic'), common objects ('needle and thread,' 'hat and coat'), states ('life and death,' 'fear and trembling'), abstractions ('good and evil,' 'law and order,' 'sickness and health'), and so forth. Series of adjectives also show compelling ordering regularities ('shiny new car,' 'long blond hair'), as do commonly paired verbs, ('cease and desist,' 'stop and go,' 'inhale and exhale'), paired adverbs ('slowly but surely,' 'not wisely but too well'). Even conjunctions have their regular orderings, 'no ifs, ands, or buts about it.'

Our strategy is to study word-orderings in two familiar but contrasting domains of occurrence: noun pairs and adjective series. Within noun pairs we begin with kin pairs and then go to food pairs, both central domains of human experience which are often

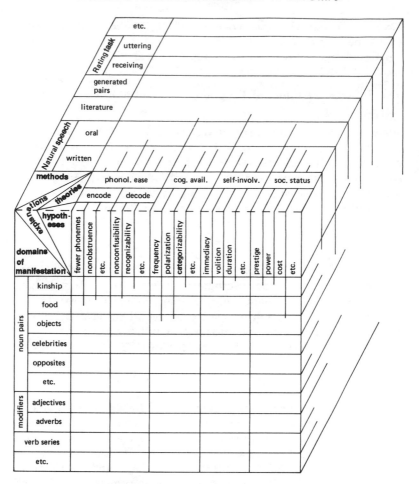

Figure 11.1 *Conceptual space within which a program of research on word-order regularities can be developed*

spoken about, making it easy to collect pairings in natural speech samples. The kin domain has a manageably small vocabulary and the food domain a rich one. A third focus of our research program is the ordering regularities in adjective series, which are hypothesized to reflect processes quite different from those determining primacy in noun pairs. The present chapter is largely confined to results on word-order regularities in kin pairs. We shall mention the data from the food-pairs and adjective-series domains only occasionally where they can help clarify an issue left ambiguous by the kin-pair data.

Multiple Categories of Hypothesized Determinants: The Independent Variables

On the second, horizontal edge of the Figure 11.1 research space we list independent variables theorized to explain primacy in word ordering. We theorize eclectically that noun-pair primacy is accounted for by five broad categories of variables. Three are semantic in that they involve characteristics of the paired concepts *per se* (rather than of their verbal labels): (1) cognitive availability, (2) affective charge and (3) sociocultural status. Two are phonological in that they involve characteristics of the concept's labels rather than their meanings: on the encoding side (4) vocalization ease, and on the decoding side (5) auditory recognizability.

Cognitive-availability variables include frequency, recency, meaningfulness, categorizability, polarization, etc. Affective-charge variables include the concepts' evaluation, closeness to self, relevance to one's needs, importance, etc. Variables in the social-status Category 3 include power, cost, prestige, ethical status, etc. As regards the two classes of phonological determinants, vocalization ease implies that primacy will go up with the label's brevity, the non-obstruence of its phonemes, its articulation simplicity, etc. Auditory recognizability variables include the familiarity of the terms' phonemes, their non-confusibility, distinctiveness of features, etc.

Multiple Methods of Data Collection

The third 'depth' edge of the Figure 11.1 research space includes our various methods of data collection such as reactive ratings, pair generation, concordances of published literature, and natural speech. The reactive rating method, the most efficient but artificial of the four, presents the respondents with pairs of expressions varying only in the ordering of two kin terms (for example, 'They like their aunt and uncle' versus 'They like their uncle and aunt') and the respondent is asked which of the two expressions sounds more natural. A second method, pair generation, yields productive rather than reactive data by asking participants to generate as many commonly paired kin terms as they can think of in the form 'kin x and kin y.'

Our third source of word-order data comes from the works of seventeenth- to twentieth-century English-language writers sufficiently eminent for a substantial portion of their work to have been made available in word-by-word concordances that list alphabetically each word used by the author, with each usage of the word shown in the context of the several preceding and following words, making it easy to calculate for each author the relative frequency of alternative orderings of a given pair (for example, 'father and mother' versus 'mother and father'). Because the authors span four centuries these concordances allow tracing historical changes in primacy in formal language production. Our fourth data-collection method analyzes word order in informal natural speech samples. We have collected a data bank of thousands of naturally occurring kin-pair expressions in children's three-minute free responses to a 'Tell us about your family' probe.

Setting Priorities within this Total Research Space
The General Sequential Plan   After sketching the total research space as blocked out in Figure 11.1, the second stage of strategic planning is to establish priorities for investigating this formidable domain. Because the horizontal edge of Figure 11.1 shows a plethora of theorized independent variables, on which little previous testing has been done, we decided at the outset to cast a wide theoretical net by including within the initial experimental design a broad spectrum of independent variables across all the five hypothesized categories of primacy determinants. From each category we selected several independent variables, often with multiple operational definitions of each variable.

Systematic investigation of each of the five categories of independent variables hypothesized to contribute to noun-pair primacy calls for five steps: (1) assembling an inclusive list of variables hypothesized to fall into that category; (2) identifying multiple indices (operational definitions) for measuring each of these variables; (3) factor analyzing matrices consisting of multiple hypothesized indices (within and across the five categories) versus a long list of kin or other terms scored on each index, in order to identify a small set of underlying dimensions; (4) selecting a few indices to measure each dimension; and (5) using this small subset of measures (singly, in combination, and in interaction with other variables) to account for word-order primacy and so give insight into thought organization and retrieval. These steps will be taken first on the kin-pair noun data, the progress on which will be illustrated below, phasing in food-pair noun data to clarify further issues, and then using adjective-series data to study other types of thought processes.

Illustrative Cognitive Availability Determinants of Primacy   We can illustrate these five steps by describing their use in identifying a set of defining variables for our first, 'cognitive availability' category of determinants of word-order primacy. We began by listing cognitive availability variables theorized to facilitate retrievability from memory. Frequency and recency of usage are obvious examples but both raise interesting problems (and opportunities). Frequency counts in written or spoken discourse (Dewey, 1923; Thorndike and Lorge, 1944; Kučera and Francis, 1967) could reflect either concept usage (a Category 1 variable) or word frequency (a Category 4 variable), but the two can to some extent be disentangled (for example, either 'Mother' or 'Mom' can be used to express the concept of the female parent, and the two labels have different written and spoken word-frequency scores). Alternatively, the convention of calling parents by kin terms and siblings by given names allows independent manipulations of concept- and term-frequencies.

Other hypothesized cognitive availability variables, beyond frequency and recency, include concreteness, imagery, categorizability, meaningfulness, number of attributes, and familiarity, on each of which Toglia and Battig (1978) have collected rating norms for 280 common nouns. Their concreteness, meaningfulness, and imagery norms can be cross-validated with Paivio et al. (1968) and Emmerich's (1979) norms (separately on children and adults) and with Noble's (1952) norms obtained by the production rather than rating method. Rubin and Friendly (1986) include norms on kinship terms. Brown (1976) and Bradshaw (1984) list over a dozen sets of published norms for several popular cognitive dimensions – concreteness, meaningfulness, etc. Other hypothesized cognitive availability variables include ease of definition, ease of recall (Christian et al., 1978), and various indices of associative difficulty (Brown and Ure, 1969), including number of associates evoked (Mayzner et al., 1965; Locascio and Ley, 1972; Glanser, 1962; Postman and Keppel, 1970), latency of associates (Ley and Locascio, 1970; Taylor and Kimble, 1967), and ratings of associativity (Cieutal, 1963). The literature on 'animateness' (Berrian et al., 1979) and 'vividness' (Tulving et al., 1965; Taylor and Thompson, 1982) provide additional Category 1 variables, as do the activity and potency dimensions in the Osgood et al. (1957) semantic differential approach.

Compiling these normative atlases will yield a data matrix with the nouns as the row headings and the measures of these numerous cognitive dimensions as column headings, with each cell entry being the score of the row noun on the column cognitive-availability dimension. From this noun × cognitive-variable data matrix we can calculate a cognitive-availability correlation matrix, a factor analysis of which will identify the dimensions underlying this spectrum of cognitive-availability measures and allow selection of a small subset of indices that describe the whole category economically and diagnostically. Similar factor analyses of each of the other four categories of hypothesized primacy determinants will serve to identify its underlying dimensions and a few indices that efficiently measure the whole category, a yield that is valuable not only in the word-order work described here, but also in other types of research in which any of these five categories of variables are used. To enhance its general usefulness, the compilation and analysis should be made generally available on a PC disk that would begin with a compilation of existing atlases (Bradshaw, 1984; Brown, 1976) in the form of a matrix of row nouns scored on a wide variety of these column cognitive-availability variables (or on variables in the other four categories). The disk should also include the derived matrix of correlations among the variables in the cognitive availability (or whichever) category and also an orthogonal (varimax) factorial solution of this correlational matrix.

Kin-Pair Primacy Effects of Variables from the Five Categories

The obtained results on the primacy effects of variables in each of the five categories hypothesized to affect primacy in noun pairs will be illustrated by our reporting how the predicted relations are empirically supported for some but not other variables in each category. Because of space limitations we shall here concentrate on the obtained data only for kin-pair nouns, and on kin-pair data obtained by just one of our four general methods, the rating data. We shall refer to results obtained by the other three methods (pair generation, natural speech, and concordanced literature), and to ordering within food pairs or adjective series, only where these other data are useful for clarification.

The kin-pair rating data were obtained by sending by post a questionnaire to 650 persons selected at random from county directories for four widely separated USA communities. Of these, 163 returned by post a completed questionnaire (a 25 per cent return rate). The questionnaire included 68 pairs of simple sentences, each pair made up of opposite orderings of a kin pair (for example, 'Their niece and nephew like them' and 'Their nephew and niece like them'). For half of the pairs the task was to rate which of the two paired expressions 'sounded better' to the rater; and for the other half, which of the two the rater 'would usually say.' The verb 'like' was used in half of the sentence pairs and 'know' was used in the other half. In half of the pairs the kin pair appeared as the subjects, and in the other half as the objects of the sentences

('Their niece and nephew like them' versus 'They like their niece and nephew'). For half of the pairs the rater's task was the passive one of checking off the preferred sentence of the pair; for the other half the task was the more active one of writing out the preferred sentence. We shall report the effects of these counterbalanced method variables, and of dispositional variables like sex and age, only when they made a difference in the preferred ordering of the kin pairs.

The 68 kin pairs that the respondents rated on the questionnaire (two of which were repeats for a reliability check) included 60 different kin terms, among which were the 13 basic English kin terms (mother, father, brother, sister; husband, wife, son, daughter; uncle, aunt, niece, nephew; and cousin) plus generic terms (parent, spouse, etc.) and the 13 basic terms' prefixed compounds (foster-sister, grandfather, etc.) and suffixed compounds (son-in-law, etc.) plus quasi-kin terms (friends and relatives, ladies and gentlemen, Mr and Mrs, etc.). The more common and more theory-relevant of the kin terms were used more often in the 66 pairs. Most of the 66 pairs consisted of two parallel kin terms likely to be said together frequently (for example, 'grandmother and grandfather,' 'father and son') rather than uncommon pairings (such as 'grandfather and nephew').

Primacy Effects of Variables in Category 1, Cognitive Availability

The first three of the five categories of hypothesized variables are semantic determinants of primacy (cognitive availability, affective charge, and social status); the last two categories are phonological ease variables (encoding vocalization ease and decoding auditory recognizability) that concern the verbal label rather than the concept *per se*. Category 1, cognitive availability, predicts that the person in uttering pairs of nouns will retrieve first the one that is more meaningful in some sense. Category 2, affective charge, predicts that the person will access first the more personally involving or better liked of the pair's members. Category 3, social status, predicts that the person will access first the pair's member with the higher societal evaluation. We will illustrate the effect of each of these three semantic categories by reporting the obtained primacy relations for several of its variables.

Illustrative cognitive-availability variables are frequency of occurrence and polarization in meaning space. For each of the kin terms on our rating questionnaire we defined the dependent variable primacy score as the proportion of all expressions in which the given term appeared in the questionnaire where the expression was rated as preferred when the given term appeared first. Each kin term was scored also on multiple Category 1 independent variables that served as partial definitions of cognitive availability; then primacy scores were correlated with scores on each cognitive-availability variable across the kin terms. Primacy was found to correlate significantly with, among others, frequency indices (Thorndike and Lorge, 1944; Kučera and Francis, 1967), with the activity (but not the potency) scale on the semantic differential (Osgood et al., 1957), and with Toglia and Battig's (1978) categorizability and with a polarization score calculated across their six cognitive scales.

Primacy Effects of Variables in Category 2, Affective Charge

The influence of the affective-charge category in determining kin-pair primacy can be illustrated by the effects of two interestingly contrasting variables, genetic closeness and voluntariness of the relationship. Evolutionary theorizing implies that attachment should increase with genetic closeness. If, as we hypothesize, retrievability increases with affective charge, then the genetically closer kin in the pair should be said first. Thirteen of the 66 rated pairs were relevant to this prediction in that both members of the pair would be genetically related to the reference person but with different degrees of gene-pool sharing. In 12 of these 13 pairs the expression was sizeably ($p < 0.05$) preferred when ordered so that the more closely related kin was said first, regardless of seniority (for example, 'son and grandson' is preferred over 'grandson and son' by 93 per cent of the raters, 'mother and grandmother' by 68 per cent), and even when number of syllables is controlled for (for example, 'uncle and nephew' is preferred to 'nephew and uncle' by 81 per cent and 'uncle and cousin' by 79 per cent).

A second hypothesized Category 2 affective-charge variable, the reference person's volitional choice in the relationship, presents an interesting contrast. With regard to the first variable, genetic closeness to the rater, we predicted that the closer the genetic relationship, the greater the affect and the more primacy in ordering. But now we are predicting that voluntarily selected significant others (with no genetic relationship at all) have higher affect and higher primacy over significant others who are closely related genetically. The rating data confirm this predicted autonomy primacy. For the 14 pairs out of the 66 where a volitionally chosen significant other (spouse, friend, etc.) is paired with a genetically linked kin (brother, daughter, etc.), the expression in which the chosen other is named first is preferred in 12 of the 14 pairs (p<0.05). For example, 'friends and relatives' is preferred (p<0.05) to 'relatives and friends' by 62 per cent of the raters. One's spouse, while genetically unrelated to the self, is clearly the closest kin there is by the criterion of primacy. One's spouse has its greatest primacy preference when paired with one's offspring – 'wife and daughter' preferred to 'daughter and wife' by 94 per cent of the raters, 'husband and son' by 82 per cent, 'wife and son' by 76 per cent. Spouse also has sizeable, if lesser, primacy over one's siblings (which matches the pair's members for generational seniority): 'husband and brother' preferred by 80 per cent, 'wife and brother' by 60 per cent, 'husband and sister' by 53 per cent. One's spouse even has some slight primacy over one's parent, pairs in which seniority plus genetic overlap are pitted against volition: 'husband and father' is preferred by 59 per cent, 'husband and mother' by 56 per cent, 'wife and mother' by 59 per cent. One sees here an overriding Category 2 volitional determination of word-order primacy with some underlying determination by seniority, a Category 3 variable. Volition's enhancement of primacy is much greater (in all six relevant pairs) for within-sex than for between-sex pairs – for example, for 'wife and sister' (91 per cent) versus 'wife and brother' (60 per cent), – suggesting that for opposite-sex pairs the primacy choice may already have been made on the basis of sex, before voluntariness comes into consideration. The primacy decision may be made on a step-wise variable-by-variable process, rather than by a multi-variable weighted procedure.

Primacy Effects of Variables in Category 3, Social Status

The role of social status in determining primacy in kin pairs will be illustrated by the effects of two plausible variables, age and maleness. On the assumption that generational seniority confers status, respect, power, and so forth, on a family member, we predicted that the older kin would be said first. Among the 66 pairs rated on our questionnaire there were 17 pairs in which both members were of different generations but were related equally closely to the reference person. For all 17 pairs the expression was strongly preferred (p<0.01) with the older member mentioned first, for example, 'father and son' was preferred over 'son and father' by 0.97 of the raters, 'mother and daughter' by 0.93, and 'mother and son' by 0.93. Seniority enhances primacy also outside the family, but not as strongly as within: 'man and girl' (0.77), 'adult and child' (0.73), 'Mrs and Miss' (0.67), 'Mrs and Ms' (0.68), suggesting that age dominance is even stronger in the family domain than in broader society.

We also predicted that because males dominate society and exercise more power within the family there would be male primacy in kinship pairs. However, evidence for overall male primacy was weak. Among the 66 rated pairs, 21 satisfied the criteria of having members equally close to the rater genetically, of the same generation as one another, and of different sexes. Of these 21 pairs, 12 were preferred with the male first and 9 with the female first. Thus there was little male primacy overall, but individual pairs tended to manifest highly asymmetrical sex-primacy preferences. There was considerable male primacy within spouse, offspring, and sibling pairs, the 'husband and wife' ordering being preferred over 'wife and husband' by 0.87 of the raters, 'son and daughter' by 0.79, and 'brother and sister' by 0.77. However, there was as pronounced a female primacy in other pairings, with 'mom and dad' preferred by 0.82 of the raters, 'niece and nephew' by 0.80 and 'aunt and uncle' by 0.76. Outside the family male primacy is more pronounced: 'Mr and Mrs' (0.98), 'male and female' (0.93), 'sir and madam' (0.74) (although the possibly patronizing 'ladies and gentlemen' was preferred by 0.92). The family appears to be more of a woman's world than is the broader society.

Primacy Effects of Variables in Category 4, Vocalization Ease

That one says the easier word first is conjectured by the oldest hypothesis in word-order theorizing, called 'Panini's law' after the Sanskrit grammarian who proposed it two and a half millennia ago, which predicts that in such discretionary pairs one tends to say the shorter word first. Panini's law is supported by our obtained -0.31 correlation ($p < 0.05$) between number of syllables and primacy among the kin terms that appeared on the rating questionnaire.

The kin-pair domain is not a good one in which to test the role of word length because in most of the frequently paired kin terms (except for avuncular pairs) both members have the same number of syllables in English, so we looked at primacy in common food pairs, the labels for whose members vary more widely on Category 4 variables like number of syllables. In general, people generating 'food 1 and food 2' pairs tend to say first the one whose label has fewer syllables; for example, among vegetables, the 'peas and carrots' order is used by 0.92 of those generating it, and 'carrots and celery' is used by 0.95 showing declining primacy with number of syllables. Other Category 4 ease-of-vocalization characteristics that enhance primacy are labels starting with vowels rather than consonants, with less obstruent consonants, and with fewer consonants.

Primacy Effects of Variables in Category 5, Auditory
Recognizability
The basic assumption underlying this category is that a speaker
who has to communicate a series of related noun concepts will
start with the one whose label is the more recognizable, thus
providing a context that facilitates recognition of the less clear,
later label. Recognizability is defined as increasing with variables
such as distinctiveness of the phonemes (as regards their formants,
their places and manner of articulation, etc.), their noncon-
fusibility, the familiarity of the label's sounds, etc. In our kin
pairs, recognizability-enhancing familiarity – as measured by
English-language frequency of initial phonemes – did contribute to
primacy. An interesting theoretical complication is that these
Category 5 recognizability assumptions often lead to opposite
predictions from the Category 4 vocalization-ease assumptions.
For example, frequency of the label's phonemes should enhance
ease of vocalization via a practice effect and so by Category 4
theorizing should make for primacy; but phonemes' frequency
would also decrease distinctiveness and so, by Category 5 theorizing, should militate against primacy.

Research on Primacy Decision Processes and Interactions

We illustrated the first phase of this research program on thought
processes exhibited in word-order primacy by sketching how
variables in each of five categories of hypothesized determinants
acted separately in determining primacy. Still needed is the identification of factors and a small subset of variables that efficiently
define each of the five categories. Meanwhile, we turn here to the
second phase of our research program which aims to reveal
thought processes by investigating how variables in each of the
five categories interact with one another and with situational or
dispositional variables in determining word-order primacy.
Because in the previous section we illustrated the isolated effects
of variables from each category by means of rating data we shall,
for variety, in the sections that follow illustrate interaction effects
mainly with data collected by the other three methods – generated
pairs, natural speech, and formal literature.

Obtained Process Anomalies
Weighted-regression versus Step-wise Combinatory Models The
results reported in the previous sections indicate how numerous
variables from each of the five categories affect primacy

individually, when the other variables are held constant. More complicated questions arise regarding cognitive algebra used in combinatory cases when several variables (from the same or different categories) vary simultaneously, and push the relative primacy between the pair's members in opposite directions. For example, when 'spouse' and 'parent' are paired, the Category 2 volitional variable predicts spousal priority, while the Category 3 age-seniority variable predicts parental primacy. Volition and seniority have each been shown to enhance primacy strongly when the other is held constant. How do their opposite effects on primacy combine when they vary orthogonally?

One combinatory possibility is a weighted regression model such that the effects of each of the determinants concurrently varying between the pair's members are factored in, weighted by the contrast between the members on it and its importance under currently relevant dispositional and situational conditions. Another combinatory possibility is an all-or-nothing stepwise decision process, as in 'elimination by aspect' models, such that one determinant at a time is considered, and the primacy decision is made on it when a sufficient triggering level is reached, considering the contrast between the pair members on that determinant and the determinant's importance under existing conditions. For example, Category 3 status variables may be considered first in abstract circumstances, and the Category 2 affect variables may be considered first under more concrete circumstances. We find in the rating data that when abstract generic terms like 'parent' and 'spouse' are used, then age-seniority (Category 3) dominates primacy, with 73 per cent preferring the 'parent and spouse' ordering. However, when concrete terms focusing on individuals are used (wife, husband, mother, etc.) then the Category 2 volitional variable dominates primacy, with 60 per cent of the respondents preferring 'wife and mother', 'husband and mother,' etc.

Nontransitivity and other Logical Peculiarities in Primacy   Word-order data show intriguing departures from simple logical relations. Nontransitivity of kin-pair orderings is common in natural language free descriptions of one's family, as illustrated by the orderings of 'mother,' 'father,' and 'sister.' 'Mother and father' is the order in 0.80 of the parent pairings occurring in the oral and written family descriptions, and 'father and sister' is the order used in 0.79 of the pairings of these two terms. Hence transitivity requires that 'mother' have vast primacy over 'sister'; but on the contrary, the reverse 'sister and mother' order is used in 0.59

(p<0.05) of the pairings. Comparable intransitivity is found in the mother–father–brother triad. Such nontransitivities may reflect a decision-by-dimension cognitive algebra, with the entry of the different determinants changing with contexts (in this example, when we go from opposite-sex pairs to same-sex pairs).

A similar decisional process may be operating in the previously mentioned primacy of volitionally chosen over genetically related significant others. This volitional primacy is considerably stronger when the two kin are of the same sex (for example, 'wife and sister' is preferred to 'sister and wife' in 91 per cent of the choices but 'wife and brother' by only 60 per cent; similarly, the 'husband and brother' ordering is preferred by 80 per cent but 'husband and sister' by only 53 per cent). It may be that when there is a sex difference between members of the pair some speakers make the primacy decision on the basis of sex without ever getting to consider the volitional variable; but when both members are of the same sex, then speakers order on the basis of volition.

Interestingly, nontransitivities like this illustrative mother–father–sister case, while appearing strongly in the natural speech samples, do not occur in formal literary writing, where the concordanced literature shows a predominant (0.89) 'father and mother' ordering reflecting the Category 3 status variable (as contrasted to the 0.80 'mother and father' orderings in informal speech reflecting the Category 2 personal-attachment variable). Hence, the mother–father–sister triad mentioned above as showing intransitivity in informal speech shows transitivity of primacy in formal written literature.

Another type of primacy asymmetry can be illustrated by word orderings of parents and siblings. In pairings that occur in natural speech descriptions of one's family, the male parent has primacy (p<0.01) over siblings ('father and brother' (0.72), 'father and sister' (0.79)), but siblings have primacy (p<0.05) over the female parent ('sister and mother' (0.59), 'brother and mother' (0.58)). This asymmetry, surprising in itself, is especially paradoxical because when the two parents are paired in natural speech 'mother' has strong (0.80) primacy over 'father' so that any asymmetry should go in the direction opposite to that found. We shall try to account for such paradoxical reversals in terms of decision models and the contrasting contexts in which these several kin pairs tend to be mentioned in natural speech.

Communicating by Violating Primacy Conventions Listeners probably draw little inference about a speaker's personal cognitions, feelings, or behaviors when he or she follows conventional word-ordering, but may draw inferences from violations of the usual ordering. For example, when polar opposite terms are paired, the socially desirable one is typically said first ('good and evil,' 'rich and poor,' 'life and death,' etc.); when this convention is violated, as on a sheriff's reward poster announcing 'Wanted: dead or alive,' the sheriff is probably communicating that he would prefer to receive the desperado in a moribund condition.

Obtained Interaction Effects

Methods Interactions   In this research program we have used four diverse methods for gathering kin-pair primacy data: reactive ratings, generated pairs, occurrence in informal speech, and occurrence in concordanced formal literature. Each of the four methods was used with variations. For example, the reactive rating tasks included 'which sounds better' versus 'which do you usually say'; generating pairs asked for frequently versus infrequently paired terms; free descriptions involved responding in written versus oral modes; concordanced literature involved contemporary authors versus those from several centuries back. This multimethod approach provides both methodological information (for example, about cross-methods' robustness of obtained relations, and about whether simpler methods may be safely substituted for more onerous methods) and also substantive information (for example, interaction effects on primacy between methods variables and variables from the five categories).

Primacy Differences as a Function of Formality   Primacy within the parental kin pair is an illustrative case of conflicting determinants. Maleness, a Category 3 status determinant, would predict the 'father and mother' ordering (as in 'Honor thy father and mother'), while the Category 2 affective-attachment determinant would predict the 'mother and father' ordering. Rather than inferring from this mutual-cancellation analysis a null hypothesis prediction, it can be used more powerfully to predict interaction effects: for example, that the male-primacy (Category 3) status determinant will show up more strongly in enhancing the male-parent-first ordering to the extent that the eliciting context is formal; conversely, the maternal-attachment intimacy (Category 2) determinant will be stronger in evoking the mother-first ordering to the extent that the eliciting context is more affectionate.

These interaction predictions are borne out by the data. Formality of context was manipulated across four methods: (1) least formal was to score primacy in parental pairing occurring during oral or in written descriptions of one's family; (2) more formal was to ask respondents to judge which sounded better between pairs of sentences containing contrasting orderings; (3) still more formal was the comparative frequencies of the two orderings in contemporary (nineteenth and twentieth century) literature; and (4) most formal, the orderings' comparative frequencies in seventeenth and eighteenth century classical literature. Across these four levels of increasing formality, the proportion of parental pairs in the more formal 'father and mother' order (rather than 'mother and father') increased steadily ($p<0.001$) from 0.20, to 0.47, to 0.71, to 0.89. A second prediction implied by the hypothesis that female-parent primacy increases in more affectionate contexts was also confirmed. Female primacy was higher ($p<0.05$) when the affectionate 'mom and dad' terms were used than with 'mother and father' at each level of data-collection formality. For example, in oral and written accounts of one's family, 0.20 of all parental pairings using the formal terms are in the 'father and mother' order, while only 0.12 of all pairings using the affectionate terms are in the 'dad and mom' order. When respondents reactively rated the suitability of the two orderings, 0.47 preferred male-parent priority when rating the formal terms ('father and mother') versus only 0.18 when the informal terms ('dad and mom') were rated.

Historical Changes in Word-Order Primacy   On the assumption that family relations in England and the United States have grown more egalitarian over the past several centuries, we predicted that Category 3 status variables, such as maleness and age seniority, would be less determining of primacy in the literature of recent centuries than of earlier ones. Our concordance data on seventeenth and eighteenth century English-language authors, versus nineteenth and twentieth century authors, do show a reliable decline in male primacy. For example, the proportion of 'father and mother' ordering has declined ($p<0.05$) from 0.89 to 0.71, and the proportion of 'brother and sister' ordering is down from 0.86 to 0.64. However, the literature concordance data show no decline in the age-seniority primacy bias (for example, the 'father and son' order remains constant at 0.91 across these four centuries). The youth rebellion may be too recent to be reflected in such twentieth century literature as has entered the Establishment Canon.

Speaker Characteristics as they Affect Word-Order Primacy   Kin pairs often involve age or sex contrasts between the two concepts and so allow study of how speaker's age or sex interact with kin-term age or sex in determining primacy. That word-order regularities stabilize early in life is shown by the finding that speaker's age from 6 to 70 years has little effect on primacy within kin pairs. Speaker's sex produces a slight Category 2 egocentric own-sex bias in ordering within kin pairs of opposite-sex people of the same generation and genetic closeness to self. For example, the 'mother and father' ordering is preferred by 0.58 of female raters and only 0.46 of male; 'mom and dad' is preferred by 0.86 of the females and 0.76 of the males. However, this own-sex primacy bias is stronger in actual-speech data than in rating data, which may reflect better ability to monitor and purge the egocentric own-sex bias in reactive rating than in one's spontaneous speech.

Linguistic Context Effects on Word-Order Primacy On the assumption that core term primacy could be smothered by linguistic embeddedness, we predicted that adding prefixes or suffixes to the core kin words would depolarize the primacy asymmetry between them. This effect was found but was slight in magnitude and barely reached the 0.05 level of significance. Across seven basic core pairs without prefixes and suffixes 'mother and father,' 'brother and sister,' 'father and son,' etc.) the mean primacy polarization was 0.92. When we added suffixes ('-in-law') or prefixes ('step-,' 'greatgrand-,' 'foster-') the mean polarization declined only slightly (p = 0.05) to 0.85.

Extensions to Further Subject-Matter Domains
So far we have discussed primacy almost entirely in terms of the kin-pair material. We shall conclude by mentioning briefly further issues regarding the thought-process implications of word-order regularities that can be studied conveniently in two further domains – in noun pairs involving foods, and in adjective series.

Proposed Research on Primacy in Food Pairs Between the kin pairs and the food pairs, many of the determinants in the three semantic categories correspond analogously. For example, the Category 2 kin variable of affective charge may correspond to the food variable of flavorfulness, or the Category 3 kin variables of power and status may correspond to the food variables of price and fashion. Finding more abstract characteristics that will embrace both of the analogously corresponding across-domain variables can advance one's grasp of the deeper psychological significance of the variables. Also some variables can be studied better in the food than in the kin domain, especially Categories 4 and 5 phonological variables, because the members of common food pairs tend to vary more on the linguistic characteristics than do frequently paired kin terms.

One can also investigate the operation of new factors with the food pairs. Our current data indicate that ordinarily in food pairs meats are said before non-meats ('ham and eggs,' 'franks and beans'), but that if the non-meat has been transformed by human effort, it gains in primacy (for example, 'devilled eggs and ham,' 'baked beans and franks'). This suggests the operation of a Lévi-Straussian raw/cooked, nature/culture dimension, or of a Ricardo/Marxian labor theory of value as another variable to be investigated among the Category 3 social status determinants. For example, we can pit against one another the Lévi-Straussian and Ricardo/Marxist interpretations by cross-varying transformed versus nontransformed foods with cases where the transformation adds versus subtracts ('overcooked,' etc.) value. Other issues raised by food pairs are the need to account for the high primacy of fruits, the low primacy of vegetables, and the middling primacy of sweets (desserts).

Proposed Research on Primacy in Adjective Series Primacy in adjective series, such as people's almost unanimous tendency to say 'old oaken bucket' and 'dirty old man' rather than 'oaken old bucket' and 'old dirty man' we hypothesize to reflect quite different thought processes from those that determine primacy in noun pairs. Our preliminary data indicated that primacy declines progressively across the following six adjective classes: number, size, evaluation, time, sensory quality, and materials, as in 'Three large dilapidated old red brick houses.' This abstract-to-concrete ordering seems a maladaptive communication strategy because starting with the most abstract adjectives aggravates their vagueness. The reverse ordering of saying the more concrete, imaginable adjectives first would provide needed context for specifying the abstract adjectives had they come later. A possible explanation is that the hearer stores the successive adjectives in a push-down list until the noun arrives and then pulls out the adjectives for processing relative to the noun with a last-in, first-out ordering. This hypothesis that the privileged position for adjectives is not primacy in vocalization but closeness to noun implies that the preferred ordering of adjectives will reverse when they follow rather than precede the noun, for example, 'A dirty old man . . .' ordering should reverse when the adjectives come after the noun, 'A man, old and dirty . . .'.

This push-down stacking – with its last in, first-out processing – may account also for other ordering oddities in communication, such as the person's tendency to describe the location of an object in an inefficient micro-to-macro sequence, as by saying 'You will find the scissors under some papers on the left side of the top drawer of the table in the dining room,' where the first-named clues provide little guidance until the later ones are heard, suggesting again that information is processed by temporary storage in push-down lists.

This last issue illustrates how, in an organized research program, relations that start out as questions can gradually become answers. In this word-order research we began by asking what variables affect word-order primacy and, as answers become clearer, we increasingly use word-order primacy to throw light on other processes. A critic might grant that the ubiquity of these highly polarized and consistent word-order regularities are amusingly interesting but protest that they seem to have little bearing on burning issues of theory or practice. Our claim for the topic is that getting a better understanding of this widespread and neglected primacy phenomenon promises to reveal interesting cognitive processes that are operative also in more significant domains, and can provide an efficient tool for studying other questions in social cognition.

References

Berrian, R. W., Metzler, D. P., Kroll, N. E. A. and Clark-Meyers, G. M. (1979) Estimates of imagery, ease of definition, and animateness for 328 adjectives. *Journal of Experimental Psychology: Human Learning and Memory*, 5: 435–447.

Bever, T. G., Fodor, J. A. and Weksel, W. (1965a) On the acquisition of syntax: A critique of 'contextual generalizations.' *Psychological Review*, 72: 467–482.

Bever, T. G., Fodor, J. A. and Weksel, W. (1965b) Is linguistics empirical? *Psychological Review*, 72: 493–500.

Bradshaw, J. L. (1984) A guide to norms, ratings, and lists. *Memory and Cognition*, 12: 202–206.

Braine, M. D. S. (1965) On the basis of phrase structure: A reply to Bever, Fodor & Weksel. *Psychological Review*, 72: 483–492.

Brown, A. S. (1976) Catalog of scaled verbal material. *Memory and Cognition*, 4(1B): 1S–45S.

Brown, R. W. and Bellugi, U. (1964) Three processes in the child's acquisition of syntax. *Harvard Educational Review*, 34: 133–151.

Brown, W. P. and Ure, D. M. J. (1969) Five rated characteristics of 650 word association stimuli. *British Journal of Psychology*, 60: 233–249.

Buium, N. (1974) An investigation of the word order parameter of a parent–child verbal interaction in a relatively free order language. *Language and Speech*, 17: 182–187.

Christian, J., Bickley, W., Tarka, W. and Clayton K. (1978) Measures of free recall of 900 English nouns: Correlations with imagery, concreteness, and frequency. *Memory and Cognition*, 6: 379–390.

Cietual, V. J. (1963) Association indices for 446 randomly selected English monosyllables, bisyllables, and trisyllables. *Journal of Verbal Learning and Verbal Behavior*, 2: 176–185.

Cooper, W. E. and Ross, J. R. (1975) Word order. In R. E. Grossman, L. J. San, and T. J. Vance (eds), Papers from the parasession on functionalism, pp. 63–111. Chicago: Chicago Linguistic Society.

Dewey, G. (1923) *Relative Frequency of English Speech Sounds*. Cambridge, MA: Harvard University Press.

Donaldson, M. (1987) Language: learning word meanings. In R. L. Gregory and O. Zangwill (eds), *Oxford Companion to the Mind*, pp. 421–423. New York: Oxford University Press.

Emmerich, H. J. (1979) Developmental differences in ratings of meaningfulness, concreteness, and picturability. *Developmental Psychology*, 15: 464–466.

Enkvist, N. E. and Kohonen, V. (1976) Reports on text linguistics approaches to word order. Abo, Finland: Text Linguistics Research Group.

Glanser, M. (1962) Grammatical category: A rote learning and word association analysis. *Journal of Verbal Learning and Verbal Behavior*, 1: 31–41.

Greenberg, J. H. (1966) Some universals of grammar with particular reference to the order of meaningful elements. In J. H. Greenberg (ed.), *Universals of Language*, 2nd edition, pp. 73–113. Cambridge, MA: MIT Press.

Jakobson, R. (1971) Implications of language universals for linguistics. In R. Jakobson, *Selected writings II: Word and Language*, pp. 580–591. The Hague: Mouton.

Kučera, H. and Francis, W. N. (1967) *Computational Analysis of Present-Day American English*. Providence, RI: Brown University Press.

Ley, R. and Locascio, D. (1970) Associative reaction time and meaningfulness of CVCVC response terms in paired-associate learning. *Journal of Experimental Psychology*, 83: 445–450.

Locascio, D. and Ley, R. (1972) Scaled-rated meaningfulness of 319 CVCVC words and paralogs previously assessed for associative reaction time. *Journal of Verbal Learning and Verbal Behavior*, 11: 243–250.

McGuire, W. J. (1983) A contextualist theory of knowledge: Its implications for innovation and reform in psychological research. In L. Berkowitz (ed.), *Advances in Experimental Social Psychology*, vol. 16, pp. 1–47. New York: Academic Press.

McGuire, W. J. (1986) A perspectivist look at contextualism and the future of behavioral science. In R. Rosnow and M. Georgoudi (eds), *Contextualism and Understanding in Behavioral Science: Implications for Research and Theory*, pp. 270–301. New York: Praeger.

McGuire, W. J. (1989) A perspectivist approach to the strategic planning of programmatic scientific research. In B. Gholson, W. R. Shadish, Jr., R. A. Neimeyer and A. C. Houts, *Psychology of Science: Contributions to Meta-science*, pp. 214–245. New York: Cambridge University Press.

Mayzner, M. S., Tresselt, M. E. and Wolin, B. R. (1965) Tables of pentagram frequency counts for various word-length and letter-position combinations. *Psychonomic Monograph Supplements*, 1(5, whole no. 5).

Moeser, S.D. (1975) Iconic factors and language word order. *Verbal Learning and Verbal Behavior*, 14: 43–55.

Noble, C. E. (1952) An analysis of meaning. *Psychological Review*, 59: 421–430.

Osgood, C. E., Suci, G. J. and Tannenbaum, P. H. (1957). *The Measurement of Meaning*. Urbana, IL: University of Illinois Press.

Paivio, A., Yuille, J. C. and Madigan, S. A. (1968) Concreteness, imagery, and meaningfulness values for 925 nouns. *Journal of Experimental Psychology*, Monograph Supplement, 76 (no. 1, pt. 2): 1–25.

Pinker, S. and Birdsong, D. (1979). Speakers' sensitivity to rules of frozen word order. *Journal of Verbal Learning and Verbal Behavior*, 18: 497–508.

Postman, L. and Keppel, G. (eds) (1970) *Norms of Word Association*. New York: Academic Press.

Quine, W. V. O. (1987) Symbols. In R. L. Gregory and O. L. Zangwill (eds), *Oxford Companion to the Mind*, pp. 763–765. New York: Oxford University Press.

Rubin, D. C. and Friendly, M. (1986) Predicting which words get recalled: Measures of free recall, availability, goodness, emotionality, and pronounceability for 925 nouns. *Memory and Cognition*, 14: 79–94.

Taylor, J. D. and Kimble, G. A. (1967) Association value of 320 selected words and paralogs. *Journal of Verbal Learning and Verbal Behavior*, 6: 744–752.

Taylor, S. E. and Thompson, S. C. (1982) Stalking the elusive 'vividness' effect. *Psychological Review*, 89: 155–181.

Thorndike, E. L. and Lorge, I. (1944) *The Teacher's Word Book of 30,000 Words*. New York: Teachers College Bureau of Publications, Columbia University.

Toglia, M. P. and Battig, W. F. (1978) *Handbook of Semantic Word Norms*. Hillsdale, NJ: Erlbaum.

Tulving, E., McNulty, J. A. and Ozier, M. (1965) Vividness of words and learning to learn in free-recall learning. *Canadian Journal of Psychology*, 19: 242–252.

Waugh, L. R. (1977) *A Semantic Analysis of Word Order: Position of the Adjective in French*. Leiden, The Netherlands: Brill.

12

Speaking and Understanding from Viewpoints: Studies in Perspectivity

Carl F. Graumann

The Problem and Concept of Perspectivity

If two observers watch a social episode in which two actors are somehow engaged in a conflict, it may happen that, afterwards, we not only get two different accounts of the episode by the two protagonists, but also get different reports by our two witnesses. This is a well-known fact, familiar to parents trying to settle their children's quarrels, to judges in court listening to witnesses' testimonies, or, for that matter, to students of attribution. It is also a favorite means of novelists, playwrights and scriptwriters to present one and the same plot from different viewpoints. Less well-known is where, when and how such differences of perspective occur and, above all, what 'perspective' basically means. Although the psychological and, mainly, the social psychological nature of such questions should be evident, theory and research in the field of social cognition and interaction have hardly taken notice of the problem of perspectivity.

It is in reaction to this deficit that this author and his research group have undertaken the task of theoretically and empirically reconstructing the perspectivity of such everyday scenarios as the one outlined above (Graumann 1960, 1978, 1989; Graumann and Sommer 1988; Sommer and Graumann, 1989). Being generally interested in the social psychology of language, we focused on the problem of the linguistic manifestation of perspectives. On the basis of a general (phenomenological) theory of perspectivity (Graumann, 1960), we experimentally reconstructed conflictuous everyday scenarios by the production of video features presented to subjects who had been instructed to put themselves in either the protagonist's or an opponent's position. In a series of experiments we studied (1) the hypothesized perspective-specific variation in the subjects' description of an episode; (2) the hypothesized long-term memory effect of a perspective taken; (3) the effects of a perspective set by linguistic means (text perspective); and (4) the effects of a habitual (for example, professional) versus a situational (for example, experimentally induced) perspective on language production. In these experiments (to be described below) the dependent variables were linguistic, and it was in these linguistic features of language production that the effects of the perspectives taken by our subjects were found. Since to our knowledge these studies were the first experiments in which the influence of perspective on language production could be demonstrated and was systematically varied, it seems appropriate to address the background conception from which these studies were developed.

Whoever acts – and for the psychologist speaking is acting – does so from a given position, from a point of departure; and, in Lewinian terms, acting is locomotion toward a goal or point of destination, be it in physical, social or mental space (Lewin, 1936). Nobody has ever challenged the basic fact that seeing something always means seeing it from a given viewpoint or, in a correlative term, in one of its aspects and being referred to other (potential or future) aspects of the same (object or person). Phenomenological analyses have shown (Husserl, 1973; Graumann, 1960) that in a structurally related sense this also holds for non-sensory cognitive experience. One and the same problem can be 'approached' from different 'sides' with different 'appearances' or 'aspects' corresponding to each approach. (Although philosophers sometimes resent the spatial character of terms like 'approach' or 'side', 'position' or 'aspect', psychology cannot be done without the use of spatio-temporal metaphors.)

It is possible (and has traditionally been the elementary approach) to elaborate the full-fledged structure of perspectivity with its elements of viewpoint, aspect, and horizon on a strictly individualistic level. But since this has been reviewed elsewhere (Graumann, 1989; Graumann and Sommer, 1988) and the present context is 'Language, Interaction and Social Cognition', the topic of perspectivity shall be approached on the social, or rather the interpersonal, level.

If there is a speaker then, usually, there is a hearer. Contrary to a certain linguistic (and psycholinguistic) tradition our basic model is not one individual who is a so-called speaker/hearer but (at least) two individuals communicating. In other words, our 'point of departure' is social interaction, which not always but often enough is speaking and understanding speech in turns or simultaneously.

The study of social interaction has been on the research agenda of social psychology for about half a century, but psychologists' 'interaction' has remained kind of deaf-mute: in almost every

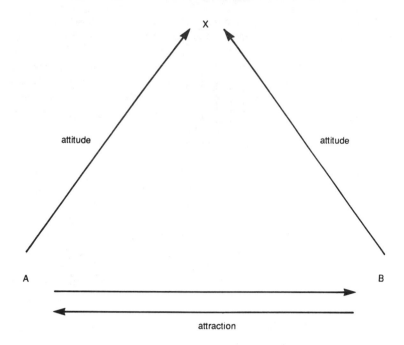

Figure 12.1   *Newcomb's ABX model (Newcomb, 1953: 394)*

traditional dyadic model, *Ego* and *Alter*, Person and Other, A and B, are said to interact, to communicate, but they do not speak.

One of the 'pioneers' of social psychological communication studies is Newcomb (1953/1962). His ABX model (Figure 12.1) is well known: a person A is (positively or negatively) 'attracted' by a person B with whom A maintains a 'co-orientation' with respect to something, called X. For the present purpose, it is not necessary to discuss Newcomb's dynamic (ultimately homeostatic) hypotheses about such ABX relationships but it is important to consider two of his complementary assumption. The first one states that 'the orientation of any A toward any B . . . is rarely, if ever, made in an environmental vacuum' (1962: 150–151) – a warning against a purely interpersonal conception of social interaction which disregards the fact that there is always something (an object, an event, a state of affairs or another person) with respect to which persons communicate. The complementary assumption states that 'the orientation of any A capable of verbal communication about almost any conceivable X is rarely, if ever, made in a social vacuum. There are few if any objects so private that one's orienta-tions toward them are uninfluenced by others' orientation' (1962:

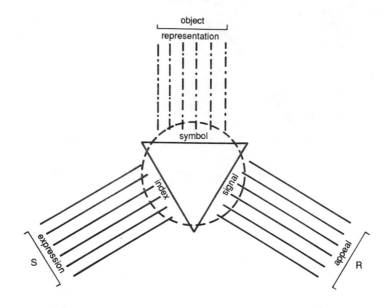

Figure 12.2   *Bühler's organon model (Bühler, 1934/1965: 28)*

151). Differing orientations of A and B toward X as well as A's 'co-orientation' toward B and X imply both 'cathetic and cognitive tendencies' (1962: 150). They are perspectives from a given position A or B with respect to X, including the dynamically interesting case that A discovers B to hold a view of X different from A's viewpoint (which induces in A a 'strain toward symmetry' with B).

Although Newcomb, commenting on his model refers to 'A and B as they communicate about X' (1962: 151) and interprets the 'strain toward symmetry' in terms of attempts 'to influence another toward one's own point of view' (1962: 153) or of A 'trying to persuade B to his own point of view' (1962: 155), the language of 'influence' and 'persuasion' does not enter this model of 'communicative acts'. It is semiotically empty. Newcomb's model is, however, only one of the many models of 'communication without language' which Moscovici (1967) critically contrasted with those of 'language without communication'.

That A relates to B by talking about X is also the basic rationale of another model developed earlier by Karl Bühler (1933, 1934) in his theory of language, mainly in 'The axiomatization of the language sciences' (1982). The so-called organum model (Figure 12.2) rests upon Plato's dictum that language is an *organum* for one person's communicating with another about things. Again we

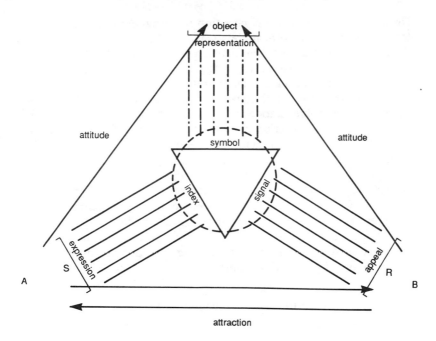

Figure 12.3   *A combination of Bühler's organon model and
Newcomb's ABX model*

have a triangular model with two persons and one object (or state
of affairs) involved, but instead of three, it consists of four parts:
its center is the *sign*. By means of three functions the sign binds
A (the sender), B (the receiver) and X (here: objects and states of
affair) together. With respect to the sender the sign is 'index' or
'symptom'; with respect to the receiver it is 'signal'; with respect
to the object it is 'symbol'. In the same vein, the sign is the
sender's 'expression'; to the receiver it is 'appeal'; for the objects
it is their 'representation'. There is no doubt that Bühler's is a sign-
centered model of language, not a model of communication.
Nothing happens between the persons nor between persons and
object unless mediated by the central sign. That people are
attracted by each other, that they are (cognitively) oriented toward
objects without language (for example, perceptually), is none of
Bühler's concern. Hence, we have a model of language without
communication (cf. Heger, 1971).

Contrasting these two models one may say that while Newcomb's is semiotically empty, but dynamically 'hot', Bühler's is
dynamically empty, but semiotically rich. What we need, however,

for a social-psychological conception of verbal communication is at least a synthesis of both models (Figure 12.3), indicating both the dynamics of mutual communication with respect to the environment and the expressive, appealing, and representative power of the language mediating such communication.

For the special topic of speaking and understanding from viewpoints, the combined model illustrates not only that one and the same object X is experienced differently from different positions (to be found out by and giving rise to communicative acts). It also indicates that the way reference to an object is understood by a 'receiver' depends on the signs used by the 'sender'. This is of special importance if the object talked about is not part of a common perceptual situation. Hence, we may hypothesize that the divergence of perspectives or orientations, which in Newcomb's model are cognitive and cathectic, but speechless, may also be found in a differential use of language by people talking from different positions or viewpoints.

Perspective in the Study of Language and Cognition

Studies on perspective are widely scattered in psychology and in linguistics, as a rule without (explicit) reference to perspective theory. Neither for psychology nor for linguistics can we refer to a comprehensive critical review of the field. Limited selective overviews are given in Graumann (1989) and in Canisius (1987). For the present purpose of giving the background from which our own experiments were developed, it will do to exemplify where and in which respects perspective and viewpoint have been discovered and acknowledged as a topic of research. Since for psychologists studies of perspective in developmental and social psychology will be familiar (for a brief summary see Graumann, 1989) we shall in what follows accentuate seemingly remote linguistic and literary studies of perspective and viewpoint and only very selectively refer to such psychological investigations as have an immediate bearing on our studies. This amounts to a liberal interpretation of the general topic of this volume in an interdisciplinary attitude, trying to bring approaches to the problem of perspective from literary analysis and linguistics, as well as from language and social psychology, toward a convergence. The convergence and divergence of perspectives, however, is a central issue of the field we have just entered.

Perspective in Language
Although historically and systematically linguistics may be a closer relative to social psychology than the study of literature, for the

exemplification of perspective in language its treatment in literary analysis is a good point of departure. But for the student of social psychology the discussion of an initial question may be in place. Why be interested in literature and literary theory? Is not literature mostly fiction while social psychology – as a science – has to deal with facts? If this is true it is only half the truth. There are several good reasons for an active interrelationship between social psychology and literature (for example, Potter et al., 1984; Shotter and Gergen, 1989). They need not be reiterated here. Two general arguments, however, may precede a more specific look into narratology.

First, one should not overemphasize the notorious distinction between fiction and fact for two reasons:

1 A large part of the social information we receive and 'process' in our everyday life is not immediate sensory experience, for which seeing may be believing. It is narrative and second-hand. We learn about others from different others, about 'third persons' from 'second persons', more precisely from the stories B tells A about X (in this case X being the third person). Since most of what we nowadays prefer to call 'social cognition' refers actually to the information one individual gets about other individuals, we have – at least to a large extent – to do with the processing of texts, texts in whose veracity we may trust or not. Texts mainly of the story type, as enjoyable or thrilling as they may be, very often keep us in suspense as to how much fact, how much fiction they carry. Even in social psychological experiments we have developed a penchant for fictitious target-persons, personality descriptions, cover stories and the like. In the special field of so-called person perception we rarely confront our subjects with real 'live' persons (occasionally actors), but with drawings, photographs, films and video-clips instead. Almost professionally and for methodological reasons we have made it a habit to cross the border between fact and fiction.

2 Another reason against dichotomizing between fact and fiction may be taken from research on social cognition. If it is true that in schemata, prejudice and stereotypes there is an imaginary element (not reducible to past experience) there must also be a fictitious element in our everyday orientation and, above all, co-orientation.

The second argument comes from literary theory. Texts of a narrative or dramatical structure represent actions and dialogues that can properly be called social actions since usually we are presented with two or more actors whose activities are somehow interrelated, in love, jealousy, rivalry, strife, adventure. Very often we have a main character, the protagonist, around whom the whole plot is centered, and a counteracting antagonist. Hence, the rule in such stories and dramas is that one and the same situation is seen and dealt with differently by different actors, undoubtedly so in situations of interpersonal conflicts, the subject-matter of most dramas. If the story of a typical human conflict is well written or convincingly performed, the topic of fact or fiction, of real or imaginary life, does not come up, at least not for the listener, reader, spectator. What they see and hear is human experience.

Conversely, it happens occasionally in everyday life that we become first-hand witnesses of events that are so weird, phantastic, dreamlike or just incredible that we must put in an extra effort to pinch ourselves that this is real life.

Taking both arguments together leads to the conclusion that social psychologists should not exaggerate the necessary distinction between the factual and the fictitious, the real and the imaginary. That literature, at least for the study of perspective in social cognition, is a source of psychological stimulation and (maybe) insight shall briefly be indicated in the next subsection.

Perspective in the Study of Literature If we, quite generally, accept that the use of language, among other things, has the communicative function of bringing a hearer (B) to attend to what a speaker (A) has in mind (for example, X), the question is how this is accomplished. (And if we replace the words 'bringing B to attend' by 'influencing' or 'persuading' B, the social psychological interest in this topic should be evident.)

The author of a narrative text has different techniques available to establish perspective(s). The author may either introduce himself or herself as the narrator (in the first person singular) or, less immediately, let someone else be the narrator (in the first or third person) or let one of the main characters of the story present the essential position. Or, as Bakhtin (1973) has convincingly demonstrated for Dostoevsky, different world-views are brought forward by different 'voices' in a kind of verbal 'polyphony'. Finally, it can be the construction of the text as a whole that conveys the author's 'message' to the reader. But who is the reader? Fowler (1982: 214) criticizes Uspensky's theory of point of view (1973) for not being precise about the reader: Is he or she a real person, an ideal, an average reader or merely implied in a text to be read? A pure linguist like Fowler himself prefers the 'reader' to be 'an abstract property of the compositional (i.e. linguistic) structure of the text', meaning that perspective can be linguistically pervasive without being allotted to individual personified voices. I emphasize this conception since we approached our own experimental analyses with the heuristic assumption that a still unknown number of linguistic features may be indicative of perspective. Psychologically relevant is Uspensky's early distinction of four different conceptions of point of view, namely,

1   as 'an ideological and evaluative position';
2   as 'a spatial and temporal position of the one who produces the description of the events';
3   'with respect to perceptual characteristics'; or
4   'in a purely linguistic sense'.

For the social psychologist the first and the third level of analysis are important.

Conception 1: Whether explicitly stated or merely implied, viewpoints are evaluative or value-expressive. If, as sociologists and psychologists, following Mead and Piaget, maintain, perspective-taking is a prerequisite for communication, we may expect that taking the perspective of another is not evaluatively neutral. In our own experiments as well as in related ones (for example, Mummendey et al., 1984a,b) it was found that the protagonist with whom subjects had been instructed to identify was valued more positively than the antagonist. This differential evaluation became manifest in both spontaneous assessments 'He is okay', 'I like the way he did it') and in solicited responses to question ('Who is right?', 'Whom did you like more?'). Although the everyday character of the interactions presented to the experimental subjects was not conducive to a hero versus villain interpretation, the evaluatively differential treatment of protagonists and antagonists was consistent.

Conception 2: Since the conception of viewpoint as the spatial and temporal position of either author or reader, speaker or hearer, is a special topic of the general linguistic study of deixis (see below), we may rather attend to Uspensky's conception and Fowler's elaboration of *Conception 3*, the 'perceptual' sense of point of view. Since it is here that literary analysis comes closest to psychological research we should at least consider a few of the major distinctions, some of which may sound quite familiar to a psychologist.

There is mainly the distinction between *internal* and *external* perspectives. The author may either have or imagine access to the mental life of one of his or her characters (the internal perspective). Or, the author views (or lets view) a character from outside (the external perspective). Here Uspensky, probably unknowingly, rephrases Dingler's distinction of 'autopsychology' (first-person psychology) and 'allopsychology' (third-person psychology) (see, Holzkamp, 1964: 70). For the internal perspective, not only beauty but the whole world is 'in the eyes of the beholder' who talks about his or her experience in the first person or voices his or her inner monologues (like Leopold Bloom's stream of consciousness in *Ulysses*). Or, a second possibility, 'the narrator comments on or describes the mental processes . . . of the characters' (Fowler, 1982: 222) using what Uspensky called *verba sentiendi* – that is, words denoting mental states and processes. In both cases, the author acts like an empathizing psychologist.

Also for the external perspective two alternatives have been suggested (by Uspensky and Fowler). A character and his or her behavior may be described impersonally in a quasi-objective 'behavioristic' account, in which even the narrator remains hidden. Or the narrator becomes a dominant figure as the story-teller who control the plot, comments, interprets, passes judgment and evaluation, be it in sympathy with or in a critical attitude toward a character.

If the comprehension of narrative texts has to do with the reader's or listener's adoption of a point of view as some theorists say, we have here qualitatively and experientially quite different modalities of perspective-taking. Sometimes, in modern prose we go through them in rapid shifts of perspective. Sometimes, we are offered a synthesis of internal and external perspective as is the case in a 'literary experiment' done by Walter Jens (1961), in which a story is produced written from the perspective of an octogenarian who both remembers a past experience and reflects upon it with the wisdom of his old age. Being both actor and observer he unites 'the immediacy of the personal perspective with the auctorial power of disposal' (Jens 1961: 86).

Perspective in Language Use While in the analyses of literature the focus is on stylistic means to convey viewpoints, the topic of perspective in linguistics is much more fundamental. A brief quotation from Joseph Grimes's *The Thread of Discourse* may illustrate the problem:

> The more we look at it, the more evident it becomes that everything we say is phrased from a particular perspective, just as everything that a cinematographer shows on the screen is photographed from a particular perspective. He sets his camera in a definite place and trains it principally on one character, in speech we choose one element that we are referring to as the point of departure for the relationships to all other

elements. This affects word order, choice of pronouns, and decisions concerning subordination. (1975: 260)

Linguistic means of ordering have pragmatically and psychologically also to be understood as means of orienting whomever speech is addressed to. As may be developed from Bühler's *organum* model, a speaker uses a sign to draw a hearer's attention to a nonlinguistic referent. Since, in principle, A has a choice of signs to identify X (for B), one and the same referent may be identified by different signs. In order to account for such differences Jim Wertsch (1985: 167–176) introduced the notion of *referential perspective*. It is 'the perspective or viewpoint utilized by the speaker in order to identify a referent' (1985: 168).

Perhaps the most elementary semiotic means of referring someone to something are *deictic* expressions. Without going into any details of this well-researched and broad linguistic and psycholinguistic problem area, a 'cognitive' qualification may be suggested. Traditionally, the study of deixis has been restricted to personal, spatial, and temporal reference: I–you, here–there, now–then, come–go, are the most common examples for the identification of positions, directions and movements. But while spatial deixis is usually considered with respect to (a common) visual space, temporal deixis already transcends the present perceptual field. But even 'figural' deixis in cognitive space, in which I may refer my interlocutor to different positions, different approaches and goals by means of deictic terms, may be just as unambiguous as orientation by pointing in the *Zeigfeld* (index field) (Bühler, 1933/1976), provided the referent is in my partner's 'field of consciousness'. The explanation may be found in the pervasive spatial and spatio-temporal metaphors without which psychological discourse would be very poor (and a chapter on viewpoints impossible).

Perspective in Cognition

The major interest of literary analysis and linguistics in viewpoints is with respect to texts and text-production. The fact that texts are usually produced to be read, that language has to be understood, seems to concern psychologists rather than linguistics. Hence, when psychologists deal with perspective it is mainly as a feature of language processing or, more generally, of information processing on the receptive rather than productive side.

Since it has been done elsewhere (Graumann, 1989) we need not review the different fields of psychology in which perspective has been studied, such as the field of perspective-taking in cognitive and moral development, the study of perspective in interpersonal

communication, whose 'pioneer' is Ragnar Rommetveit (1974); the
field of attitudinal judgment as covered by Upshaw's and Ostrom's
'variable perspective approach' (see Upshaw and Ostrom, 1984),
plus Eiser's modifications (see Eiser, 1986); the field of attribution
as far as the so-called actor–observer divergence of perspectives is
concerned (Jones and Nisbett, 1972); the social psychology of
aggression, where Mummendey and her associates (1984a,b) have
demonstrated that actors and victims hold divergent perspectives of
the same critical episode; or finally the topic of memory perspective.

This last type of research may reemphasize the convergence and
complementarity of literary and psychological studies. The fact
underlying studies on point of view in personal memories (Nigro
and Neisser, 1983; Frank and Gilovich, 1989) has been known for
a long time: people remember biographical events from different
visual perspectives. Either they have 'observer memories', seeing
themselves from the outside, or they have 'field memories': they
remember a scene as it was available to them in the original situation. Nigro and Neisser, who introduced this distinction, show that
subjects are more likely to adopt an observer perspective when
asked to recall events they experienced further in the past whereas
'recent events . . . are more likely to appear as field memories'
(1983: 477). In addition, it could be demonstrated that 'events
involving a relatively high degree of emotional self-awareness are
likely to produce observer memories' (1983: 477). Since original
experiences are normally in a 'field perspective', later 'observer
memories' of the same experience must be considered to be
reconstructions, some of which may be of the Freudian 'screen
memory' type (1983: 468).

Perspective in Language Production and Comprehension

In all these psychological studies the critical questions are: Which
position does a person take with respect to an event or issue? How
can the adoption of a position or viewpoint be accounted for in
terms of the situation or of the person? With the exception of
Rommetveit and of the Eiser group with their interest in the value
connotation of judgmental labels (in response scales) the role of
language in the adoption of viewpoints was largely ignored. Even
in the studies of the role of perspective in story comprehension and
recall (Pichert and Anderson, 1977; Anderson and Pichert, 1978)
there is no strictly linguistic description or definition of a perspective (nor any other theoretically satisfactory definition).

Convinced that it is possible to combine linguistic, psychological

Table 12.1   *Experiment 1: Perspective and text production*

Dependent variable

Macro-level	Micro-level	Additional questions
Summary (*)	Grammatical subject (*)	Fairy tale opening (*)
Episode structure (*)	Event-specific verbs (*)	Who is right? (*)
	Verba sentiendi (*)	Whom did you like
	Verbs of spatial	more? (*)
	orientation (*)	Estimated value of the
	Event-specific words (*)	car (*)
	Terms of spatial	
	orientations (−)	
	Perspectival qualifications	
	(−)	
	Perspectival use of direct	
	speech (−)	
	Perspective-related slips	
	of the tongue (+)	
	Nominalisms (−)	
	Passive constructions (−)	
	Metastatements (−)	

(−): no significant differences (p>0.05)
(*): significant differences (p ⩽ 0.05) between or within groups in the predicted
    direction
(+): significant difference between experimental groups and control group

Source: Graumann and Sommer, 1988: 206

and phenomenological knowledge about perspectivity (Graumann,
1978, 1989), we theoretically derived and operationally established
linguistic indicators of perspectivity to find out which of these
means a speaker uses in order to convey a perspective a listener is
invited to adopt. Variables that we considered to be indicative of
perspective are on two levels (Table 12.1): on the macro-level we
worked with summaries (as manifestations of macro-structures)
and with episode structures (written in macro-propositions); on the
micro-level, depending on the specific task, the variables were
grammatical subject, event-specific verbs, *verba setiendi*, verbs of
spatial orientation, and later on words and phrases indicating
violation of norms and accounting for it.

The method to induce a given perspective (our independent
variable) was to present subjects with a video feature of a
controversial social episode with always a protagonist and an opponent. Subjects were instructed to take the perspective of either
character.

The major findings of the first four different experiments (1) on perspective and text production, (2) on perspective and memory, (3) on a comparison between text perspective and reader perspective, and (4) between speaker and hearer perspective were:

1 a confirmation of previous findings that a reader's perspective influences text comprehension;
2 that perspective also affects text production;
3 that these results can be reproduced after an interval of eight weeks;
4 that perspective affects not only the recall of idea units but specific semantic and syntactic variables;
5 that by means of such text variables a reader can be induced to take a given perspective.

In a fifth experiment with a different video feature we examined a hypothesis which had come up in the preceding studies, namely, that we should distinguish between situational and habitual perspectives. Situational perspectives are induced by somebody else or by some event in the present situation as, for instance, by experimental instruction or by persuasion to do something. Habitual perspectives, on the other hand, are brought into the situation by the person who has acquired them in the course of his or her biography (or 'learning history') or as part of the shared stock of social knowledge (as in social representations). The way we manipulated habitual perspective as our independent variable was by confronting two experimental groups of people (versus a control group) with a videotaped conflictuous social episode, the groups being E1, professional drivers, such as cabbies, E2, habitual and committed (almost 'militant') cyclists, and C, a group of non-motorists and non-cyclists. The situational perspective was, as usual, induced by the instruction to identify with the car-driving or bike-riding protagonist of a video film featuring a (professional) driver and a (convinced) cyclist on their different ways through town with encounters and mutual annoyances. Including a 'neutral' instruction this yielded a 3×3 design (N = 141) (Sommer and Graumann, 1989).

The overall finding of this study is the dominance of the habitual over the situational perspective, less so on the macro-level than in micro-level variables such as grammatical subject, *verba sentiendi*, spatial and cognitive orientation, and in the perspective-specific qualification of norm-violations, with the drivers 'discounting' the driver's violations but augmenting those of the pedalling character. In all these variables the effects of the situational viewpoint was either insignificant or clearly weaker than those of the habitual perspective.

Finally, and in order to further validate our approach we did a linguistic (re)analysis of data raised by Amélie Mummendey and her group within their studies of aggressive interaction (Mummendey et al., 1984a,b). They had asked their subjects to watch a video feature of an argument and quarrel between two highschool students and to take the perspective of one of the pupils. The character to empathize with was either, in one episode, the 'actor' or 'initiator' of a verbal or physical attack against the other one, the 'victim'. Or he became, in a subsequent episode, the target of the former victim now retaliating as the 'reactor'. Evaluations of the experimental perspective manipulations revealed that 'subjects from the actor's perspective evaluate the actor's critical behavior as more appropriate and are less likely to label it as aggressive' (1984a: 94).

Leaning on these findings of an actor–victim divergence in aggressive interaction, we transcribed and analyzed Mummendey's tape-recorded verbal material in terms of the dependent measures that we considered to be indicators of perspective. While the full report on this 'secondary' analysis is still in preparation, some preliminary results can be presented:

1   The hypothesis was confirmed that the protagonist whose perspective is taken becomes the grammatical subject more often than the antagonist.
2   Also confirmed was the hypothesis that words designating mental states and processes (*verba sentiendi à la* Uspensky) are preferred for the person identified with.
3   Confirmed also was that verbal indications of the appropriateness or inappropriateness of emotional reactions are perspective-specific.
4   Also, the discounting versus augmenting of norm-violations proved to be a function of the perspective taken.
5   As already mentioned, the figure identified with was valued more positively than his opponent.
6   Partly confirmed was the hypothesis that initiators tend to account for their own actions in terms of external attribution, while reactors prefer internal accounts of the initiator's action.

No significant differences were found between the two perspectives in the variables' spatial and cognitive orientation and norm-compliance, which may be due to type and brevity of tests.

For further details and a discussion see the full report (Sommer et al., in preparation). The theoretical and methodological interest in this reanalysis is evidently that we have been able to accomplish two things: (1) to extend the validity of perspective theory to independently obtained data; and above all, (2) not only to corroborate but to differentiate the findings about actor–victim divergences of perspective by means of analyzing free-speech verbal protocols.

We now feel encouraged to probe deeper into the territory of free speech and discourse, so far left to ethnographers of communication and discourse analysts. After a first pilot study on perspectival structure and dynamics in dialogues (Graumann, 1990) we are presently trying to reconstruct the basic elements of perspectivity as defined by (our reading of) variable perspective theory, namely, own position, range, end-anchors and grain of a personal 'scale' (that is, subject-created) 'scale' of reference, in the field of persuasion, which we conceptualize as the effort to approximate a target person's perspective towards one's own (Sommer, 1990).

Conclusion

To conclude and as an interim balance one can summarize the ideas and findings from literary, linguistic, and social-psychological studies of perspectivity in language and cognition in terms of a few postulates and hypotheses for further research:

1   Irrespective of whether all knowledge is perspectival, as philosophical, sociological, and psychological perspectivists say (see Apel, 1973; Mannheim, 1936; McGuire, 1984), there are sufficient reasons to assume that whenever we communicate whatever we have to say to someone about something, a position from which or with respect to which is either implied or explicitly addressed.

2   Hence, as students of social interaction (or, for that matter, of social cognition), we should be prepared to discover signs of positions with respect to which an utterance or another social action makes sense.

3   Perspective, although a basically cognitive term (of orientation and co-orientation toward persons, objects, events and states of affairs), has its firm and objective place in language. Hence, the language we (have to) speak, often predisposes the way we approach a subject.

4   To the degree that language is not only the medium but also the boundary condition (potential as well as constraint) of a large part of social interaction, giving perspective to individual acts, a social psychology disregarding language (as condition, medium or product of interaction) keeps missing the chance of becoming a *social* science.

5 Social interaction can only be fully understood if we succeed in discovering how, in spite of differing viewpoints, interlocutors attain mutuality of perspective. The frame in which this discovery is to be made is the *dialogue* rather than individual (speech-)acts.

Note

The experiments referred to in this chapter were made possible by a grant of the Deutsche Forschungsgemeinschaft to the Sonderforschungsbereich 245 'Sprechen und Sprachverstehen im sozialen Kontext' (Speaking and Understanding in Social Context). The author wishes to express his thanks to Gün Semin and C. Michael Sommer for valuable help and suggestions.

References

Anderson, R. C. and Pichert, J. W. (1978) Recall of previously unrecallable information following a shift in perspective. *Journal of Verbal Learning and Verbal Behavior*, 17: 1–12.

Apel, K. O. (1973) *Transformation der Philosophie*, vol. 2. *Das Apriori der Kommunikationsgemeinschaft*. Frankfurt: Suhrkamp.

Bakhtin, M. M. (1973) *Problems of Dostoevsky's Poetics*. Ann Arbor, MI: Ardis.

Bühler, K. (1933/1976) *Die Axiomatik der Sprachwissenschaften*, 2nd edition. (Introduction by Elisabeth Ströker) Frankfurt: Klostermann. (Engl. trans. in R. E. Innis (1982) *Karl Bühler: Semiotic Foundation of Language Theory*. New York: Plenum.)

Bühler, K. (1934/1965) *Sprachtheorie*. Stuttgart: Günter Fischer.

Canisius, P. (ed.) (1987) *Perspektivität in Sprache und Text* [Perspectivity in Language and Text]. Bochum: Brockmeyer.

Eiser, J. R. (1986) *Social Psychology*. Cambridge: Cambridge University Press.

Fowler, R. (1982) How to see through language: Perspective in fiction. *Poetics*, 11: 213–235.

Frank, M. G. and Gilovich, T. (1989) Effect of memory perspective on retrospective causal attributions. *Journal of Personality and Social Psychology*, 57: 399–403.

Graumann, C. F. (1960) *Grundlagen einer Phänomenologie und Psychologie der Perspektivität* [Foundations of a Phenomenology and Psychology of Perspectivity]. Berlin: de Gruyter.

Graumann, C. F. (1978) Interpersonale Perspektivität und Kommunikation. *Phänomenologische Forschungen: Studien zur Sprachphänomenologie*, 8, pp. 168–186. Freiburg: Alber.

Graumann, C. F. (1989) Perspective setting and taking in verbal interaction. In: R. Dietrich and C. F. Graumann (eds), *Language Processing in Social Context*, pp. 95–122. Amsterdam: North-Holland.

Graumann, C. F. (1990) Perspectival structure and dynamics in dialogues. In: I. Markovà and K. Foppa (eds), *The Dynamics of Dialogue*, pp. 105–126. New York: Harvester.

Graumann, C. F. and Sommer, C. M. (1988) Perspective structure in language production and comprehension. *Journal of Language and Social Psychology*, 7: 193–212.

Grimes, J. E. (1975) *The Thread of Discourse.* The Hague: Mouton.

Heger, K. (1971) Zur Standortbestimmung der Sprachwissenschaft. *Zeitschrift für romanische Philologie,* 87: 1–31.

Holzkamp, K. (1964) *Theorie und Experiment in der Psychologie.* Berlin: de Gruyter.

Husserl, E. (1973) *Experience and Judgment* (trans. by J. S. Churchill and K. Ameriks). Evanston, IL: Northwestern University Press.

Jens, W. (1961) Die Perspektive im Roman. *Jahresring,* 61/62. Beiträge zur deutschen Literatur und Kunst der Gegenwart. Hrsg. vom Kulturkreis im Bundesverband der Deutschen Industrie; bearb. von Rudolf De La Roy u.a., pp. 63–86. Stuttgart: Deutsche Verlagsanstalt.

Jones, E. E. and Nisbett, R. E. (1972) The actor and the observer: Divergent perceptions of the causes of behavior. In: E. E. Jones et al., *Attribution: Perceiving the Causes of Behavior,* pp. 79–94. Morristown: General Learning Press.

Lewin, K. (1936) *Principles of Topological Psychology.* New York: McGraw-Hill.

McGuire, W. J. (1984) Perspectivism: A look back at the future. *Contemporary Social Psychology,* 10: 5/6: 19–40.

Mannheim, K. (1936) *Ideology and Utopia: An Introduction to the Sociology of Knowledge.* New York: Harcourt Brace.

Moscovici, S. (1967) Communication processes and the properties of language. In: L. Berkowitz (ed.), *Advances in Experimental Social Psychology,* vol. 3, pp. 226–271. New York: Academic Press.

Mummendey, A., Linneweber, V. and Löschper, G. (1984a) Aggression: From act to interaction. In: A. Mummendey (ed.), *Social Psychology of Aggression,* pp. 69–106. New York: Springer-Verlag.

Mummendey, A., Linneweber, V. and Löschper, G. (1984b) Zur Perspektiven-divergenz zwischen Akteur und Betroffenem in aggressiven Interaktionen. *Zeitschrift für Sozialpsychologie,* 15: 290–303.

Newcomb, T. M. (1953) An approach to the study of communicative acts. *Psychological Review,* 60: 393–404. (Reprinted in: A. P. Hare, E. F. Borgatta and R. F. Bales (eds) (1962) *Small Groups – Studies in Social Interaction,* pp. 149–163. New York: Knopf.)

Nigro, G. and Neisser, U. (1983) Point of view in personal memories. *Cognitive Psychology,* 15: 467–482.

Pichert, J. W. and Anderson, R. C. (1977) Taking different perspectives on a story. *Journal of Educational Psychology,* 69: 309–315.

Potter, J., Stringer, P. and Wetherell, M. (1984) *Social Texts and Context – Literature and Social Psychology.* London: Routledge & Kegan Paul.

Rommetveit, R. (1974) *On Message Structure: A Framework for the Study of Language and Communication.* London: Wiley.

Shotter, J. and Gergen, K. J. (eds) (1989) *Texts of Identity.* London: Sage.

Sommer, C. M. (1990) In their own words: Some experiences with subject-created reference scales. (Paper read at the Budapest meeting of EAESP.)

Sommer, C. M. and Graumann, C. F. (1989) Perspektivität und Sprache: Zur Rolle von habituellen Perspektiven. *Arbeiten aus dem Sonderforschungsbereich 245 Sprechen und Sprachverstehen im sozialen Kontext,* Nr. 9.

Sommer, C. M., Freitag, B. and Graumann, C. F. (in preparation) Aggressive interaction in perspectival language. *Arbeiten aus dem Sonderforschungsbereich 245 Sprechen und Sprachverstehen im sozialen Kontext.*

Upshaw, S. and Ostrom, T. M. (1984) Psychological perspective in attitude research. In: J. R. Eiser (ed.), *Attitudinal Judgment*, pp. 23–41. New York: Springer.

Uspensky, B. (1973) *A Poetics of Composition.* Berkeley, CA: University of California Press.

Voloshinov, V. N. (1973) *Marxism and the Philosophy of Language.* New York: Seminar Press.

Wertsch, J. V. (1985) *Vygotsky and the Social Formation of Mind.* Cambridge, MA: Harvard University Press.

Subject index

Name index